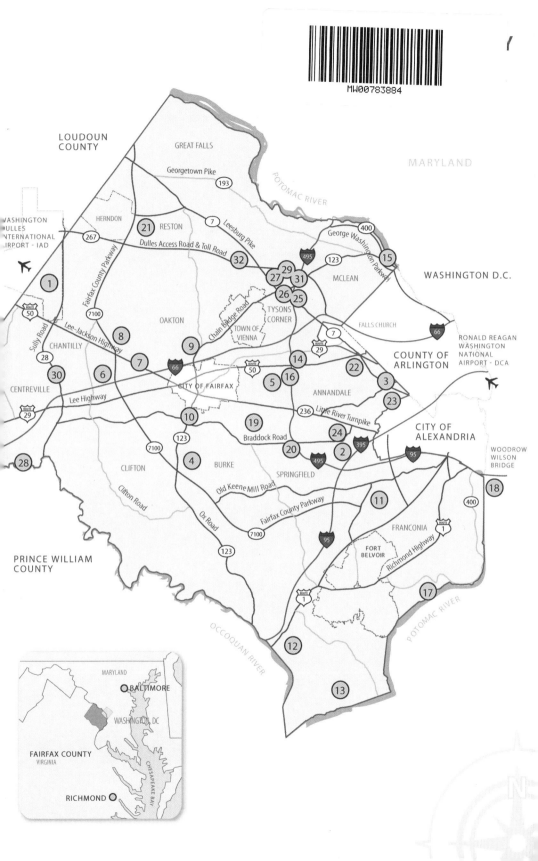

THE FIGHT FOR
FAIRFAX

A Struggle for a Great American County

THE FIGHT FOR
FAIRFAX

A Struggle for a Great American County

RUSS BANHAM

PREFACE by JOEL GARREAU

GMU
PRESS

THE FIGHT FOR FAIRFAX: A Struggle for a Great American County
By Russ Banham

Copyright © 2009, GMU Press

Published by GMU Press, Fairfax, Virginia.

Book design by Spectrum Creative, LLC, Fairfax, Virginia.

Printed and manufactured in the United States of America.

Cover photography: Crossroads Market, Tysons Corner, c. 1955, Photographic Archive, Fairfax County Public Library; Dulles Greenway Toll Road, © 2009, Dewberry; and CIT Building, The Center for Innovative Technology.

First printing, June 2009

Library of Congress Control Number: 2009924442

ISBN: 978-0-9818779-5-2

This book is dedicated to the many
hard-working, tenacious, and visionary men and women
who endeavored to build Fairfax County
over the past fifty years
into the extraordinary place it has now become.

Preface

Note to a Future Historian
BY JOEL GARREAU

"Victors write the histories," Winston Churchill is credited as saying.

Except sometimes that's not true.

The planet has been going through the biggest revolution in two centuries in how it builds cities. Every urban area worldwide that is growing is growing like Fairfax, Va., with multiple urban cores far beyond the old downtowns. I call them "Edge Cities." You see the pattern everywhere— not only in Dallas, Portland and Boston but now Sydney, Lagos, Cairo, Bangkok, Djakarta, and Kuala Lumpur. (Not to mention Stockholm, London, Amsterdam, Paris, Toronto, and Milan.)

Many writers about cities, however, hate these vast new job centers, refusing to study them seriously, wishing them away, villifying them as "sprawl."

Sigh.

Given that these Edge Cities are now the standard form of global urbanism, and given that they are unquestionably our centers of commerce, industry, and wealth creation, from Silicon Valley, California, to Buckhead, Georgia, to Fairfield County, Connecticut, this is sad.

But a new generation is coming. Doubtless its members will be interested in understanding how they grew up. They will want to know how it came to be that "Edge Cities" were the places in which the vast majority of ordinary people in the early 21st century came to live, work, play, pray, shop, educate themselves and die. They will want to know what the people who created these places thought they were doing. When that day arrives, they may be grateful for *The Fight for Fairfax*.

So, consider this a note to a future historian.

The Fight for Fairfax is not the politically correct version of history, nor is it the the the cosmic overview. But it is the version created and paid for by the people who actually did the deed. They knew that what they accomplished was important, and before they all passed on, they wanted to leave a record. *The Fight for Fairfax* is it.

Without a doubt, Fairfax is an amazing place. Its lessons echo globally. In two generations, Fairfax went from a rural backwater little changed since the Civil War, to one of the richest, best employed, best educated, most diverse, safest, million-plus population urban areas on earth. It sports five Edge Cities—one of the densest concentrations in the world—each of which is bigger than downtown Memphis and some bigger than downtown Minneapolis or Seattle. In fact, Fairfax now routinely brags that it is the center of the Washington metropolitan area, with the District of Columbia being only the ceremonial and entertainment periphery.

Those who fought tooth and nail against this transformation, and were vanquished, are treated politely in this book. But they are not its focus. This book is about the people who made it happen. That is its value.

It's about crazy old one-eyed Marcus Bles and George Johnson and Sid Dewberry and Jerry Halpin and Milt Peterson and Earle Williams and of course, Til Hazel—the man who did more to shape the built environment of the Washington metropolitan area than any man since Pierre L'Enfant, and I'm not so sure about L'Enfant.

In the late 1980s when, as a callow young *Washington Post* hard charger, I first started reporting on the phenomenon I would christen "Edge City," my plan was to find out who was "doing this to us," and get somebody indicted. It seemed to me that Fairfax and its ilk was the epitome of everything that was wrong. But as it became obvious to me that the generation that created this new world was far more in touch with the desires of the American people than their intellectual critics, I softened. I particularly remember the day I interviewed one participant who said, "Go a little easy on these guys. When they started, they didn't know that what they were doing was possible."

So shoot me. I find I have a place in my heart for people who invent the future out on the new frontier, without waiting for anyone to tell them what they should do. It's what Alexis de Tocqueville saw as the heart of what it meant to be an American.

The Fight for Fairfax is their story, told their way.

Joel Garreau is a student of culture, values and change and the author of *Edge City: Life on the New Frontier.*

Acknowledgement

Gratitude must be expressed to all who contributed their time in lengthy and often multiple in-person and telephone interviews and email correspondence. Heartfelt thanks to my dear editor, Betsy Holt, in appreciation of her constant encouragement that the manuscript had merit, and to my research assistant, Richard "Dick" Harless, for putting in yeoman's hours digging up hundreds of documents thought lost to antiquity. Kudos also to Jerry Gordon and the Fairfax County Economic Development Authority for letting me rootle around in their archives for days on end, and to George Mason University for its unwavering support of the project. This book was a two-year labor of love made sweeter by the support of my wife Jennifer Sue Johnson, and children Isabelle, Charles and Mia.

Foreword

T his is the story of a remarkable place that lies at the junction of the Old South and the New South. In just sixty years, this place—Fairfax County, Virginia—has awakened from the centuries old remnants of tobacco plantations and dairy farms to become the technological leader of the New South. Thirty thousand people lived here in the 1930s; today, the population exceeds 1.1 million. Fairfax County rivals Silicon Valley as a technological haven, but it surpasses its California cousin in most quality of life respects. This vibrant economic hub is blessed with modern industries, high paying jobs, superior public schools, high educational attainment, a multicultural workforce, low unemployment, great housing stock, numerous open spaces, and superb medical facilities. And yet it could have turned out much differently.

Fairfax County's modern history serves as an exemplar of economic prosperity and an archetype of the Information Age. Located midway between the rural Blue Ridge Mountains and the nation's political epicenter in Washington, D.C., Fairfax initially benefited from the expanding postwar federal government and the lucrative contracts Uncle Sam dispensed across the Potomac River. In the 1950s and 1960s, it became Washington's bedroom as hordes of bright, young newcomers planted stakes in the region.

The established political machine, however, soon took umbrage with this momentous influx and tried to curtail the expansion via an array of questionable growth-control measures. Had it succeeded, this book might instead be about Montgomery County in Maryland, also on the perimeter of Washington, D.C. Fortunately, a handful of visionary leaders in Fairfax County's private sector—a zoning attorney, a university president, a few defense contractor CEOs, and several real estate developers, engineers, and homebuilders—saw what the county could become.

This close group of civic-minded individuals perceived Fairfax not as Washington's bedroom, but as an economic axis all its own. Under their leadership, Fairfax County became more than simply a prototypical "edge" suburb in which citizens relied on jobs in the adjacent city (in this case, the nation's capital). Instead, the paradigm was reversed, and the county became the place where city dwellers sought employment. The edge became the axis, and today the number of available jobs in Fairfax County dwarfs employment in the District of Columbia. Job growth now outpaces population growth, a ratio that is expected to persist through at least 2030.

Historically, the private sector has been America's economic engine, but in recent decades growth has become a pejorative word, interpreted outside the context of what it can provide economically, socially, and culturally. Back in the 1960s and 1970s, Fairfax County's government embraced this notion and thus failed to accept the power of the human survival instinct: that is, people go where the jobs are. Washington had them aplenty, and Fairfax was next door. But instead of accommodating the newcomers, the local government tried to push people elsewhere—an impossible quest.

As the county's population burgeoned, this intrepid group of business leaders realized they had the rare opportunity to build something vital and robust from the ground up. They saw themselves not as stewards preserving the status quo, but as engineers of a modern Mesopotamia. They understood that more commerce and industry in Fairfax translated into more dollars to pay for vital infrastructure, thus reducing the tax burden on all residents.

While fighting no-growthers in the local arena, these leaders also courted Main Street politicians in the state capital of Richmond for the county's fair share of financial resources to build roads, schools, and sewers. They created a major institution of higher learning at George Mason University that would catalyze the region's economy in much the same way that Stanford University had with what is now Silicon Valley. They reinvented land use and zoning, building superb residential communities and erecting virtual cities like Reston and Tysons Corner that stand as tributes to modern planning. They put their touch on hospitals, education, and a score of cultural attractions and parks. Their imprint is indelible, and their story serves as a lesson to other municipalities on the brink of a new destiny.

Certainly they could have made their fortunes and said to hell with Fairfax. Instead, they devotedly built the county brick by brick against enormous odds, fighting populist politicians, turning the tax base on its head by luring hundreds of major technology companies to the region, and opening the channels for the rich quality of life features that followed. They invented Fairfax County, nurturing it into a place where its citizens could see tomorrow.

Table of
Contents

U.S. Highway 1 intersected with an unpaved Gum Springs Road between Alexandria and Mount Vernon in 1930.

CHAPTER 1

The Great
Migration

I n the aftermath of the Second World War, many urban cities in the United States underwent a major shift in population. City dwellers, many of them returning servicemen who received low-cost housing benefits from the federal government, uprooted their families and migrated to new, relatively inexpensive suburban housing developments that were sprouting outside city borders.

One bright summer afternoon in 1945, John Tilghman Hazel Jr., a broad-shouldered, precocious lad just two-and-a-half months shy of his fifteenth birthday, spied the first of these new developments in Fairfax County, Virginia. Til, as he was called, was at work on his family's dairy farm, hauling hay in a neighbor's field. Hearing the unfamiliar buzz of construction at an adjacent property, he immediately grasped its significance. He was an especially bright boy who knew all about the war, reading up on it daily and impressing his teachers at Washington–Lee High School—named for Virginians George Washington and Robert E. Lee— with his aptitude in many subjects. In his spare time between homework and tending the 110-acre farm, located west of Arlington County and south of the Potomac River about a mile from the crossroads in McLean, he pored over encyclopedias.

As a boy, John Tilghman "Til" Hazel Jr. labored on chores and operated heavy equipment on the family farm.

His father, John Tilghman Hazel Sr., had purchased the initial acreage from his father-in-law, Will W. Douglas, a successful businessman. John built a small house on the property and ordered a series of pamphlets on subsistence farming from the U.S. Department of Agriculture, which Til studied intensely. John had grown up hungry in nearby Georgetown during the First World War and had fretted about the war clouds gathering in Europe and the threat of food rationing it posed at home. Property was the antidote to his worries, offering land for growing crops and grazing livestock.

John's father, William Hazel, was the more intrepid type. He had joined the 7th Cavalry as a teenager in the 1890s, a few years after the famed unit massacred the Sioux Dakota tribe at Wounded Knee, the battle that ended the Great Indian Wars. Upon his return East around 1906, William took employment as a stable manager at Chestnut Farms Dairy in Washington, D.C. In the 1920s, he started his own dairy farm near Falls Church, Virginia, and fully expected his son to join him in the business.

John had other ideas. He became the first member of his family to finish college and entertain such grand ambitions as a career in medicine, serving as a resident at the Georgetown University School of Medicine through 1930. He married Ruth Douglas around this time, and on October 29, 1930—exactly one year after the stock market crash of 1929—Til was born. John then moved his family to Boston, where he spent five years with the Public Health Service at the Merchant Marine Hospital in Chelsea, Massachusetts. In 1935, he opened an office on Wilson Boulevard in Clarendon, a small subsection of Arlington County. Attached to it was the family home.

Four years later, in 1939, John purchased his father-in-law's farm. But while the farm assuaged his anxiety about putting food on the table, he spent very little time there, and the family never lived in the farmhouse. It was inhabited by a hired man and later by John's parents. In 1944, Ruth managed the family and farm enterprises while John took a two-year surgical service at the Mayo Clinic. Ruth, who had been born and reared in Arlington, had roots in southern Maryland. Her grandfather was a drummer boy in a Confederate unit from southern Maryland during the Civil War. Several times a week, she left Clarendon for the farm, overseeing the efforts of her son, who was assisted by his aging grandfather William and the hired man.

Til left the house in Clarendon after school and during the summers, traveling eight miles to the farm, sometimes by bicycle. He was a strong, capable boy, driving tractors and trucks at the age of twelve, and physically built to handle the rigors of farm work. At fifteen, he operated a small, four-foot combine and a baler hitched to a borrowed tractor. It was a substantial improvement over the draft horses and teams of mules that he had labored behind in previous summers. His farm chores forged a bond with his father, who was otherwise absorbed in his medical work, tending to his patients and co-founding Arlington Hospital—one of the first hospitals in northern Virginia—in the 1940s. "Dad was all doctor: 150 percent medicine," says Til. "Farming gave us something to talk about."[1]

That late summer day while hauling hay in 1945, Til glimpsed the initial dig at what would become the Pimmit Hills subdivision, the first sin-

A farmer harrows a cornfield on a dairy farm in Fairfax County with a horse and mule team, c. 1940.

gle-family home community built in Fairfax County after the war. On quarter-acre lots, hundreds of rectangular one-story, three-bedroom frame houses would redefine the landscape, many purchased by returning war veterans leveraging their G.I. Bill loans. "It hit me that the area was changing," says Til, "and this was a good thing."

New Subdivisions Spring Forth

The change occurring in Fairfax County was in fact the most pronounced the region had experienced since the first colonists had arrived at the dawn of the seventeenth century. The impetus was Washington, D.C., the postwar capital of the Western world. The federal government had grown to meet the exigencies of the Second World War, continuing to expand during the ensuing Cold War with the Soviet Union. Thousands of new employment opportunities cropped up in the District, and soon there were so many people working in Washington who wanted to live in Fairfax County that an acute housing shortage transpired. Local real estate developers and home builders like George Offutt—who built the first sections of Pimmit Hills—George Yeonas, M. T. Broyhill, Carl Hengen, Vernon Lynch, and Edward Rutledge Carr struggled to construct houses quickly enough to satisfy demand. (George Yeonas's son, Steve, would later build the Yeonas Building Company into an area powerhouse.)

Edward Carr's real estate interests in Fairfax were located in Springfield, a rural tract of scattered abandoned homes with no water or sewer services. During the war, Carr had erected subdivisions in Arlington County. Carr had selected Springfield as the location for his newest subdivision because it was the last sizable tract of undeveloped land close to Washington, D.C. It was also to be intersected by the Henry Shirley Memorial Highway, named for the state's former highway commissioner. "Many of the military buyers [have] located in Springfield with a view toward settling there in retirement," *The Washington Post* reported. "It's a natural place for members of the armed forces to live—near Fort Belvoir [and] straight down Shirley Highway to the Pentagon."[2] Still, when Carr announced his strategy, "people thought he was nuts—it was too far out," says his son, builder Edward Carr Jr.[3]

The four-lane Shirley Highway was developed to provide egress to federal employees traveling from the Pentagon in Arlington County to Washington. Built in 1943, the Pentagon—the highest-capacity office building in the world at 3.7 million square feet—was one of the first federal government entities to locate outside the District, although its mail-

Pimmit Hills, built after the Second World War, was one of the first subdivisions of its kind.

ing address remains Washington, D.C. In 1944, a two-and-a-half mile section of Shirley Highway opened from the Pentagon road system to Route 7. Five years later, the highway was fully open to passenger cars, and state highway officials bragged that their new expressway would save 617,000 gallons of gasoline and 1,500 tires, sparing commuters seven million miles of travel each year.[4]

Carr drew a series of concentric circles around the District, saw that a ring intersected Shirley Highway at Springfield, and purchased the largest piece of land available. "Dad bought a 3,200-acre-tract from the Lynch family in 1946, built some roads and then a mile-and-a-half-long 'trunk' to get sewerage and water into the area by the 1950s," says Edward Carr Jr.[5]

The first house in the subdivision, a brick rambler that sold for less than $18,000, was built in 1948.[6] By 1955, more than two thousand houses dotted the landscape, including one for the Carr family. Presciently, Carr had drawn up a Master Plan for the community that included schools, churches, shopping centers, and parks, making Springfield a veritable oasis in a desert. Beyond the subdivision was "absolutely nothing," notes Carr's son. "Just dirt and second growth timber. That, and the road to Washington."

Colonial Times and the Other Washington

Dirt and second growth timber describes much of Fairfax County prior to the Second World War. The county dates its colonial history to 1607, when Captain John Smith arrived and founded the settlement of Jamestown, part of what later became James City County in the Commonwealth of Virginia. Both Jamestown and James City County were named for England's King James I, who ruled from 1603 to 1625 and is remembered for the King James Bible. Jamestown itself was funded by the Virginia Company, a group of venture capitalists in England who believed the area lay claim to vast deposits of gold and silver like Mexico.

It was not to be. Most of the 104 original colonists perished from typhoid, dysentery, and other diseases caused by the mosquito-infested area's contaminated water. The high death toll explains why the local

Tsenacomoco Indians led by Chief Powhatan resisted attacking the colonists: he figured the settlers would eventually die out.[7] But the chief was mistaken. Another six thousand colonists arrived in Jamestown between 1607 and 1624. Although seventy-five percent of them died within a few years—most succumbing to water-borne illnesses—those who survived gave birth to the country's first industry: a glass-making factory.

By the 1620s, tobacco had replaced glass as the colony's chief industry, with nearly fifty thousand pounds exported to England annually. Unfortunately, tobacco, more than virtually any other plant, can deplete nutrients from the earth. Although the Indians had grown tobacco for centuries, they planted it in small quantities alongside corn, potatoes, squash, and other vegetables. Driven by high demand for the leaf overseas, the colonists employed monoculture agricultural methods, harvesting large fields of tobacco that would eventually wear out the land.[8]

Gradually the Tsenacomoco were displaced by the newcomers. Many perished from smallpox, malaria, and other diseases unwittingly brought to the New World by the colonists. With few Indians left by 1649, King Charles II granted several English noblemen the deeds to all the land between the Rappahannock and Potomac Rivers: nearly 5.3 million acres in northern Virginia.

Seventy years later, most of this land had come into the possession of Thomas, Sixth Lord of Fairfax. Lord Fairfax built a home for his family on the property of Belvoir, the ruins of which today lie on the grounds of Fort Belvoir, purchased by the U.S. Army Corps of Engineers in 1910. In 1748, Lord Fairfax made the acquaintance of surveyor George Washington, a distant relative then just sixteen years old. Impressed by the young man's energy and talents, he employed Washington to survey his lands west of the Blue Ridge mountains. He granted Lawrence Washington, George's older half-brother, a large tract of land in what Washington would name "Mount Vernon," which George inherited upon Lawrence's death in 1752. Lord Fairfax also deeded a sizable parcel in 1754 to George Mason, a close friend of his cousin William. Mason later called his land Gunston Hall.

Successful businessmen and tobacco planters, Mason and Washington attended the Constitutional Convention in Philadelphia in 1787, where Washington, previously commander-in-chief of the Continental army in the Revolutionary War, presided. At the convention, Mason insisted that a bill of rights detailing the specific rights of citizens be included in the proposed Constitution of the United States. Although Mason lost this battle at the time, his Virginia Declaration of Rights is said to have influenced James Madison in drafting the bill of rights that was passed two years hence at the First Federal Congress of the United States in New York. On December 15, 1791, the U.S. Bill of Rights was ratified by three-fourths of the states. The French Declaration of Rights of Man and the Citizen, issued after the French Revolution, is also based on Mason's pioneering work.

Dedicated to their land and the county they inhabited, both men continued to direct their farming operations during the war. Washington wrote a lengthy letter to his farm manager regarding the spring planting season on the night before the Battle of Trenton, and Mason refused political office several times because of the demands of his Gunston Hall farm. Such intertwining of business and the land would become a theme that coursed throughout the history of the county.

Cultivating the Land

The county had been named for Lord Fairfax three decades before the war. In 1742, the Virginia legislature carved it out of Prince William County, naming the town of Springfield near present day Tysons Corner as the seat of government. [9]The new county was bordered on the north, east, and south by the Potomac River, and on the southwest by the Occoquan Creek. In 1757, Loudoun County was created from the county's northwestern section, and in 1789, an eastern portion of Fairfax became part of the District of Columbia, which was designated the new nation's capital in 1790. The city of Alexandria was also cleaved from the county as a separate entity and ceded to the U.S. government to become part of the District in 1801. Today, Fairfax County encompasses 407 square miles, of which 12 square miles is water.

These trans-Potomac sections were eventually returned to Virginia in 1846, becoming the twenty-six-square-mile Arlington County and the city of Alexandria, respectively. At present, Fairfax County is located south and west of Washington, separated from the District by the city of Alexandria and Arlington County to the south and west, and by the Potomac River, which rolls seaward for fifteen miles through rocky gorges and forested hills along the county's northern border.

Much of the county in the mid-1700s was virgin wilderness intersected by rivers and streams. Tobacco remained the economic mainstay and chief export, and tobacco notes were the primary form of currency for purchasing goods and paying debts.[10] Most of the county's five thousand people were involved in the growing, harvesting, packing, and selling of tobacco; one-third of them were African slaves toiling on the tobacco plantations and serving as domesticated help. [11]

To provide egress for the bustling tobacco trade, forests were cleared and "rolling roads" were sliced out of the countryside. The term referred to the large wooden barrels called hogsheads that were filled with tobacco leaves and then pulled by oxen to tobacco warehouses and landings along the Potomac and Occoquan rivers for shipment to England. Many of the county's small towns were built or expanded along these gently sloping roads, including Fairfax, Falls Church, Chantilly, and Centreville.

By the early 1800s, however, several factors had conspired to cause the demise of tobacco cultivation. The constant overplanting had ruined the soil and the abolition of primogeniture laws had dissolved the old tobacco plantations. The county evolved into a more conventional farming district with scattered small farms producing corn, wheat, rye, oats, and potatoes. Cattle, sheep, and hogs were other main sources of income,

Thomas, Sixth Lord Fairfax. The painting by Sir Joshua Reynolds hangs in the Alexandria Washington Masonic Lodge No. 22, Alexandria Virginia.

In 1752, George Washington inherited a large tract of land in Mount Vernon that was once owned by Lord Fairfax. The Potomac River is visible from the house.

as was the timber harvested in the southern and central parts of the county where the acidic soil had largely prevented tobacco growth and other agricultural pursuits.

The loss of tobacco depressed the local economy, paring the county's population from 13,317 in 1800 to about 9,200 in 1830. Another twenty years would pass before the county again numbered ten thousand inhabitants. Travelers described Fairfax County in the 1840s as desolate, with "scrub pine, overgrowing abandoned tobacco fields, deserted houses on small farms that could neither keep nor sustain their occupants, and poor conditions of overland travel."[12]

Still, the county saw improvements. Many of its first post offices were established in the 1840s and 1850s, including Burke's Station Post Office and Fairfax Station Post Office. By the beginning of the twentieth century, three railroad lines were in operation, all of them ending in Alexandria. The lines stretched south toward Richmond and west through Fairfax Station toward Manassas. With such improved transportation, larger farms sprouted along the rail lines, and wealthy

Washingtonians bought summer homes near rail stops and the old rolling roads. Unfortunately, the Civil War would soon put a halt to such prosperity and budding growth.

Restarting the Economic Engine

On May 23, 1861, Virginia seceded from the Union and thereafter Fairfax County was squeezed between Confederate troops occupying the western region and Union troops occupying the regions to the north and east. Soldiers from both camps traversed from one side to the other, destroying private properties and businesses en route. Centreville was a staging area for the pivotal First and Second Battles of Manassas— both won by the South. The Union army took over the railroads to transport soldiers and supplies, and an estimated one third of county residents fled to safer harbors in the north or south. Area nursing centers—several established by Clara Barton—heaved with the wounded, and mortuaries overflowed with the dead. The sight of President Abraham Lincoln reviewing seventy-five thousand Union troops at Bailey's Crossroads in November 1861 stirred local resident Julia Ward Howe to write "The Battle Hymn of the Republic." After the war, discarded cannons and other weaponry were a common sight along rutted roads.

The county's economic engine restarted once Virginia was readmitted to the Union in 1870. At the time, Fairfax featured two railroads: one that ran from Alexandria to Mount Vernon, and another that shuttled between Arlington and Leesburg—now a bike trail and powerline corridor. As soon as the railroads were back in operation, the roads were cleared and agricultural commerce was reestablished. Although ranked twenty-ninth in size among Virginia counties in 1870, Fairfax was first in dairy production, second in potatoes, fourth in hay, and fifth in all market products combined.[13]

By 1900, the county's population had reached 18,580 residents, though it was still just a fraction of the Greater Washington Metropolitan Region's four hundred thousand inhabitants.[14] Most of its residents lived within six incorporated towns, "all reached by one or more railroads, and all in a thriving and prosperous condition," boasted *A 1907 Industrial and Historical Sketch of Fairfax County,* published by the Fairfax Board of Supervisors, the county's governing body, which represented each of its six magisterial districts at the time. (A seventh magisterial district was formed in 1953 with a seventh supervisor to eliminate the problem of a tie.)[15]

Among the incorporated towns was Falls Church, which claimed 1,100 citizens and an excellent connection to Washington, D.C., via the Washington, Arlington, and Falls Church Electric Railway. Electric trolley lines also connected commuters from the towns of Fairfax, Herndon, Vienna, and Clifton to the District. "Verily, Fairfax County, old in its history and hoary in its traditions, is throbbing with a new life of activity and enterprise," the Board of Supervisors waxed lyrically in 1907. "Certainly no other section [of Virginia] extends a more cordial welcome and more attractive inducements to the investor and home-seeker . . . She is attracting settlers from all parts of the Union and even from foreign countries."

In reality, Fairfax grew only slightly over the next twenty-five years. Despite the federal government's expansion during and after the First World War, the county's population increased by just five thousand residents in 1910 to twenty-five thousand inhabitants in 1930, a mere doubling from 1790.[16] In contrast, Santa Clara County in California, home to what would someday be called Silicon Valley for the semiconductor chips of silicon that were manufactured in the area, certainly had a head start, population-wise. Santa Clara boasted 145,000 people in 1930—approximately 120,000 more inhabitants than Fairfax County counted. Nevertheless, expectations remained high for future growth, and plans were put in motion to prepare for it.

New Industry and the New Deal

Fairfax County began laying the groundwork for expansion in the 1920s. The county established a school board and public health department, and Virginia Governor Harry Byrd earmarked significant state funds to pave old roads with asphalt and construct the state's first highways, an activity overseen by the new Virginia Department of Highways. By 1928, improved, hard-surfaced roads connected twenty-five of the thirty-four communities shown on maps of Fairfax County to Washington. Railroads serviced twenty-two of these communities.

As improvements were made, local officials increasingly began to view land use control as the government's responsibility. Later, the Board of Supervisors passed an ordinance requiring that subdivision plans be approved by the County Engineer. Another ordinance dictated that roads linking subdivisions to the general road system must be a minimum width. A sewer ordinance was also passed, although many years would elapse before the sewer system was integrated[17]; by 1955 only less than half of the county's residents would be served by trunk line sanitary sewers.[18]

The Great Depression of the 1930s precipitated the county's first real population jump. President Franklin Delano Roosevelt's response to the country's financial freefall—his "New Deal"—significantly increased federal programs and bureaus, causing a spike in the number of federal employees. While dairying was still the major industry in Fairfax in 1938, accounting for more than $2 million in industry, more and more county residents were now finding work in the nation's capital. Plans were put forth to build what would later become Interstate 66, a major highway connecting commuters in northern Virginia to Washington. But Arlington County residents met the plans with opposition and litigation, effectively postponing construction for decades.[19]

The surge in new residents compelled the Board of Supervisors to appoint, via state-enabling legislation, an independent, nonpartisan Planning Commission in 1938 to create more comprehensive zoning regulations. Each supervisor appointed a member to the commission. Meanwhile, the local Chamber of Commerce appointed a special committee on property assessment procedures to map all county land and create a new system for describing properties and their sales histories. Land books previously indicated only whether property was owned by "white" or "colored" people, and if it was "improved" or "unimproved."[20] These actions launched Fairfax County into the modern era of land use planning.

The Board of Supervisors also took the lead in establishing public services for the forty-one thousand residents, including a countywide library system in 1939 and a police department in 1940. The following year, the county adopted its first zoning ordinance with input from the Planning Commission.[21] The ordinance segregated incompatible land uses, regulating home construction and renovations by requiring building permits and imposing penalties for noncompliance. Although it made only a crude distinction among residential, commercial, industrial, and agricultural uses, it represented another significant foray by the local government into land use planning.

The new ordinance zoned the densely populated eastern third of Fairfax into three residential districts permitting a minimum lot size of one-half acre or less, and the western two-thirds for minimum lots of one-half acre or more. In 1956, the Board of Supervisors amended the ordinance based on a suggestion by Supervisor Joseph Freehill, restricting the western two-thirds to lots of two acres or more, a veritable quadrupling in lot size. The Board's obvious intent through the Freehill Amendment was to impede the building of homes in the western region.[22]

While the Second World War added more than five hundred thousand people to the Greater Washington Metropolitan Region, the population of Fairfax County experienced slower growth. After the war ended, however, the fuse was lit for a significant boom in population. Suddenly, job opportunities generated by the postwar expansion of the federal government made Washington, and its outskirts the third fastest growing region in the country—although most of the growth occurred in Arlington and Alexandria counties. Housing construction soared, prompting the Board of Supervisors to issue another new ordinance in 1947 governing subdivisions of low density, single-family homes.

By 1950, ninety-nine thousand people called Fairfax County home, a virtual quadrupling in twenty years and a 140 percent increase within the last decade.[23] The onset of the Korean War and mounting tensions over the threat of a nuclear war with the Soviet Union encouraged further government expansion. According to a study by consultant Homer Hoyt for the county's Planning Commission, by 1953, 90 percent of county workers were federal employees or working for service industries contracted by the federal government.[24] That year, Uncle Sam employed more than two million civilians, up from 699,000 in 1940.[25] These workers needed to live somewhere, and the choices were limited. It had to be Washington, D.C., Montgomery County, Maryland—or Fairfax County, Virginia.

Establishing Vital Public Services

As the decade of tail-finned automobiles, drive-in movie theaters, and rock 'n' roll drew near, Til Hazel was a crew cut sixteen-year-old still toiling at his family's dairy farm during summers and school afternoons. His maternal grandmother had given the Hazels a one-and-a-half-ton Dodge truck to haul sugar corn to the wholesale farmer's market on Maine Avenue in the District of Columbia and sacked wheat to the Wilkins-Rogers Milling Company at the Georgetown waterfront. While Til tended to the farm, his brother Bill—who was four years younger—hawked produce from the farm's small vegetable plot at a stand not far from where the Hazels lived in Arlington County. "The farm was the subsistence operation Dad had always envisioned, producing food primarily for the family, with surplus eggs, ham, milk, and so on going to friends and neighbors or [being] sold," Til says.

Thanks to the wise counsel of his class sponsor, a much-admired Latin teacher at Washington–Lee High School, Til decided to attend Harvard University rather than Iowa State, where he had pondered majoring in agriculture. In 1947, he left for Cambridge, Massachusetts, to study American history, returning occasionally to the farm in the summertime. One year he helped Bill streamline operations by enlarging the dairy barn by an additional ten stanchions. Til graduated cum laude from Harvard in 1951, and received a Juris Doctor degree from Harvard Law School three years later.

During this time Fairfax underwent extraordinary change. The county's rapid residential development and its related demands for additional schools, police, parks, and services required more sophisticated land use planning, more roads, and more public services. To assist in these needs, a new executive form of government was installed, replacing the former executive secretary government. The new system, passed by the electorate in 1950 and effective in January 1952, called for the Board of

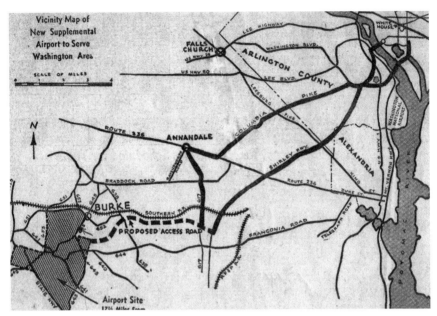

A map illustrating the original airport proposal site in Burke, Virginia, was published in *The Evening Star*, June 14, 1951.

Supervisors to appoint a County Executive responsible for managing local government in conjunction with the Board. In effect, the County Executive was responsible for administrating all county affairs under the Board's authority, such as criminal justice, social and health services, waste treatment, taxes, and business and economic development.

In 1950, the Board created the Fairfax County Park Authority. The Park Authority was entrusted with preserving environmentally sensitive land resources, and later, preserving areas of historic significance as well as purchasing land for recreational parks and facilities. The Board's initial goal in creating the authority was to reserve fifteen acres of parkland per one thousand county residents, an objective it ultimately exceeded. In 1959, the Park Authority hired its first salaried professional director, Fred M. Packard. Unfortunately many parks in the 1950s and 1960s were limited to whites. For example, African Americans were barred from Great Falls Park—which had been bought with county funds and operated by the Park Authority—because the Commonwealth of Virginia required separate facilities for blacks.[26]

In 1950, the U.S. Congress passed the Second Washington Airport Act, a nod to the growing need for businessmen and government officials to travel to and from the nation's capital. The act set aside funds for the creation of an additional international airport to relieve congestion at Washington National Airport, built in 1941. In 1951, the U.S. Department of Justice posted a notice at the Burke's Station Post Office that 4,520 acres in Burke would be condemned to make way for the new airport. James Wilding, former president and CEO of the Metropolitan Washington Airports Authority, recalls, "There was some money on Capitol Hill to make things happen—and before you knew it, Burke, which had good access to the District via the Shirley Highway, was selected as the site."[27]

An Officer and a Bona Fide Virginia Gentleman

Of these assorted developments, none was more important than the 1951 decision by the Board of Supervisors to develop the county's first long-range Master Plan. A major reason for the plan was the large number of septic tank failures, as well as the need to provide sewers to new residents. Intermittent water shortages and the lack of a unified water system were other factors. "[We need] a comprehensive plan for orderly land development, a public improvement and services program, the control of land uses, and the control of land subdivision, with full provision for needs of recreation," stated County Supervisor Anne Wilkins, a leading advocate of strict government controls at the time.[28]

The Board hired a consultant, Francis Dodd McHugh, to direct the Planning Commission's technical staff and the new County Comprehensive Planning Office it had created when developing the Master Plan. McHugh—who had previously executed a similar plan for Westchester County, New York[29]—was given two years to publish the Master Plan. Among his new hires in the Planning Office was civil engineer Rosser Payne. "We provided McHugh with the field network to check the topography, soil, and water supply, which he integrated into his plans for what the county should look like," Payne says. "We forecast that four hundred thousand people would reside in the county within twenty

Fairfax County Executive Carlton C. Massey raises a flag at the 1959 ceremonies during the construction of Fairfax Hospital.

years. Arlington County was basically full. Alexandria also was pretty full and was a historic city with not much room to grow anyway. Fairfax was where the action was."[30]

The Board also hired its first County Executive in March 1952. The appointee was a bona fide Virginia gentleman, Carlton C. Massey. Born in Post Oak, a crossroads in Spotsylvania County, Massey had served the previous eight years as manager of Henrico County, which surrounds the state capital of Richmond. His father had been a member of the Virginia House of Delegates, and he was an honors graduate of the

Virginia Polytechnic Institute, earning a bachelor's degree in civil engineering in 1928.

Level headed and self-effacing, the pipe-smoking Massey set a tone of professionalism in county government for nearly twenty years. He was committed to the proposition that the needs of citizens must be accommodated by a progressive government. Massey created several new government departments to oversee public services such as schools, sewer, and water systems, and established a sound financial base to fund these services via appropriate, voter-supported taxes and bonds. At Massey's urging, the Board passed a countywide sanitary sewer referendum in 1952—a reaction to the era's numerous septic tank failures. Soon funds were earmarked and a regulatory infrastructure created to build sewer lines in developing communities like Springfield.

The county's political and business leadership supported Massey virtually without hesitation. "Carlton was fully cognizant of the population growth that would occur, and was the glue that kept the Board of Supervisors together on the services and infrastructure required, from schools to sewerage," says Ralph Louk, Fairfax County's Commonwealth Attorney from 1954 to 1963. "The supervisors relied on him to lead the way."[31]

"We were very fortunate as a county to have Carlton, who was honest and professional, highly interested in planning, and had the support of Board [of Supervisors] Chairman Anne Wilkins [in the 1950s]," says Harriet "Happy" Bradley, who was elected to the Board of Supervisors in 1962. "He helped create the infrastructure to deal with the impending growth."[32]

Payne recalls staff meetings with Massey in his office every Friday morning. "There was no opposition to the county's growth at the time, just a desire to accommodate it as best we could," he says. "Washington, D.C., was growing like gangbusters, and Fairfax was envisioned as its 'bedroom community,' supplying workers to the federal government and the military."

Much of the county's growth was focused around Falls Church and Springfield, with the beginnings of expansion occurring in Annandale and Fairfax City. The remainder of the county, particularly the western

Seven Corners Shopping Center was the Washington, D.C. metro area's first major enclosed shopping mall, 1956.

two-thirds, remained largely rural. Bradley says that when she and her husband bought their first home in the area around McLean, "It was so rural, there wasn't even a stop sign at the intersection of Old Dominion and Route 123."

There wasn't much in the way of business either. The first non-agricultural company to build its headquarters in Fairfax was Melpar, an electronics contractor to the military. Melpar moved from Alexandria to Bailey's Crossroads in 1946 to conduct research on radar systems for Navy vessels, developing radar homing and warning gear for aircraft used in the Korean War. In 1952, the company built a brick campus-like office facility with rolling lawns and a small pond off Route 50 and Arlington Boulevard, a sight as foreign to local farmers as a UFO in their pastures.[33]

Other than a few grocery stores and other mom-and-pop-type operations, retail enterprises were also uncommon. For the most part, when county residents shopped, they ventured north to the District of Columbia. In preparing his economic survey of the county, Homer Hoyt noted that Fairfax residents spent $146 million a year in retail stores, but only $40 million of that total within the county. Hoyt felt certain that a regional shopping center would succeed in Fairfax. He estimated that 58 percent of the taxes received from the center would be pure profit, relieving residents of significant tax burdens.[34]

Welcome to the Neighborhoods

Rosser Payne was one of the first civil engineers in the new Fairfax County Comprehensive Planning Office.

Hoyt was right. The completion of Shirley Highway in 1951 changed the picture, and within three years, the Greater Metropolitan Washington Region's first major semi-enclosed shopping mall—Seven Corners—was built at the intersection of Wilson Boulevard, Route 7, and Arlington Boulevard near Shirley Highway in Falls Church. The mall boasted two anchor department stores, Garfinckel's and Woodward & Lothrop. To make way for the mall, the Board of Supervisors had rezoned for general business use all but one-and-a-half acres of a thirty-three-acre parcel of land owned by the Foote family. (The land had been purchased in 1865 by Frederick Foote, a former slave whose children inherited the property.[35]) After it was completed, Seven Corners was so besieged with shoppers that the Board petitioned the Virginia Department of Highways to widen area roads. Much of the shopping center was demolished and rebuilt in the late 1990s.

As businesses began to absorb some of the taxes needed to fund the county's expanding public services, the county lobbied to bring more companies into its fold. Soon residents and officials called for a revival of the Fairfax County Chamber of Commerce, which had been shuttered during the Second World War due to labor shortages and the absence of business leaders to run it. A new Chamber was formed in 1955. Unfortunately, it was largely unsuccessful in luring business to Northern Virginia, saddling more and more homeowners with the tax burden as new residents stormed the county.

Taxes were rising, and so was the volume of real estate—virtually all of it residential. From 1940 to 1954, the total value of county real estate jumped from $14.3 million to $192 million. More than $57 million in building permits were issued in 1954, with homes being completed at a rate of six hundred a month the following year. "What fifteen years ago was sleepy, 'unspoiled' Southern countryside has now become a vast bedroom and back yard for thousands lured to the world capital," *The Washington Post* stated in 1955. "And the sudden demands imposed on the county by the newcomers have stunned those charged with supervising it."[36]

The newspaper listed the county's needs as "water, sewers, education and supervision." Most of Fairfax County's housing developments followed the sanitary sewer trunk lines, as opposed to the highways. As a result, large parcels of land crisscrossed by Shirley Highway in 1955 were still undeveloped because sewers were not yet available.[37]

In 1953, Springfield—the community that Edward Carr built out of a virtual desert—celebrated its first birthday. The all-important water and sewer lines connecting 385 homes to a sewage package plant were in place. Just one year earlier, Springfield had been "a sea of mud, no roads and mostly in the planning minds" of Carr and others, stated *The Washington Post*. "Today the community is well on its way to establishment with over 1,000 inhabitants, hard surfaced thoroughfares and immediate plans for schools, shopping centers and other community facilities." Seventy-seven percent of Springfield's homebuyers worked for the federal government—not surprising given the area's proximity to the Pentagon, Fort Belvoir, and the Navy Annex.[38]

Many longtime county residents objected to the newcomers. "These New Yorkers, Californians and foreigners from the Midwest have taken over our churches," one woman told *The Washington Post*. "Their children are pushing our children out of their seats in the schools. They're buying up our choice land and razing some of our historic landmarks . . . We old Virginians just don't exist anymore."

The friction intensified as the days of old became a bygone era. By 1955, more than half the dwelling units in the county had been built since 1940, with construction most feverish in the McLean, Annandale, and Mount Vernon areas. Supervisors who expected a building boom were stunned by the proportions. From 1950 to 1955, the assessed valuation of real estate and other predictable sources of income in the county had swelled from $78 million to $265 million. And yet there was still only one office building of significant size in Fairfax.[39]

Bringing Home Big Business

Across the country in Santa Clara, California, Stanford University had funded a major research institute to buttress the region's economic development. The institute, founded in 1946, was now drawing a wide range of technology companies, including Eastman Kodak, General Electric, and Hewlett-Packard, the latter formed by William Hewlett and David Packard, graduate electronic engineers from Stanford's class of 1938. The university's Department of Electrical Engineering also kickstarted the computer age by leasing part of its facilities to nascent high-technology companies for ninety-nine years.

In the suburbs of Boston, a similar phenomenon was underway along Route 128, a sixty-five-mile-long partial circumferential highway. There, the area's major research universities, such as the Massachusetts Institute of Technology and Harvard University, nurtured the development of technological enterprises with funding provided primarily by the U.S. Department of Defense and the National Science Foundation.

Back in Fairfax, however, such businesses were slow in coming—and officials knew the county's residents would suffer for it. Once again, officials sounded a dire call for more private sector business within the county. "The county's great need," declared Planning Commission Chairman Keith Price in 1955, "is to get more industry in order to take some of the tax burden off homeowners."[40]

The Board of Supervisors envisioned that its Master Plan would establish the necessary infrastructure to attract more companies to Fairfax. In his proposal, Francis Dodd McHugh called for setting aside 4,432 acres in nine locations for light industry—all but one acre in the eastern one-third region along the railroads. His plans for the eastern portion also detailed an extensive road network and proposed the building of the Monticello Freeway from Arlington County to Charlottesville and the Jones Point–Cabin John loop (what is essentially now the Virginia portion of the Capital Beltway). The latter would provide greater access from both Fairfax County and Montgomery County in Maryland to the radial roads emanating from the District of Columbia.

For the undeveloped western two-thirds, McHugh recommended a three-to-five-acre minimum lot size to dissuade development, because he believed that the region would not have sewerage for another twenty-five years. This part of the plan, however, set off alarms in the west. Pressured by rural landowners who believed the zoning devalued the future development of their land, the Board and Planning Commission sent McHugh back to the drawing board.[41]

The controversy over the county's Master Plan underscored the two distinct views emerging about how Fairfax County should evolve. One group consisted of newcomers wanting to maintain the county's pastoral qualities; the other was comprised of rural landed gentry wishing to preserve the highest financial value of their properties. These landowners enjoyed majority representation on the Board and did not want to be hamstrung by the legislation proposed in McHugh's first draft.[42] They also had the support of real estate developers, pro-business groups like the Chamber of Commerce, and the Board of Supervisors.

These divergent forces squared off in the local election of 1955. But despite powerful backing from the pro-growth community, the suburban interests triumphed. The new supervisors on the Board aimed to slow the county's urbanization, declaring a six month zoning and residential land use moratorium in 1956 to secure time for a revised Master Plan. Two years later a "compromise" plan was unveiled, which reduced the three-to-five-acre minimum lot zoning in the western two-thirds of the county to a two-acre minimum, albeit without any supporting studies or documentation to back the decision.

The two-acre minimum lot size, suggested by Supervisor Joseph Freehill, became known as the "Freehill Amendment." The Board quickly approved it, giving no consideration to the provision of schools, transportation, and other related services and facilities in the western region. Its position was clear—the western two-thirds of the county would remain rural. Large landowners again protested the unconstitutionality of the zoning. This time they took their objections to the Virginia courts, launching a land use by litigation process that would determine much of the county's development in succeeding years—from planned roads to the provision of public services like water, sewerage, and schools.

An Attorney and Advocate

As the landowners took their arguments to court, Til Hazel also walked Virginia's halls of justice. Following his graduation from Harvard Law School in 1954, Til entered the U.S. Army Judge Advocate General's Corp, founded by George Washington in 1775. JAG, composed of army officers who are also lawyers, is dedicated to providing legal services to the army at all levels of command. After Til's honorable discharge in 1957, he returned to Virginia and became an attorney at the Arlington-based law firm of Jesse, Phillips, Klinge, and Kendrick, working out of the firm's satellite office in Fairfax. His initial task was to condemn and acquire land for the construction of two new highways: Interstate 66, and a massive circumferential highway to be called the "Capital Beltway." Both roads were funded by the Federal Aid Highway Act of 1956, also known as the National Interstate and Defense Highways Act.

The Beltway incorporated parts of the proposed Jones Point–Cabin John loop, and was planned as a sixty-four-mile artery that would circle Washington from a distance of approximately ten miles, assisting commuters traveling south and bypassing the capital in the event of nuclear attack. Much of the condemned property was abandoned farmland or otherwise vacant, and Til soon became an expert on zoning, land acquisition and eminent domain, the right of the state to take private property for public use. "Til Hazel came to know this land better than anybody," *The Washington Post Magazine* commented.[43]

Til's profound knowledge of land use and real estate development would eventually propel him to the forefront of the legal debates pitting the county's pro-business forces and landed gentry against the new suburbanites seeking to preserve a way of life they had, in fact, interrupted. More than any other Virginian since John Smith, Til Hazel—who as a young man had traversed his family's dairy farm on a borrowed tractor—would change the course of Fairfax County.

Traffic is nearly bumper-to-bumper on this four-lane stretch of the Capital Beltway (Route I-495), c. 1970.

CHAPTER 2

Crossroads of
Change

n the 1960s and 1970s, Fairfax County's government was determined to slow what was quickly realized to be an unstoppable force—people seeking jobs in the employment nexus of Washington, D.C., and wanting to buy homes and live in the less crowded, less expensive, and much safer suburb of Fairfax County.

The private sector, especially the burgeoning real estate development industry, had other ideas. Gerald T. Halpin was among this new class of visionary entrepreneurs. Where county officials only saw change, he envisioned a bright future. And wherever Jerry Halpin sensed opportunity, he quickly went after it with hard work and determination.

As a boy, he assiduously cleaned the floors at the aging elementary school in Scranton, Pennsylvania, where his father was the custodian. He always tried to finish before the winter sun dipped below the horizon, preferring a bit of daylight to deliver the Fuller Brushes that his two older brothers had hawked door to door. On weekends, Jerry made his way to Scranton's wealthier enclaves and peddled cherries, apples, and currants from his parents' small farm north of the city to earn a few extra pennies. He kept half the money and gave the rest to his family.

Born on February 15, 1923, Jerry, like many boys and girls his age, was forever marked by the Great Depression. Before taking on custodial duties, his father had been a regional sales manager at Reynolds Tobacco Company. When he lost his job he swallowed his pride and took the only work he could get. The family was close, and most everyone they knew also suffered and persevered. Work was the remedy for hardship, and Jerry never forgot it.

After graduating high school, Jerry took a job with a small plastic manufacturer to pay his tuition at St. Thomas College, where he enrolled in night classes. He soon found a better paying job as a glassblower at Radio Corporation of America, using the new lathe technology at RCA's plant in Harrison, New Jersey. When the Second World War erupted, he volunteered for the U.S. Marines, but failed the eye examination. Instead, he enlisted in the Construction Battalion of the U.S. Navy, learning carpentry and building fundamentals. He then spent about three years in the Pacific accompanying the U.S. Marines on invasions in Micronesia and Guam. Known as the "Seabees," the service's motto is "Can Do." In Jerry's case, it was an apt description.

Following his discharge in 1946, he entered Syracuse University on the G.I. Bill, painting houses to pay the tuition and saving the rest. Somehow he amassed enough cash to post a down payment on two boardinghouses. He lived in one of the rooms, renting out the rest to pay the mortgages. Jerry also obtained a newspaper franchise to deliver the Sunday edition of *The New York Times* and held down a full-time job with Retail Credit Co. When he graduated, he sold the boardinghouses and chalked up a modest profit—his first brush with the exhilarating world of real estate.

Jerry met his future bride, Helen Richter, at Syracuse, and in August 1950 they drove south to Virginia to begin their future. They had hoped to buy a small house in the new Pimmit Hills subdivision, but at $5,900, the prices were too steep. Instead, they rented a $59-a-month apartment on Bashford Lane in the city of Alexandria, three blocks from Helen's job as a secretary and accountant at Atlantic Research Corporation, a startup scientific firm. Jerry enrolled at Georgetown Law School, with a focus on real estate. Meanwhile, he kept his full-time job with Retail Credit, along with his part-time job as a carpenter at Fort Belvoir.

Then opportunity knocked. Jerry was a sharp poker player; it was a game he took to in college and had honed during the war. In 1951, after winning a game against the president of Atlantic Research, he was asked to oversee the bustling firm's business operations. Having already taken all the classes at Georgetown that interested him and with money tight, he took the position.

Fairfax County's First Headquarters

Atlantic Research was founded in 1949 by two enterprising engineers/scientists who had a $10,000 contract from the U.S. Navy to develop solid fuel propellants. As the Cold War thickened in the 1950s, the firm moved from its chemical manufacturing origins into the research and development of solid fuel rocket technology and systems. This progression was abetted by a series of acquisitions that Jerry had piloted. He was the sole businessman in a sea of scientists, managing the firm's accounting, security and human relations. He also oversaw building construction, administration, and mergers and acquisitions, and even helped the firm's partners—still his partners today—with their personal real estate investments to bolster their income on the side. As his colleagues said, Jerry had the Midas touch.

By the middle of the decade, with military orders flying in over the transom, Atlantic Research required larger manufacturing facilities. The few tracts left in Alexandria were too expensive, so Jerry shifted his gaze to Fairfax County, which boasted just one major office building at the time: Melpar, out on Route 50. He found three parcels totaling eighty-nine acres on Edsall Road and Shirley Highway—"in the middle of nowhere," he says—and bought them for $600,000.[44] What made the far-away tract feasible was its location on the road to Burke, the planned site of Virginia's second major airport.

In 1958, the firm erected its new headquarters, a novel building with a parabolic roof that looked like a bicycle seat. To shorten their daily commute, the Halpins purchased a small piece of land in Springfield for $900 in cash from real estate broker Ed Lynch, whose Virginia roots date back to the 1700s. They built a small house on the property for $29,000,

Jerry doing a fair share of the carpentry himself. "We were on our way," he says.

His path, however, was about to take a major detour. The same year that Atlantic Research moved into its uniquely shaped headquarters, the federal government nixed its plans to build a second airport at the Burke site, despite having already condemned and purchased thousands of acres in the region. The startling decision followed bitter protests from communities adjacent to Burke, and it had unforeseen ramifications for Jerry Halpin—and for Til Hazel, too. At the time, Jerry and Til didn't know each other, nor did they have any inkling how the government's change of course would alter their lives. But the abrupt adjustment would propel them both into the forefront of real estate development in Fairfax County.

A New Campus for "Cow College"

The Burke site might have been abandoned, but the rest of the county was bustling. To service the swelling population in the 1950s—from 98,500 people at the decade's onset to nearly 249,000 by its close—heroic efforts were undertaken by several public and private citizens to improve the county's education, health care, transportation, and water systems.

In June 1957, the Board of Supervisors voted to provide $25,200 in funding toward the establishment of a two-year branch college of the University of Virginia.[45] The following year University College opened with seventeen students enrolled at Bailey's Cross Roads School, a former elementary school with eight classrooms. The cows grazing in nearby fields easily outnumbered the students, prompting them to nickname their alma mater "Cow College."[46] Not that cows were an uncommon sight—dairying was still a major industry in the area. In 1956, 1,100 farms located within twenty-five miles of Washington, D.C., still operated in Fairfax.[47]

Seeking to support the fledgling institution, the town of Fairfax, led by Mayor Jack Wood, purchased and donated 150 acres for its new campus in 1958. By the time construction commenced two years later, "Cow College" had a new name: George Mason College of the University of Virginia, christened in honor of the author of the Virginia Declaration of Rights.

John Clinton "Jack" Wood was a native of New York City who had moved to Fairfax in 1944 to practice law. Six years later, Wood's eyesight had failed completely as the result of a hereditary condition, but it didn't slow him down. He served on the town council before becoming mayor, and when Fairfax was incorporated as a city in 1961, he was again elected as mayor. "Jack Wood was the driving force for arranging a campus to be located on land [adjacent] to Fairfax City, and deeding it to George Mason," says A. George Cook III, Distinguished Fellow from the School of Public Policy at George Mason University.[48] Wood later served as the first president of the college foundation and also its first rector.

The new campus's four buildings opened their doors to 356 students in the fall of 1964. Two additional buildings sprouted the following year, and plans mushroomed to acquire the school's adjacent properties to expand the campus from the original 150 acres gifted by Fairfax City. Nevertheless, the student population grew only modestly in the twenty-three years that the school was an extension of the University of Virginia. "It did not occur to the administration of UVA in the mid-sixties that a major institution of higher learning was necessary to the future of Northern Virginia, although it was vital to our future," recalls Til, who was the attorney for the Joint Governmental Control Board that acquired the school's adjacent properties.

Other crucial institutions in Fairfax County also hatched slowly. Northern Virginia had only two hospitals in the 1950s: Alexandria Hospital and Arlington Hospital, co-founded by Til's father, John, who relocated his medical practice in 1959 to the town of Fairfax, where his sons erected a medical office building for him. To raise the money to build a much-needed community hospital, County Executive Carlton Massey and Board of Supervisors Chairwoman Anne Wilkins urged the chartering of a nonprofit membership association. In motion, the Fairfax Hospital Association assembled a Board of Trustees comprised of local business and civic leaders.

One of those leaders, Grace Lucas, hosted a planning and development event at her home. Later, local leaders took their case to the streets, using a car with a loudspeaker affixed to the roof to solicit donations at crowded spots such as the Seven Corners shopping center.[49] These simple but effective fund drives were augmented by federal grants and $3 million in bonds, the latter requiring the hospital association be cleaved from county control.

On February 6, 1961, Fairfax Hospital opened at last—one half hour early to accommodate the premature arrival of a baby. The small facility, located just off Gallows Road near Route 50, had only 285 beds. Yet it was a start, growing and modernizing slowly but persistently under its first administrator, Franklin P. Iams.

Massive Reform—and Resistance

Public schools were another pressing need. As the county's population grew and the baby boom ignited, the one- and two-room rural schoolhouses that had dotted Northern Virginia for decades became inadequate to accommodate the influx of new students. In response, county superintendent Wilber Tucker Woodson advocated a building program in the 1950s that created one "classroom a day," and urged the election of government officials who supported the program. He also spearheaded bond issues, solicited federal grant monies, and worked tirelessly to create parent-teacher associations to lobby for more funding.

Woodson's efforts were remarkably successful. When he became superintendent of Fairfax County schools in 1929, fewer than five thousand students were enrolled. By the time he retired in 1961, the student population neared sixty thousand. During Woodson's tenure, the number of school buildings also increased from sixty-five to ninety-two, most of them substantially enlarged, while the value of school property increased from $707,000 to more than $72 million.[50] The county-sponsored school expansion program received national attention and was even favorably profiled in an NBC documentary in 1955.[51]

Commemorating Woodson's impact on the school system, officials named W.T. Woodson High School—the largest high school in the Commonwealth of Virginia when it opened in 1962—for the superintendent. When apprised of the tribute, Woodson humbly replied, "I appreciate the honor, but I think you made a mistake."[52]

Of course, the dark side to Virginia's education reform was its unwavering adherence to the "separate but equal" racial segregation of schools. After the U.S. Supreme Court ruled segregation unconstitutional in the landmark *Brown v. Board of Education* case in 1954, Virginia Senator Harry Flood Byrd launched "Massive Resistance," a campaign to delay and otherwise thwart desegregation. "If we can organize the Southern States for massive resistance to this order I think that in time the rest of the country will realize that racial integration is not going to be accepted in the South," Senator Byrd asserted. (The Byrds trace their lineage to the First Families of Virginia, including William Byrd II of Westover Plantation, who established the City of Richmond.)

Massive Resistance was enshrined in the state's new constitution, and several laws were passed and new public agencies created to prevent school integration. Various Virginia politicians, including Governor Thomas Bahnson Stanley, sided with Senator Byrd, and in 1956 the state General Assembly adopted a resolution of "interposition," defying the authority of the federal courts. (Under the doctrine of interposition, which is based on state sovereignty, a state can interpose between an unconstitutional federal mandate and local authorities.)

The Virginia Supreme Court fired back in 1959, ruling that Massive Resistance was unconstitutional. Virginia ultimately, if begrudgingly, complied with desegregation, and on September 28, 1960, nineteen intrepid African American students enrolled at eight previously all-white schools in Fairfax.[53] As desegregation took hold across the nation, more white families hopped on the suburban bandwagon, seeking new housing in open spaces and more desirable places to live. Unfortunately, due to economic conditions or racial discrimination, their African American counterparts were frequently unable to follow.[54]

Water Wars

Back at the turn of the twentieth century, Fairfax officials had touted the county's "pure, soft water" and its "medicinal properties," which they attributed to the water's high iron and magnesia content. "There is not a square mile of surface . . . upon which cannot be found a running stream or a bold spring," boasted officials in 1907.[55] But persistent droughts, the pollution of the Potomac River, and the population surge eventually took a toll on this legacy, causing sporadic rationing measures throughout the 1950s. By then, instead of plentiful and crystalline streams, a hodgepodge of public water systems and private wells supplied the growing county—the smallest company serving forty families, and the largest serving fifteen thousand people.[56]

To alleviate the water supply crisis, the Alexandria Water Company, an investor-owned utility serving the city of Alexandria and its immediate suburbs, opened a pumping station and a pipeline on the Occoquan Reservoir in 1954. Unfortunately, the action failed to provide enough water to meet the increasing need. Something had to be done about the unsophisticated network of competing public and private water sources—and fast.

The solution was an integrated water system. To achieve it, Massey spearheaded the formation of the Fairfax County Water Authority in 1954. Engineer James J. Corbalis was its sole employee. "The goal was to bring the twenty-six different water systems serving the county under one authority," says Fred Griffith, former director of the Fairfax County Water Authority, now Fairfax Water.[57] "Jay [Corbalis] bought each one of them, one at a time, and worked like hell to finance the acquisitions through bond issues."

The Alexandria Water Company resisted the new authority's actions, but ultimately the Fairfax County Water Authority prevailed. By the end of the 1960s, Fairfax was able to provide adequate water services to nearly all developing areas of the county. When Corbalis retired in 1985, his one-man department had ballooned to 326 employees, and the county operated four water treatment plants producing an average of eighty-seven million gallons of water each day, serving nearly 722,000 people.[58]

Lack of water wasn't the only problem created by the influx of people. More residents also meant more automobiles congesting county roads, and county officials soon clamored for additional and wider highways. Despite the overwhelming need, however, Interstate 66 stalled during the

1950s after Arlington citizens protested that it would invite too much change into their beloved county.

Paving the Corridors of Growth

Less divisive was the sixty-four-mile-long Capital Beltway. The first section, which included the Woodrow Wilson Bridge over the Potomac River near Alexandria, opened on December 28, 1961. Three years later, in August 1964, the finished road made its debut with four lanes, two in each direction. The media dubbed it "Washington's Main Street."

Fairfax officials hoped that the Beltway would prompt industry growth similar to the kind that had occurred along Route 128 in Boston. Completed in 1959, Route 128 had connected the region's growing suburbs, new office parks, and university laboratories, creating a nexus of technological advancement and entrepreneurship. As space became more limited, many businesses had moved their enterprises to the new industrial parks that sprouted on low-priced land along the highway. From 1953 to 1961, 169 businesses employing twenty-four thousand people migrated to locations adjacent to Route 128. Many others moved within close proximity, bestowing upon the road its own sobriquet— "America's Technology Highway." By 1973 the number of businesses

Cars and people crowd the opening of the Capital Beltway in 1964.

along the highway exceeded 1,200, including such high-tech pioneers as Raytheon, Sun Microsystems, Polaroid, and Compuserve.

Fairfax County's Beltway did draw some businesses to the area, but nowhere near the volume and specific type that Route 128 had. In the future, another highway would help spur this economic development. But for now, the Beltway simply provided the county's new suburbanites easy egress to the nation's capital.

An even wider and longer road, the Outer Circumferential Freeway, was also recommended in the county's 1954 Master Plan to assist in the same objective. Three years later it was reaffirmed by the state of Maryland in the 1957 General Plan for the Maryland-Washington Regional District. The 122-mile highway would encircle the Capital Beltway in both Virginia and Maryland, prompting its shorthand name, the Outer Beltway. Like Interstate 66, construction was stymied by political inaction and the protests of citizens.

In 1961, the Maryland-National Planning Commission further cited the region's urgent need to build the Outer Beltway. The commission also called for an even wider and longer circumferential highway dubbed the Outer Outer Beltway, as well as six additional radial growth corridors. These plans, too, encountered populist-driven politicians and were largely set aside.[59] A portion of the expected highway funding was instead redirected to the creation of a rail system in the 1960s, linking Washington with outlying counties.

Subdividing the Hazel Family Farm

Through it all, Til Hazel continued to support the development of roads and other necessary infrastructures. In the late 1950s, he worked tirelessly on behalf of the Virginia Department of Highways, providing right-of-way for the Capital Beltway. "His work to condemn the necessary land . . . cemented the foundation for the evolution of Northern Virginia," reported Times Community Newspapers.[60]

In the meantime, his brother, Bill, focused on the family's parcel of land. Bill Hazel had labored vigorously to make the dairy farm in McLean economically successful, living on the premises from 1950 to 1954. But that year—in part because he'd been drafted by the army and was recently married—Bill determined his best efforts were not enough, and the farm was sold. Today, a subdivision rests on the site of the Hazel's old dairy farm, with houses interspersed among the scarlet oak trees that Til planted in the 1930s and early 1940s.

For the family, the sale of the land was mostly a sentimental loss. A few years earlier, on Christmas Eve 1950, the Hazels had replaced the old dairy farm with the purchase of a much larger tract of land called "Huntley." The property—which initially comprised 760 acres in woodsy Fauquier County—had been dubbed as such since the eighteenth century, a possible reference to an early owner. After Bill was discharged from the army in 1956, he and his wife, Eleanor, moved to Huntley, and Bill took a stab at a beef cattle operation.

Four years later he switched course and started an earth-moving company, William A. Hazel, Inc., with his brother. Bill and Til were equal partners in the endeavor, and Bill ran its day-to-day operations. As Fairfax burgeoned, the firm, which performed primarily site work for streets, including water and sewer lines, also prospered.

Years earlier the brothers had built an addition to the barn at the dairy farm. Now their efforts were entwined once again. Yet neither had any inkling of the remarkable kinship they would share in the urbanization of Fairfax County.

Dewberry, GOD, and Nealon

It was the world's "largest builder of brick homes" during the 1950s, or so it billed itself. Thus when land development pioneer M.T. Broyhill & Sons decided to divest its design, construction, and engineering departments in 1955 to focus on residential dwelling units, opportunity beckoned for Sidney O. Dewberry. A design engineer, Dewberry had been hired just a few months earlier to manage Broyhill's engineering department. Now, the Northern Virginia firm was offering each of the heads of its soon-to-be divested departments the chance to buy their operations.

Tall and quietly imposing, with a patrician nose and a thatch of unruly hair, Sid Dewberry had cut his teeth as a civil engineer in Montgomery County's road department. He later worked on the Washington Aqueduct for the Washington District Corps of Engineers, leaving the public sector for the Maryland-based engineering firm of Greenhorne & O'Mara before signing on at Broyhill. With funding provided by his previous employers, Sid and fellow Broyhill surveyor Jim Nealon quickly acquired the firm's engineering division. Sid was twenty-eight years old.

On Friday, April 13, 1956, the Arlington County–based surveying and engineering firm posted its new nameplate: Greenhorne, O'Mara, Dewberry & Nealon. Unfortunately, the ominous date was prophetic. A brief economic recession soon slowed housing construction to a crawl, darkening the nascent firm's prospects. Six engineers worked for GOD & Nealon, the founders' amusing acronym, as did Sid's wife, Reva Lanier Dewberry—his high school sweetheart and the firm's bookkeeper. Within nine months, though, Reva had little to do, and Sid had to convince his partners to give him the full year to make a go of it.

Industry and hard work came naturally to Sid. Born to Albert and Katie Dewberry on December 23, 1927, he was the youngest son and the seventh of nine children. Sid's East Coast roots date back to the 1600s, when the first of his relatives arrived from England. His family owned a two-hundred-acre farm in Pittsylvania County, Virginia, part of a tobacco-growing operation once owned by his great grandfather, Ambrose Rucker. By the time it was passed to his parents, the farm produced a variety of produce. "[We] grew just about everything we consumed—except the salt and pepper," Sid jokes. "Self-sufficiency was the order of the day."[61]

He traces his early love of engineering to his father, who supervised a bridge construction crew and often took the boy with him to job sites. Although those times of togetherness were few—Albert succumbed to leukemia when Sid was nine years old—they left a lasting impression. "By age fourteen, I knew I wanted to be an engineer," Sid says.

One semester as a student, he rode a streetcar to a 7:00 a.m. class that traveled along Pennsylvania Avenue past the White House. Also up at that hour was Vice President Harry S. Truman, who took his morning constitutional, a walk up and down Pennsylvania Avenue, virtually every day, dressed in a double-breasted suit and Homburg hat, Secret Service agents ten paces behind. "The streetcar stopped to let customers off, and one day I saw him and waved," Sid recalled. "I admired him and his humble beginnings, and my family was all Democrats. Anyway, he waved back. The next day the same thing happened. It got to be pretty regular and we became waving buddies."

Following Sid's high school graduation in 1945, he enlisted for what turned out to be the final days of the Second World War and spent his two years of service stateside. He returned to Virginia, heeding his sister Dorothy's advice to enroll in college on the G.I. Bill. In 1951, he graduated from George Washington University with an engineering degree, one year after marrying Reva.

For several months in early 1957, it seemed as if time had run out for Sid's latest endeavor. One year after the firm's shaky debut, two large projects finally came its way—one a contract from Broyhill and the other an assignment to review site plans for Fairfax County. From there the firm gained momentum, and by the mid-1960s, Sid and Nealon were able to assume full ownership. They added a partner, Richard Davis, in 1966.

As the county's residential and commercial building sectors grew, many real estate developers and builders turned to Dewberry, Nealon, and Davis for engineering and surveying services. Sid knew how to appeal to developers and builders from a business perspective. "[Sid] would help them find the land," says John Fowler, a longtime employee of the firm and a member of its board of directors. "He would help them make the deals, or suggest deals to them. He would steer them to banks. He would give them breaks by deferring payments on engineering fees. Favors that made all the difference . . . He was, by far, the best."[62]

County planner Rosser Payne agrees: "Sid was one of the early members of the Arlington County Planning Commission and was instrumental in getting planning and development going in eastern Fairfax. He knew his stuff . . . and was in the right place at the right time."[63]

Land of "Amazingly Rich" Resources

The "right place," of course, was where the Board of Supervisors and the revitalized Chamber of Commerce wanted more companies to locate. In 1956, the two organizations published "What Fairfax County Offers . . . on the Virginia side of Washington!" a colorful brochure that touted the reasons companies might want to consider Fairfax as a place of business. It was the first organized attempt to encourage commerce and industry in the county, and it was led by a joint committee comprised of members from both the Board and the Chamber of Commerce—one group focused on the good of the public and the other on the interests of business. "The county needs the builders and developers, and the

Shirley Highway (Route I-395) connected Fairfax County to Washington, D.C. and other points along the way, such as the Pentagon and Washington National Airport, within minutes.

builders and developers need the county," County Executive Carlton Massey commented in a 1956 *Washington Post* op-ed. "Only through mutual understanding and cooperation can the progressive future of Fairfax County be assured."[64]

Driving both organizations was the recognition that homeowners needed relief from the escalating taxes needed to fund the increase in public services. Though the Board of Supervisors was in the midst of revising F. Dodd McHugh's Master Plan and its large lot zoning in the western part of the county, it enthusiastically endorsed commercial growth in the eastern region.

What, then, did Fairfax County offer? Not only was it one of the three fastest growing counties in America, "with opportunities amazingly rich amid suburban living exceptionally choice," the brochure gushed, "[but] most of the important federal offices are much closer in distance to the Virginia side than to other suburban areas. You can choose a plant site in a parklike semirural Fairfax County setting and be within 20–25 minutes of the heart of Washington."[65]

The primary target was light industry and, especially, the technology companies that derived the lion's share of their income from federal government contract work. "This area can become the research center of America," Melpar President Thomas Meloy asserted in the literature. Arthur Sloan, vice president of Atlantic Research, agreed, noting that the firm's "newly approved site on the Shirley Highway," was "less than eight miles from Washington, [making] this area preeminent for research."

In case the reader missed the point, a statement by planning consultant Homer Hoyt—printed three times in the brochure—underlined it: "Fairfax County has more sites suitable for laboratories and other light industry within 30 minutes of the White House than the rest of the Metropolitan Area combined."

Water purity, electric power, railroad freight service, and Washington National Airport (today, the Ronald Reagan National Airport) were listed as further inducements, as were plans to build the Capital Beltway and Outer Beltway highways. Both roads were drawn on a map under the words, "Extensive System of Speedy Highways Now and More Under Way." Fairfax County, the brochure pointed out, also offered

Dwight D. Eisenhower looks on as DCI Allen Dulles lays the cornerstone for the CIA headquarters in Langley, Virginia, November 3, 1959.

the scientific marvel of transcontinental phone dialing: "one of the first localities in America to have this ultra modern phone service."

The Central Intelligence Agency's decision in 1956 to locate its new headquarters in rural Langley, near McLean, was another attraction, at least for government contractors. While the Board of Supervisors had originally opposed the CIA locating in Langley, it had reversed its position and authorized Massey to convey its approval to the Senate Appropriations Committee evaluating the move.

The CIA had considered thirty locations before deciding on Fairfax. The city of Alexandria and Montgomery and Arlington counties lobbied strenuously to convince the nine-year-old agency to choose otherwise, as had Edward R. Carr, who offered to donate one hundred acres near his Springfield development for the purpose. But ultimately Fairfax's promise of a secure water supply from Falls Church, along with the erection of a $300,000 package sewage treatment plant, $250,000 in highway funds, and a commitment by the Virginia State Highway Department to spend a quarter of a million dollars extending George Washington Memorial Parkway sealed the deal.[66] In November 1959, President Dwight D. Eisenhower laid the cornerstone of the new CIA building.

It was just the beginning of the United States' spending on Cold War intelligence. Four years later, the U.S. intelligence budget would reach $550 million, eventually totaling $43.5 billion in 2007.[67] Over the years, the government's intelligence operations would greatly benefit Fairfax County—Tysons Corner in particular, where many buildings secretly housing intelligence operations continue to thrive.

Covering All the (Tax) Bases

Meanwhile, the Board of Supervisors waged a separate effort to encourage commercial operations by creating the Fairfax County Economic and Industrial Development Committee in October 1956. The five-member committee's primary duty, as outlined by the Board, was "to encourage the establishment within Fairfax County of desirable industrial and commercial enterprises . . . particularly enterprises having a potential benefit to the tax base." Among the favored business types were research and development, wholesale distribution, national organization headquarters, corporate headquarters or offices, and light manufacturing. Industries creating "smoke, odor, industrial waste, fire hazards, offensive noise and dust and dirt" were to be avoided.[68]

Jerry Halpin was a member of the advisory committee that decided to hire William B. Wrench, the committee's first director. Wrench had previously directed a Kentucky agency similarly charged with industrial development. When he arrived for his job interview in North Springfield, Wrench expected it to be at a city hall-type office building. Instead, he met with a panel of evaluators in the back of a shopping center, at a restaurant owned by one of the group's members. "On the way in, I kept getting lost and drove around the Washington Monument twice," he recalls. "Everywhere I looked there were trees and not much else." Indeed, more than 40 percent of the county was still forest and woodland at the time.[69]

The job provided a secretary and little else. "There was no data on the applicability of different county communities to various industries," he notes. "My initial task was to meet the leaders in the communities and assemble data relevant to the industries they were open to. I then researched potential [company] prospects and presented promotional materials to them about the community . . . I realized pretty quickly that I'd been hired as a salesman."[70]

Wrench's emerging knowledge of the power structure in various communities made him the point person during corporate site surveys. Not that all corporate prospects were met with open arms. "I learned pretty quickly about the NIMBY phenomenon—the 'not in my backyard' crowd and their government allies," Wrench says. "Ten dedicated and committed citizens can kill a plan or delay it so long the effect is the same."

He recalls that NIMBYs—a phrase commonly used to describe people who decry development in their region—nearly derailed efforts to build the county's first planned industrial park at Ravensworth, a development for which Wrench had vigorously lobbied. The park was to be located in North Springfield, just off the Beltway and close to the burgeoning Ravensworth residential community. *The Washington Post* later described the proximity of a light industrial area to suburban families in new homes as "a delicate experiment."[71] It was an experiment, however, that Wrench believed was necessary to provide homeowners with tax relief. His arguments eventually won the day. When it was built in 1959, the seventy-acre park's taxpaying tenants occupied nearly one million square feet of space.

Such attempts to build a commercial and industrial tax base in Fairfax were modestly successful, contributing to a 39 percent increase in the number of businesses operating in the county from 1951 through 1956.[72] Still, Wrench and the Board had a long way to go; less than 5 percent of the county's tax base was derived from commercial and industrial taxpayers in the mid-1950s.[73]

Nevertheless, momentum was increasing. The private and public sectors had begun to display crucial willingness to collaborate on commercial development to reduce the tax burden on homeowners, more of them arriving every day. And the buzz of residential construction was constant. In just one year, from 1956 to 1957, the Northern Virginia Builders' Association tabulated 119 new members, bringing its total membership to 589, a 25 percent increase. At least one industry was thriving in Fairfax—homebuilding.[74]

Air Supply and Demand

The federal government's detour on the planned international airport at Burke didn't end the need for a relief airport serving the Washington region. The Jet Age had just begun, and officials knew Washington National Airport would soon be incapable of serving the jet aircraft poised to make their debut. A second, more modern airport was a necessity.

Prior to the June 1941 opening of Washington National Airport, Hoover Airfield handled much of the region's air traffic. Hoover was located south of Washington on the site of the present Pentagon. When a plane took off or came in to land at Hoover in the 1930s, a guard tugged a rope across the street to halt incoming traffic.[75] Not wanting a major airport for a neighbor, residents of Burke wielded a figurative rope, ultimately preventing the federal government from going forward—despite the fact that it had already condemned and acquired 4,500 acres in the area. "The citizenry raised some serious hell," says James Wilding, former president and CEO of the Metropolitan Washington Airports Authority.[76]

The issue came to a head in the early 1950s during a floor debate in the U.S. House of Representatives on appropriations for the Civil Aeronautics Administration (CAA), the government agency responsible for airport development. The bill in question had earmarked funds for additional land acquisitions in the Burke area, provoking the ire of local residents. The bill was voted down, and in 1959 the 4,500 acres were returned to public use and sold at auction. Of that lot, nine hundred acres were provided to the Fairfax County Park Authority to create Burke Lake Park, and a significant portion was sold to the Lynch family.

Wounded by the decision to nix Burke as the site of the second airport, the CAA retreated from the subject for six years. It wasn't until General Elwood "Pete" Quesada was appointed special aviation advisor to President Dwight D. Eisenhower in 1957 that the second airport question was revived.

Born in Washington, D.C., in 1904, Quesada was an Air Corps flying cadet in the 1920s and deputy commanding general of U.S. air command forces in Africa during World War II. He directed the Allies' aerial cover in support of the D-Day invasion of Normandy, flying General Eisenhower over the area in a fighter plane prior to the invasion. The flight marked the beginning of a long friendship. When the war ended, Quesada was promoted to lead the new Tactical Air Command. And when Eisenhower became president in 1953, Quesada became his go-to man on aviation.

Quesada recognized the urgent need for a second airport, yet understood that the CAA—a backwater organization in the U.S. Department of Commerce—didn't have the clout to push a bill through Congress. So while he ardently politicized the need for a new government aviation authority, he also oversaw a bi-state (Maryland and Virginia) study of the most appropriate site for a new airport.

In 1958, Congress passed the Federal Aviation Act, creating the Federal Aviation Agency, and named Quesada its first administrator. The powerful agency (which became the Federal Aviation Administration in 1961) usurped the CAA's responsibilities and blessed the bi-state study's choice of Chantilly as the site of a second airport. Plans were immediately put in motion to acquire more than ten thousand acres in the largely rural area, which straddled western Fairfax County and part of Loudoun County.

An Airport for the Jet Age

There was only one drawback to Chantilly: road access to and from Washington. Although the FAA and local planners originally conceived that improvements to Route 50 would resolve the issue, they later decided to build a twelve-mile-long access highway connecting the airport to the planned Interstate 66 highway near Falls Church. The access highway would be built with no interchanges for local traffic, thereby offering uninterrupted egress to the capital. The planners realized that the county's nonstop growth would someday create a need for local interchanges, however, so they acquired enough right-of-way to provide a quarter-mile-wide corridor that could encompass additional lanes and interchanges for local transportation if and when the need arose.

Til Hazel was one of several attorneys that represented Chantilly landowners whose properties the government now sought to condemn. "I remember General Quesada took the witness stand and was asked why he needed ten thousand acres for an airport, which seemed like an awful lot of land and was more than twice what was bought for Burke," Til says of the 1958 hearing. "He responded that there was a new kind of airplane called a 'jet' that would revolutionize air travel, but it needed much longer runways—longer than Washington National could accommodate at the time." Within weeks a Boeing 707, the first modern jet, began service from New York to London.

A small hodgepodge of farm buildings, stores, churches, and a few homes in the rural, unincorporated community of Willard in Chantilly were torn down to make way for the new airport, which received little opposition. While some citizens protested the planned demolition of the historic Sully Plantation, built in 1794 as the home of Richard Bland Lee, one of Virginia's first congressmen (and the first congressman representing Northern Virginia), the airport's proposed perimeter eventually was altered to preserve the house and property. In 1962, President John F. Kennedy christened the site Washington Dulles International Airport, named for John Foster Dulles, Eisenhower's secretary of state. The four-lane Dulles Airport Access Road opened at the same time.

The decision to use Chantilly rather than Burke as an airport had an upside. The old site now contained hundreds of acres of parkland, including plans for a 218-acre man-made lake stocked with fish. Yet while the federal government had donated the land for Burke Lake Park, the county Park Authority still needed $35,000 from the private sector to supplement state funds of $150,000 to build, stock, and maintain the lake.

The Washington Post pleaded for the funds in a November 1959 editorial, stating, "This is too good a proposition to let pass . . . an excellent bargain." It added that the project promised "one of the most attractive recreation spots in the region."[77] Jerry Halpin read the article and pledged the $35,000 from his own wallet. "I called Carlton Massey and asked him if it was true that the county would lose the park if it didn't raise the $35,000 by the end-of-the-year deadline, and he confirmed it," Jerry recalls. Not that he had the cash. "I had just finished building my own home, doing a lot of the carpentry myself, and it was worth $29,000. I told him I'd somehow come up with the money."

When *The Post* leaked that Jerry had pledged the needed funds,[78] the media swarmed the Halpins' modest home. "My wife called me and said, 'Jerry, this has got to stop; there are photographers banging on the door,'" Jerry says. The county accepted his offer, although it later issued bonds to arrange the funding. Today, Burke Lake Park spans 888 acres and includes campgrounds, a miniature train, a carousel, outdoor volleyball courts, a wheelchair-accessible fishing pier, an 18-hole par 3 golf course, and a miniature golf course.

Jerry Halpin's role in the development of Burke Lake Park was notable—but he soon found that the switch to Chantilly would have other, more profound implications for him. Just as he had once scoured the Burke area as a potential site for his firm's headquarters, Jerry now began to take a closer look at the real estate opportunities the new airport would provide.

A Residential Revolution

As the airport issue heated up in the late 1950s, the lawsuit against the Freehill Amendment's two-acre-minimum zoning continued to wind its way through Virginia's courts. The county's zoning dispute finally reached the Virginia Supreme Court in March 1959, two months after Supervisor Joseph Freehill's sudden death from a heart attack.

It was a landmark case. Former Board supervisor G. Wallace Carper, a large landholder and dairy farmer, had challenged the amendment to F. Dodd McHugh's Master Plan, calling the 1956 zoning law of the western two-thirds of the county "unconstitutional." The amendment, he asserted, effectively prevented the development of subdivisions, thus limiting the sales value of his property.

The Virginia Supreme Court ruled in his favor, maintaining that the amendment was unconstitutional and bore "no reasonable or substantial relationship to the general welfare of the owners or residents of the area so zoned." The court also stated that the amendment was discriminatory, preventing low-income people from living in the western region while preserving the land for the benefit of "those who could afford to build houses on two acres or more." The zoning's real purpose, the court opined, was "to channel the county's population into the eastern one-third where the cost of operating the government would be more economical."[79]

The decision was a milestone. "It was one of the first judicial recognitions of the inherent conflict between land use control and the right of citizens to be adequately housed free of exclusionary land schemes," says Til, who had baled hay for Carper as a boy and watched the case closely.

Following the Carper ruling, more than 170,000 acres of the total 258,000 acres within the county—an area consisting almost entirely of wooded, agricultural, and vacant land—were upzoned to a one- or one-half acre zoning classification. Western Fairfax was immediately open to residential and commercial development, and required consequent public services like schools, fire protection, water supply, and sewerage. But while the opportunities for real estate developers and builders were bountiful, the task before the Board of Supervisors was daunting. Water, for example, had not been serviced to any great extent to the county's western region.[80]

As officials intensified their focus on land use, the Board of Supervisors increased the size and importance of the county's planning division. Meanwhile, county planners adopted the Metropolitan Washington Council of Government's "cluster" strategy as a planning premise for the western area. The concept called for the creation of urban cluster areas that would be grouped around one of the three proposed highways. The strategy was predicated on the development of a planned community, as opposed to unplanned urban sprawl. In succeeding years, several planned communities materialized, including Reston, Fair Lakes, and Burke Centre.

The Carper decision also dovetailed with other major initiatives preparing the county for the coming population boom. Thanks to W.T. Woodson, new and renovated public schools soon decorated the landscape. Under Jay Corbalis, the Fairfax County Water Authority acquired, consolidated, and upgraded a number of small water companies, providing residents with adequate water service by the end of the 1960s. The

Fairfax County Park Authority and its first director, Fred Packard, spent $20 million over the course of the decade on park acquisitions, largely for tracts that would have become the subject of conflicting land use proposals between the private and public sectors. The Beltway, too, was partially completed by 1961, while Washington Dulles International Airport, George Mason College, and the Fairfax Hospital Association began to spread their wings.

By 1960, nearly a quarter of a million people lived in Fairfax County, almost three times as many as in 1950. Nevertheless, this population growth was not unusual. Nationwide, the suburban population grew by 33 percent over the same period.[81] For example, the city of Columbus's suburban population also tripled, while St. Louis's increased by 59 percent.[82] Fairfax County would require an economic shot in the arm—local jobs—to surpass other regions of the country in population growth. For now, though, the time had come for the western region to take on major residential and commercial real estate development.

The Gorilla in Tysons Corner

In the 1930s, Tysons Corner was simply the quiet intersection of Leesburg Pike and Chain Bridge Road, two farm-to-market roads that were flanked on one side by a general store selling apples, hay, and axes for clearing land, and the other by a Gulf service station. By the 1950s, not much had changed. *The Washington Post* noted that the general store and gas station were still there, now flanked by a "beer joint." The newspaper added, "In the summer, carnival shows occasionally occupied one of the pastures around the crossroads, and you could win $50 for lasting three rounds wrestling with a gorilla."[83] When the Beltway's planned route and location of the Chantilly airport were revealed later that decade, the area's chance location—between the airport and Washington and intersected by the Beltway—was just one more factor that put it on the map.

The county's early settlers recognized the location potential of the crossroads, erecting Fairfax's first courthouse at Freedom Hill, a stone's throw from the intersection. The hill took its name from Kesiah Carter, a freed slave who settled in the area in the early 1800s. In 1852, William

Tyson purchased approximately sixty acres of the old courthouse tract, and his surname began to be associated with the crossroads that carved his property into sharp corners.

As plans for the Beltway matured, the county set aside 630 acres of undeveloped land in Tysons Corner for industrial use. The 1962 Master Plan called for another one thousand acres of prime land to be developed, inviting several multimillion-dollar proposals to transform the area into a major commercial, residential, and shopping complex.[84] Realizing the potential for even wider use once the Beltway was completed, the Board modified its plans in 1964 to provide land for offices, apartments, and a regional shopping mall.[85]

Jerry Halpin was ahead of these developments—in 1959 he was already mentally mining the area for its real-estate potential. He wasn't alone in sensing opportunity. Marcus Bles, a carpenter with a sixth grade education, had begun buying up land in the Tysons Corner area in 1949, starting with seventy-two acres he bought with $55,000 in cash from his bustling construction business. A large gravel quarry on the land offered the means for Bles to buy additional property, bringing the tally to more than three hundred acres, all of it paid in cash. "I have a horror of interest," he confided to *The Washington Post.* "If I had borrowed I could have had it all."[86]

Jerry's real estate philosophy was the converse—"OPM," as he called it, for "'other people's money,' since I didn't have any." When a 118-acre

Tysons Corner was just a quiet intersection at Route 123 and Route 7 in 1935, with not much more than a gas station and a general store.

tract of farmland on Route 123 owned by the Storm family in Tysons Corner went on the market, Jerry sensed a rare opportunity. The property lay across from Maplewood Farm roughly halfway between Washington and the new airport at Chantilly, in a triangle to be bounded by the Beltway, Route 123, and the Dulles Access Road. "It seemed like a good location," he says.

Real estate broker Ed Lynch informed Jerry that the tract was for sale at $2,500 an acre and would likely be bought by a family in Arlington unless he stepped in fast to make a deal. "I told him 'too much,'" Jerry says. "Six weeks later he came back to me and said the price had changed—it was now $3,500! He insisted it would become a valuable piece of land someday. I had to get on a plane in thirty minutes, so I told him to call Bee Smith to handle the initial negotiations."

Charles Henry "Bee" Smith was a friend and business associate who had fared well in Jerry's previous real estate investments. Intrigued by the potential of Tysons Corner, Jerry persuaded his colleagues and Smith to fund a separate, private company predicated on land development. This company, called Commonwealth Capital, bought the farmland at $3,500 an acre in 1961. Shortly thereafter, the first of several one-story and two-story buildings surfaced. The building was financed with OPM: a $57,000 check written by Prudential Life Insurance. When Jerry solicited another loan from Prudential for a second building, though, the company politely declined, saying he was "too far out in the boonies."

But Jerry and Tom Nicholson, a colleague at Atlantic Research who had joined him at Commonwealth, knew they were on the threshold of something big. They began to mull the development of a planned business park consisting of offices, research and development space, and apartment buildings both on the existing parcel and possibly a neighboring tract of Tysons Corner: Maplewood Farm.

Opening the West*Gate to Washington

Owned by the Ulfelder family since 1925, Maplewood was actually made up of two farms that encompassed 512 acres. A stately 1870s-era, twenty-two-room mansion sat on the land, built in the manner of the Second Empire, an elaborately ornamented architectural style inspired by the Louvre museum in Paris and the former British Embassy on Connecticut Avenue in Washington.[87] German immigrant and former U.S. Army colonel Rudolph G. Seeley, his wife, Martha Ulfelder, and their three children lived in the sprawling house.

Maplewood had been a very successful dairy farm and had enjoyed a modest side business selling peaches from a thirty-acre orchard. However, after the Second World War, difficulties attracting skilled labor became an ongoing problem, as did the farm's high taxes.[88] The farm eventually became "an economic burden," wrote Seeley.[89] Seeley had been trying to sell Maplewood since at least 1950. By the end of the decade, as the buzz of highway construction diced the property into fragments, farming had become impossible and selling the land imperative.

Around the time Jerry and Tom began to mull expansion, Ed Lynch called again. "[Ed] said that the people across the street from our Storm tract, were, in fact, looking to sell their land," Jerry says. "We approached Rudy [Seeley] and apprised him of our plans to build the business park. He said he was interested in joining us, but we would have to meet with Ethel Ulfelder in Mexico." In 1962, the Ulfelders and Commonwealth Capital formed a joint venture to develop the business park. The Ulfelders provided 142 acres, and Jerry and his partners provided 118. Commonwealth Capital was absorbed into the new venture, called West*Gate Corporation (a nod to Tysons Corner's budding position as the "western gate" to Washington, D.C.).

Halpin, Nicholson, Seeley, and a fourth partner, Charles Ewing, cofounded the company. A graduate of West Point and former army officer in the Corps of Engineers, Ewing had met Jerry at Harvard Business School in 1951 and worked with him as assistant at Atlantic Research. The four men were a close bunch who joked that the name of their company should have been HENS, an acronym for Halpin, Ewing, Nicholson, and Seeley. Ewing handled development and construction; Nicholson, who had graduated from the Massachusetts Maritime Academy and also went to Harvard Business School, was the financial officer who assisted Jerry in putting together deals; and Seeley, an outgoing and well-liked gentleman eight years older than Halpin, was the "front man"—the liaison with the business community and government agencies. As for Jerry, "he called the shots, making the big, strategic decisions," Ewing says. "We were never big on titles."[90]

It was touch and go for the developers in the beginning. "We had to pledge our houses and furniture to pay the taxes on the land and the interest on the loans," Ewing says. "Unlike other developers that did 'one-off' projects, seizing an opportunity and then waiting for the next one, we had all this land to develop and some pretty sizable dreams."

After receiving zoning approval from the Board of Supervisors to build the West*Gate Research Park, the founders sold off a few small parcels of land to generate money to build the roads, water, and sewers. They also deeded twenty-five acres to the county for schools, parks, and other amenities. "Our plan was to attract government organizations and the companies that catered to them like defense contractors and research firms," Ewing says. "It wasn't a hard sell. We were a very pretty girl, right between Dulles Airport and the District [and] intersected by several roads and highways. You'd have to trip over us to get to Washington."

One of their first important transactions was building the new head-quarters of Research Analysis Corporation, a U.S. Army think tank and subsidiary of Princeton Labs chaired by General Omar Bradley. At 150,000 square feet, the building was the largest office structure of its kind in the county. Inside, the scientific company conducted secret experiments for the federal government. The deal marked the beginning of many covert real estate transactions on behalf of Uncle Sam, which Jerry won't discuss. "I don't want to get shot," he jokes.

The first private corporation to lease a building at the office park was Mars, Inc., the candy empire run by Forrest Mars Sr. Mars had created M&M's candies and lived in the horse country of Middleburg, Virginia, in Loudoun County. "Forrest always said he chose Tysons Corner because we had the only office building between the airport and his house," Ewing says.

Many of the original office buildings, designed by architect Charles Goodman, were maintained for the company's own account—real estate parlance for owning, leasing, and managing the buildings. Jerry had a passion for green space and, assisted by his son Peter, built berms and planted trees and shrubs along the streets that had been carved into the old farmland. Tysons Corner soon flourished into cool, green naves that shaded the office buildings from passersby. In 1965, *Industrial Development* magazine wrote that at West*Gate, "there is a concern for things like architectural continuity, high standards of construction and protection and care of the natural assets of the area. They haven't just bulldozed everything away. They've left such things as the trees and the natural rolling slope of the land. It's all very encouraging."[91]

A scant four years earlier, the county's Planning Commission had worried that Tysons Corner, if developed, would become "a colossal slum of the worst kind . . . a bedlam of unrelated, individually-planned land uses."[92] Jerry Halpin, the earnest kid who had peddled cherries, apples, and currants as a boy, eased their worries.

By 1972, West*Gate Corporation controlled over six hundred of the 1,700 acres in Tysons Corner. The quiet rural intersection of two farm-to-market roads was no longer. The old Gulf gas station was gone, as was the general store. Even the Ulfelder mansion was headed for the wrecking ball. The Wild West of Fairfax was being tamed. And for the first time, major companies seriously eyed the western part of the county as a place to do business. By 1970 twenty research-oriented businesses had set up shop in West*Gate Research Park.[93]

Washington's bedroom community was on its way to becoming an economic nexus of its own. Visionary developers like Jerry Halpin, assisted by engineers like Sid Dewberry and construction mavericks like Bill Hazel, were ready to erect office buildings to house the anticipated influx of companies as well as houses and apartments for their executives and employees. Civic-minded men and women had stepped forward to guide the necessary increases in public services.

And then a new Board of Supervisors took hold and vowed to slow the development dead in its tracks.

Dark clouds over a Fairfax County residential subdivision seem to portend the coming political storm.

CHAPTER 3

Closed for
Business

I n the great postwar exodus from the cities to the suburbs, local governments like the Fairfax County Board of Supervisors suddenly
found themselves with enormous responsibilities that their prewar
predecessors would have marveled at. The pressure on the supervisors
was extreme, given the relentless influx of people and their demands for
housing, transportation, schools, sewerage, water, and the other amenities of the American Dream.

When Til Hazel made his first appearance before the county Board
of Supervisors in a 1960 zoning case, he learned a regrettable consequence of this extreme pressure: influence peddling was a factor in Board
decisions at the time. "We had a land use system based upon politics and
individual politicians' votes," he says. "While the procedures were reasonably superficial, it was clear that influence with supervisors was critical. I did not accept that premise then or ever—there had to be 'rules' for
me to remain engaged. If you don't have rules, there is no preventing the
potential for corruption."[94]

Yet as Til soon found, corruption already had quite a foothold. The
influence peddling that swept the Board of Supervisors in the mid-1960s
marks one of the more unfortunate eras in the history of the county. The
stage was set during the early 1960s when President John F. Kennedy, in

a highly controversial decision, appointed his younger brother Robert F. Kennedy as attorney general. RFK soon seized headlines with his relentless pursuit of organized crime figures, and the Anti-Racketeering Act was passed as a result.

Federal officials then leveraged the Anti-Racketeering legislation in an investigation of alleged corruption by the Fairfax Board of Supervisors. The investigation was prompted by plans to build a subdivision—a medium-rise apartment complex—in the Dranesville district off Route 123. First Lady Jacqueline Kennedy's stepfather, Hugh Auchincloss, owned a large estate nearby called "Merrywood" that overlooked the Potomac River at Chain Bridge Hill, as did a member of JFK's cabinet, U.S. Secretary of the Interior Morris Udall. RFK also owned a prime piece of property a few miles away, near McLean. Consequently, when a rezoning application for the apartment complex came before the Board, the Kennedys and Udall paid close attention.

Opponents of the rezoning request, who argued that the land had significant scenic and historic value, took notice, too. Supervisor A. Claiborne Leigh publicly came out against the development . . . at first. But when the rezoning went to the Board for a vote, he gave his approval. Something didn't fit, and the local office of the Internal Revenue Service decided to audit the tax returns and bank accounts of several supervisors to find out what it was. "A can of worms suddenly opened," says William Wrench, former director of the Fairfax County Economic and Industrial Development Committee.[95]

Officials subsequently called a federal grand jury to investigate if bribery was a factor in the supervisors' zoning votes. On September 20, 1966, the jury handed down twenty-four zoning bribery conspiracy indictments against fifteen county officials, developers, and zoning attorneys. Of those fifteen, eight were convicted, including Leigh and his fellow supervisors Robert Cotton and John Parrish.[96] "They were taking bribes . . . for things like trailer parks, which [is income] you can't declare on your income tax," remembers James H. Dillard, who joined the Virginia House of Delegates in 1971. "The other thing they would do is they would say, 'I'll vote against this new development in my district, but you all vote for it so it will pass—[and then] I can still claim I voted against it to please my constituents.'"[97]

A Black Mark on the Board's Record

Among those indicted was former Virginia state senator and zoning attorney Andrew W. Clarke. Clarke was charged in four counts of state bribery and two counts of federal bribery conspiracy. Audrey Moore, who joined the Board of Supervisors in 1972 representing the Annandale district, says that Clarke's bookkeeper "was very precise and made sure that everyone who took a bribe [was] paid after the rezoning so it would not look like a bribe."[98] Next to each one of the suspicious zoning cases, Clarke's bookkeeper apparently had written the words "cost of zoning." The term allegedly referred to bribes paid to the supervisors by Clarke on behalf of certain developers.

Til, who successfully handled Clarke's defense, got an inside look at the goings-on, despite defending someone whose integrity was suspect. On the federal charges, he argued that the alleged conspiracy had occurred prior to passage of the Anti-Racketeering Act, under which the indictment came. "The statute, originally passed as a means to thwart organized crime, allowed the use of tax returns in criminal prosecutions," he explains. "[Clarke's] tax returns provided the basis for the prosecution, but these returns were filed in years prior to the legislation."

On the state charges, Til persuaded the judge to exclude Clarke from trial based on his failing health. Clarke suffered from Parkinson's disease and had endured several strokes. "I brought in the chief pathologist from Georgetown Hospital to testify that Andy was, indeed, a very sick man and couldn't stand trial," Til says. "I believe his sickness clouded his judgment."

According to a source familiar with the case, Clarke's illness was just part of his pathetic fall. He had also been a powerful politician who lost his position and clout. "He [had been] a Napoleonic figure in the county, and everyone bowed to him," the source comments. "Once he figured out that a few hundred dollars here and there could guarantee supervisor votes on select zoning cases, he felt like he was back in charge." Clarke died in March 1968 and never had to stand trial.

The highly publicized trial stained the reputation of the Board of Supervisors, despite the relatively piffling amounts of money involved. "After the IRS came in," says Moore, "it was apparent that the bribes were so little. It is pitiful when you see major things happen because of so little money."

Joseph Alexander, who joined the Board representing the Lee district in 1964, recalls the difficulty in managing the county in the wake of the scandal. "We had a meeting where we told those who had been indicted that we could not sit with them anymore," he says. "They weren't too happy about that, but we explained we [couldn't] do the people's business with them still in the room. Several supervisors resigned and others were appointed to fill their terms out."[99]

Alexander and Harriet "Happy" Bradley, elected to replace Leigh as the Dranesville supervisor in January 1964, were among the few Board members not touched by the bribery and allegations of conflict of interest. Bradley had previously served a five-year stint on the county's Planning Commission, ending it as its chairwoman. During her tenure, she had been made privy to inside information indicating the names of individuals who may have participated in the zoning scandal, which she had passed on to the authorities. As a supervisor, Bradley was pro-business and favored the continuation of orderly growth in the county. "Everyone else on the Board at least pretended that they were still interested in planning and observing the Master Plans that had been put together," she says. "No one wanted to be caught not being interested in planning."[100]

Nevertheless, development in Fairfax was direly affected by the allegations. "The scandal gutted the development process," says county planner Rosser Payne. "It created a stigma on the whole process. We in the planning department didn't know what to do or how we would recover." Payne left the department as a result. He recalls, "I told [county executive Carlton] Massey that I didn't want to spend half my life building this up and then in one fell swoop it would be gone."[101]

As time went on and several new supervisors were elected or appointed to replace those disgraced, the Master Plans painstakingly put forward by Payne and his colleagues were dismissed—particularly as they related to future transportation needs. "There was disbelief on the part of the Board that the growth was going to happen like Rosser said," Alexander explains. "He kept arguing that growth will come and we needed to plan for it, but some Board members felt he was pushing development . . . Yet what he was predicting was correct."

The scandal was a serious black mark on the record of Fairfax County and was soon leveraged by anti-growth forces to allege widespread corruption in government. Nevertheless, other than the individuals involved in the Clarke case, both politically and administratively, the county has since been remarkably free of even the slightest suggestion of corrupt behavior.

In September 1966, a citizen's committee was formed and charged with studying the county's zoning procedures and land use system. The eight-member Zoning Procedures Study Committee, comprised of representatives from the business and development communities and the citizen constituency, conducted extensive hearings on changing the zoning system to make it more "fair and efficient." One year later, the committee—of which Til was a member—produced a report that suggested substantial alterations in land use policies and practices, including changes in who should have final authority on zoning questions. For the first time, the primacy of the Board of Supervisors in land use decisions had been challenged.[102]

The committee's report required and generated enabling legislation from the Virginia General Assembly, but reform was still a long way off. "Unfortunately," Til wrote in 1976, "the legislation and suggested changes were largely unsupported by the Board of Supervisors and proved to be merely an interesting discussion topic, despite substantial lip service to the contrary. The supervisors . . . did not wish to divest themselves of the power of decision in land use matters at the zoning level."[103]

So the Board retained its solitary grasp. And thanks to the bribery scandal, an increasingly vocal crowd of individuals opposed to growth found a receptive audience with voters and county officials.

An Answer to Urban Sprawl

Although later tainted by the bribery scandal, prior to 1967 the Fairfax Board of Supervisors had been responsible for a number of important initiatives preparing the county for its systematic growth. Between 1963 and 1967, an additional ninety thousand people had moved to Fairfax, raising the population to four hundred thousand. As *The Washington Post* commented, the Board "took a number of dramatic, farsighted moves to meet the problems of the county's tremendous population growth."

Among its achievements was the approval of several bonds to build a more modern infrastructure, including $58.5 million for new schools, $18 million for parkland acquisitions, $32.5 million for new hospitals and medical facilities, and "additional millions for libraries, a 13-story County Administration Building and college classrooms," *The Post* stated. The newspaper further commended the supervisors' role in consolidating the county's fragmented water systems, passing ordinances to reduce soil erosion and air pollution, moving to protect several historic sites, redistricting the county "to almost everyone's satisfaction," and most presciently, "master planning most of the County to guide development through the Year 2000." Although the supervisors rezoned less than those on predecessor Boards—"which dismayed developers," said *The Post*—on the whole the developers were treated "quite fairly."[104]

One such developer was Robert E. Simon Jr. A real estate investor from New York, Simon had inherited Carnegie Hall, one of the city's great cultural institutions, from his father. In 1960, he sold the entertainment venue and moved forward with bold plans to invest the proceeds into building a "new town" in Fairfax County. But first he needed rezoning approval from the Board of Supervisors.

One blisteringly hot July afternoon in 1962, the whippet-thin, forty-eight-year-old financier made his tenth visit to the Board to argue his case for a utopia in the middle of nowhere: a single place where people would live, work, and play in clusters of mixed-use buildings surrounding public plazas that encouraged a sense of community. It was Simon's antidote to urban sprawl. Nine times the supervisors had sent him home, hat in hand. The tenth time would prove a charm.

Simon had recently purchased the 6,750-acre Sunset Hills Farm, located on the county's western perimeter, for $13 million. Ironically, Dr. Carl Adolph Max Wiehle had also considered the area to be the ideal site for a planned community in the 1890s, but his plans never came to pass. Instead, the eponymous town of Wiehle, as it was later called, ended up in the hands of Abram Smith Bowman, who arrived from Kentucky in 1927 and bought four thousand acres from Wiehle.

Bowman subsequently purchased another three thousand acres, established a dairy, and renamed the entire tract Sunset Hills Farm. When prohibition was repealed in 1934, he built a distillery on the property slightly north of the Washington and Old Dominion Railroad track. Three years later, Bowman and his sons released their first label, *Virginia Gentleman* bourbon, followed by the less successful *Fairfax County* bourbon. (Bill Hazel recalls that the same mash used for making the whiskey "was fed to cattle from Route 7 to Herndon."[105]) Simon bought all but sixty acres of the Bowman tract, leaving enough land for the family to continue operating their distillery, which they did until 1988, when the company relocated to Fredericksburg, sixty miles south of Sunset Hills Farm.

Now, at 3:30 in the afternoon, the latest owner of Sunset Hills stood before the Board to present his most recent plans: seven European-style villages, connected by miles of trails, acres of open space, manmade lakes, and commercial, industrial, cultural, and civic functions. Each village would be home to about ten thousand residents of all income levels and races—still a radical concept since *Brown v. Board of Education* was only a few years old. Simon's new town would also be open to "racially mixed" couples, even though interracial marriage was prohibited by statute in Virginia and fifteen other states (the U.S. Supreme Court overturned the statutes in 1967).

Reston's Roots

Reston was undeniably the largest and most audacious project ever to have come before the Board of Supervisors, and an extraordinary undertaking for one man. Simon's inspiration for the project came from his own past. Over the years, he had lived in two radically different environments: Manhattan and Syosset, a rural area on Long Island, New York, where he and his wife owned five woodsy acres. "We believed we were living the 'American Dream,'" he says. "Once we began living the dream, however, my wife found herself chauffer to the children. The kids found it difficult to get together with their friends. And my commute to Manhattan took more than an hour, and frankly I was fortunate in that we lived only four minutes from the Long Island Rail Road. Nevertheless, I'd get home at 7:00, 8:00, and be exhausted."[106]

On numerous occasions, Simon had driven through Long Island's Levittown, a planned community built in the early 1950s by Abraham Levitt and his sons. Although sometimes derided for its inexpensive, small ranch-style houses built on concrete slabs, Levittown deeply affected him. "I'd see these kids streaming all over the place in the cul de sacs, and our kids would look out the car window at them longingly," he says. "Even though the houses were 750 square feet, they were affordable. It had an impact on me."

He began researching other experiments in utopian communities, such as Radburn, an idealistic effort in 1928 to build a self-sufficient town within two square miles of Fair Lawn, New Jersey. "My father was an investor in Radburn, and as a teenager I learned all about it," says Simon. "One of the games we played with my father was coming up with names for the streets." Radburn had been based on England's so-called Garden City model, and was envisioned by developers Clarence Stein and Henry Wright as a small city that would support its twenty-five thousand inhabitants with its own industry. Homes would be gathered around a central open area to encourage pedestrian traffic, while the back sides of houses would face service streets. Unfortunately, Radburn would ultimately succumb to the Great Depression—only 408 houses were built and any hopes of an industry were dashed by the economic situation.

This early rendering illustrates the "new town" of Reston, Virginia—brainchild of developer Robert E. Simon Jr.

As Simon read from a yellow pad of paper scrawled with information on all he had learned about garden cities and new towns, the supervisors listened intently. The new town, Simon said, would be called "Reston," its first three letters representing his initials. The location was virtually perfect: only eighteen miles from Washington and close to Washington Dulles International Airport, whose main terminal foundations were being laid that year. Additionally, the Beltway was nearly completed and would assist in travel to the area.

There was just one problem. As *The Washington Post*, which covered the development, explained, "The county's one- and two-acre zoning had to be scrapped, to be replaced by a new concept—zoning by population density." *The Post* continued, "Simon asked for flexibility. As long as he didn't intend to cram more people onto his land, why couldn't the developer cluster the houses as he wished, breaking up the monotonous suburban grid and surrounding houses with woods, parks and pathways that would bring homeowners together."[107]

To grease the rezoning wheels, Simon promised to buy water only from the county and to provide ten acres of parkland per one thousand residents. That day, the supervisors voted unanimously in Simon's favor, creating a new type of zoning written by Simon's attorney Ed Pritchard called a "Residential Planned Community."

An Uncommon Community

The zoning modification was the first of its kind in the nation and a land use milestone, permitting denser development patterns. While single-family, low-density housing had been the norm, thanks to Simon's vision and tenacity, multi-family, townhouse development, and flexible planned communities became a growing trend.[108] The decision marked a "historic detour from half a century of suburban tract development," *The Washington Post* reported. "No minimum lot size, no minimum setback lines, no maximum percentage of lot coverage. And, totally foreign to suburbia, commercial uses could mix with multi-family dwellings." The newspaper concluded, "Just as in small towns, people could live above the store."[109]

As part of Reston's 40th birthday celebrations in 2004, a bronze statue of Robert E. Simon Jr. was placed on a park bench in Washington Plaza on Lake Anne.

But convincing prospective homeowners to do just that proved more difficult. The first of Reston's mixed-use clusters—Lake Anne Village Center, dedicated in December 1965—resembled a European coastal village with balconied apartments overlooking retail shops, restaurants, and a central plaza with a burbling fountain. Simon's vision called for people to upgrade their housing needs as they aged, so he also built contemporary townhomes fronting manmade Lake Anne. These were the first townhomes to be built in Virginia in more than a century.

The atypical living arrangement and environment were a far cry from the typical suburban bedroom community, and many potential homebuyers considered this a drawback. "We had put this large sign on Route 66 promoting the new town that said, 'Welcome to Reston, Population _____,'" says developer Charles A. Veatch, a salesman in Reston's early days. "It took a long time for that sign to read '1,000.'"[110]

Simon soon faced mounting financial problems. "Bob had a very ambitious program and had never been a large-scale developer," says Veatch, who was also Reston's first postmaster at $1 a year. "He was trying to make breakthroughs, not the least of which was social. But realtors would tell interested people, 'You don't want to live there—your neighbors could be black and that could hurt your property values.' The irony is that there was little interest among African Americans to live in Reston because it was so remote."

Luring non-smokestack businesses and industries to the area was equally challenging. "It wasn't until Sperry Systems moved in and the U.S. Geological Survey bought a huge piece of property and built its headquarters in Reston in 1971 that viable employment was available," Veatch says. "By then, Bob was gone . . . He needed a lot more money than he ever anticipated it would take to complete Reston, and gradually became overextended [on his loans]."

Although Simon was initially successful in acquiring additional funds from the project's primary investor, Gulf Oil, as well as from John Hancock Insurance Company, the slow pace of home sales and rentals took its toll. According to U.S. Census Bureau figures, 487,000 homes were sold nationally in 1967, down from 560,000 in 1963.[111] So in 1967,

Simon reached a financial arrangement with Gulf and handed over control and management of the project.

Gulf Reston, the new developers, honored Simon's dream, though the houses built were more in tune with popular styles. "Bob's vision was great, but his practicality was not," says Jim Todd, who oversaw Reston's development from 1970 through 1984.[112] "Bob was hung up on this extreme contemporary urban statement not being sullied by traditional Virginia-style housing. But there was a small market for a Mies van der Rohe contemporary statement in the middle of pastoral scenery." Todd continues, "Bob deserves credit for forward thinking; the master plan is his. [But] the product—a beautifully planned residential neighborhood in the country—belongs to others."

With new developers at its helm, Reston—along with the adjacent rural town of Herndon—gradually bloomed. As the community grew, Dewberry & Davis was one of the firms that provided its engineering and design services to various projects. By 1988 more than seventeen thousand housing units in Reston were in place, as were schools, a library, hospital, parks, and recreational facilities. At present, more than sixty thousand residents call the old "new town" home. Still spry despite his ninety-plus years, Simon lives with his wife in an apartment at Lake Anne. A short distance away is a life-size bronze statue of him sitting on a park bench. The sculpture was dedicated at the community's fortieth anniversary in 2004.

New Infrastructures Take Flight

While Bob Simon was dreaming up plans for Reston, Til Hazel's own vision for Fairfax County was continuing to take shape. In 1961, the work that had consumed much of Til's time—acquiring right-of-way for the Beltway—culminated in the opening of the circumferential highway's first section. That year, Til left the firm of Jesse, Phillips, Klinge, and Kendrick, the law firm that represented the Virginia Department of Highways, to become a Fairfax County Associate Judge. He practiced zoning law on the side, renting two rooms across the street from the Fairfax courthouse.

Three years later, the finishing touches were put to the Beltway, and this section became Washington's Main Street, even though the route coursed through Maryland and Virginia. The Beltway was not only an important connecting link for many localities in Fairfax, it also was a well-worn bypass for travelers driving up and down the East Coast.[113] Zoned residential land along the highway quickly became expensive, worth $16,700 an acre on average in 1964, up from an average of $1,900 an acre in 1950.[114]

Yet the Beltway wasn't the only public infrastructure being birthed in Fairfax. On a gray and chilly November 19, 1962, on the county's western boundary, Washington Dulles International Airport was christened. More than fifty thousand people attended the dedication ceremonies, including the widow of John Foster Dulles, for whom the airport was named.

A military band played as the Thunderbirds flying team performed above, and President Kennedy and former President Eisenhower both spoke at the dedication. Kennedy traveled to the airport by helicopter. He was several minutes late, and he drew laughs when he remarked about his quick journey from the White House. His hair blowing in the wind, Kennedy extended praise to General Pete Quesada for his visionary planning and unflagging efforts to bring about the airport's development and completion. "This is a great airport at a great time in the life of our country," the president concluded.[115] It was an apt remark. Just the previous month, Kennedy had scored a major public opinion coup with his adroit handling of the Cuban Missile Crisis.[116] A spirit of optimism, if not nationalism, prevailed during this period, dubbed "Camelot" by the media.

Washington Dulles International Airport was owned by the federal government and overseen by the Federal Aviation Administration, but unlike most other federal infrastructures, the airport was celebrated as a masterpiece of mid-century modernism. Famed architect Eero Saarinen, who designed the main terminal and died just one year before its completion, considered it his best work. And his "mobile lounges," used to transport passengers between the terminal building and aircraft parked a half-mile away, were equally novel.

Still, only five airlines were in residence at Dulles, and the number of passengers remained small for many years. Of the twenty-eight thousand people who used both Dulles and Washington National airports in 1966, only three thousand of them utilized Dulles alone. "For years Dulles was a federal joke," says Leo Schefer, president of the Washington Airports Task Force.[117] And while *The Washington Post* lauded the airport as "one of the most beautiful in the world," the newspaper commented that its ticket counters were "barren of business, its skycaps idle, its escalators with no more than a trickle of suitcases."[118] In her book *Images of America: Washington Dulles International Airport,* author Margaret C. Peck concurs: "The space between the counters and the exterior wall was wide open. One and all had the privilege of going about as they desired."[119]

The best way to get to the airport from Washington was on the Dulles Airport Access Road. The four-lane freeway, christened the same day as the airport, was built to service high-speed airport traffic from the capital. Consequently, its on-ramps traveled only to Dulles, and its off-ramps solely toward the capital. Although the access road connected the airport to the Beltway and to Route 123 near McLean, it excluded local commuter traffic, which the federal government felt would impede airport-only traffic.

Anticipating the county's continuing population growth, the FAA obtained enough right-of-way (more than four hundred feet as opposed to the typical 250 feet) for parallel roadways to someday be built with multiple interchanges on either side of the access road. The right-of-way also included a median strip adequate for future rail use. In the meantime, the access road and its exclusion of local traffic became the subject of rancorous debate for two decades.

The debate pitted the Virginia Department of Highways (renamed the "Virginia Department of Transportation" in 1974), which sought use of the road for local traffic, against the FAA, which wanted to preserve the road for airport-only traffic. Budding communities like Reston also sought local use. "The access road whacked the Sunset Hills farm in two, which resulted in Reston being sliced across the middle," says Jim Wilding, at the time a junior engineer on the Dulles project. "Bob Simon and then Gulf lobbied to open the road up to local traffic. They really went to work, but General Quesada, who firmly believed in the exclusive use of the access road, pushed back."[120]

Blocking the Flow of Growth

Yet the debate over parallel roadways paled in comparison to the acrimony over another critical piece of county infrastructure: sewerage. While land around the Beltway had increased sharply in value in the mid-1960s, parcels in the county's central, central-south, and western regions were still relatively inexpensive and ripe for development at that time. Unfortunately, those areas also lacked much-needed public facilities like roads, water, and sewers.

Unlike the other public services under the county's control, sewers must be provided in advance of development. So when the new Board of Supervisors took office in 1968, it latched onto a cunning device to slow growth in the county—the provision of sewerage. "The Board had the ability to create policies by which it could release or not release a scarce resource, such as sewer capacity," asserts former Fairfax County attorney Lee Ruck.[121] Whether or not the Board's position was legal soon became another contentious issue.

Back in 1955, only half the county's residents were served by trunk line sanitary sewers, most of them in the northern region closest to the District of Columbia. In fact, *The Washington Post* stated at the time that if development continued in the southern part of Fairfax, "the county [would] have a terrific problem" because of the cost of installing sewers, then estimated at $50 million. The newspaper didn't bother commenting on the western two-thirds of Fairfax, which was expected to remain agricultural.[122]

The situation remained virtually unchanged until 1964, when the Potomac Interceptor opened to receive its first sewage flows from Dulles Airport and Fairfax and Loudoun counties. This major trunk sewer connected northern watersheds in the county, as well as watersheds in parts of Loudoun and Montgomery counties to the Blue Plains Treatment Plant on the north side of the Potomac River in Washington. The District of Columbia charged the counties for the sewer treatment. Residents located in the south and south-central regions of the county were either served by just a handful of small sewer treatment facilities—including the Little Hunting Creek Plant, Dogue Creek Plant, and Westgate Plant—or no sewer treatment at all.

"All the sewer lines had their own individual treatment plants, based on the particular district," says Millard Robbins, former executive director of the Upper Occoquan Sewage Authority, which now serves the western and southwestern parts of Fairfax County. "If a developer wanted to develop a property, he'd get permission to install his own treatment system and would form what's called a 'sanitary district.' Consequently, the county was populated by numerous independently operating sanitary districts."[123]

There was a significant problem with this approach. "The philosophy was to do things as cheaply as you could and the state would allow," Robbins explains. "Consequently, the sewer systems—when they worked—provided minimum treatment, at best." Til agrees: "The small plants were ineffective. Given the state-of-the-art at the time they were constructed—in the late 1940s and early 1950s—they didn't provide the highest level of treatment."

One potential solution was to declare Fairfax County a city. In 1964, state senator Omer Hirst argued as such, claiming that Fairfax had reached "the end of its rope" as a county and needed city powers to serve residents wanting urban services like a unified sewer system.[124] A city government would eliminate the parochial interests of supervisors elected by constituents in different districts, who each had their own needs in mind and not necessarily the best interests of the county. A city charter would also allow Fairfax to pursue and fund its own transportation agenda, rather than be under the aegis of the Virginia Department of Highways (which had jurisdiction over counties and not cities). "The idea was to eliminate the 'balkanization' of a government run by supervisors that were emperors of their own kingdoms," says Bill Wrench.[125] But the bid to become a city failed in the Virginia Senate, as did an attempt by the city of Alexandria to annex 8.3 square miles of the county in 1969, another effort predicated on providing more effective public services to residents.

Thus, the Urban County executive form of government persists to this day. It was slightly altered in 1967, after a study by George C. Kelley Jr.—who was appointed to be Massey's deputy county executive in 1968—recommended that the seven magisterial districts be refashioned into eight districts, with an additional supervisor and a chairman elected by county citizens to serve as a vote tiebreaker.

Treating the Water Problem

Its power now secure, the new Board rationalized that the best way to slow growth was to simply deny zoning and development plans on the basis that there was no sewage plant capacity in the Pohick. Ruck contends, "In the general realm of public policy, what the Board did was legitimate, hoarding a scarce resource and dribbling it out."

Ruck may have considered the Board's actions legitimate, but developers found them frustrating. When homebuilder Tom Cary acquired approximately five hundred acres west of Springfield, he applied to the Board for rezoning and expressed the need to build a small "package" sewer plant for his planned development. The Board denied the request, and so Cary asked Til to represent him in a lawsuit against the county.

In addition to his courtroom duties, Til was managing the 1964 senatorial campaign of Democrat Harry F. Byrd Jr., son of Virginia's longtime senator and former governor Harry F. Byrd. ("Young Harry," as he was called, won the election and served until 1983.) Nevertheless, Til took Cary up on his offer to sue Fairfax. "It was better to be respected than loved," he explains.

Cary was far from the only developer having trouble obtaining rezoning. That same year, Abe Pollin, a developer who had built houses primarily in Washington and Maryland, purchased 903 acres along Pohick Road and Keene Mill Road, a tract of land adjacent to Cary's holdings. Pollin applied for rezoning to build a subdivision of more than one thousand homes on the property. The Board initially rebuffed him. "I was completely stymied," he says. "I just couldn't get it approved and this was the largest piece of land we had ever assembled."[126]

County executive Carlton Massey stepped in to broker the divide. A civil engineer, Massey understood the need for adequate sewerage, but he believed the answer lay in a single, large plant that would absorb the inadequate treatment provided by the small package plants serving the watershed east of the Pohick. "Carlton was concerned that a proliferation of small plants would be bad for the county, and I quickly agreed," says Til. Massey asked both Cary and Pollin to defer their rezoning applications to give him time to prepare an alternative, and the developers acquiesced.

As Massey mulled plans for a larger treatment plant, the hodgepodge of package plants became even more overloaded, discharging 80 percent above their allowable pollutant load. The small Westgate Plant, for instance, received three to four million gallons of sewage a day above its eight-million-gallon capacity.[127] The lower Potomac soon became a cesspool, with more raw sewage suspended in its waters than the river had absorbed in the early 1930s when the county had no sewage treatment plants.

Finally, in June 1970, the Virginia State Water Control Board awoke from its slumber and imposed a moratorium on new sewer hookups in the county. The moratorium was designed to compel the county to upgrade its inferior and overloaded sewage plants. The Board of Supervisors fired back, insisting that the plants could not be improved to the Water Control Board's standards. In response, Til filed a bevy of lawsuits against the county on behalf of builders in northern Virginia, and arrived in court with technology that proved the plants could indeed be upgraded.

A Watershed Decision

The technology came courtesy of Noman M. Cole Jr., a nuclear engineer who was active in local environmental causes, including a successful crusade to preserve Mason Neck—a sparsely populated wilderness at the southernmost part of the county—as a state park. In the process, he had fought powerful real estate interests that were seeking to build a satellite city of twenty thousand people in the area. Today, most of Mason Neck remains as it did when its namesake, George Mason, met George Washington in a carriage along the shoreline to ride to church services at Pohick Chapel on Sundays.[128]

Cole thus had no political ax to grind in assisting Til and the developers, and his research was compelling. It indicated that the plants could provide quality treatment if certain chemicals were used to accelerate the removal of pollutants like phosphorus. Cole further recommended the installation of pure oxygen systems and the provision of nitrogen tertiary treatment. "The no-growth forces were trying to use the sewers as a means of controlling new growth in the Washington metropolitan area," Cole wrote in 1980. "Their theory: if you have no new sewer capacity, the plants will remain overloaded, make a big mess of the Potomac, and thereby be the basis for calling a halt to new development . . . What really suffered was the Potomac itself."[129]

Til's lawsuits were a success, forcing the county to immediately upgrade and improve the small package plants. Both Cary and Pollin were able to move ahead with their developments, with Pollin assisted by Sid Dewberry, who had moved the offices of Dewberry & Davis from Arlington to Fairfax County in 1965. "We got the permit from the State Water Control Board to build a package treatment plant for Abe's 903 acres," Sid recalls.[130] The permit was predicated on Pollin connecting his system to the Pohick Trunk Sewer when it was completed. Pollin did, and later built the MCI Center (the Verizon Center today), a major sports arena in the heart of Washington.

Supervisors could no longer use sewers to thwart growth, at least for the time being. "[County attorney Lee] Ruck never succeeded in establishing that sewer legally could be released by the Board as a scarce resource," says Til. And abetted by Cole's technology, the small plants actually did their job. Sewage in the Potomac was dramatically reduced. "Til and Noman moved the focus away from . . . controlling growth to the fact that we had to do something for the environment," says Jimmie Jenkins, director of the Fairfax County Department of Public Works.[131]

The small plants were soon replaced with a major trunk sewer extending up the Pohick Valley to the new Lower Potomac Treatment Plant near Fort Belvoir. Finally, the region had the state-of-the-art unified sewer system that Carlton Massey had envisioned would provide the most efficient and effective wastewater treatment to Fairfax County.

The private sector had lit the fuse for the new plant. "As it turned out, the issue over sewer permits was one of the main motivators for the Board moving to build the larger treatment plant," Sid says. "It [was] just another example of how the business community forced the Board to move off dead center and do something important. [The] business community provided the impetus for the local governing body to be more aggressive in just about everything—from K–12 [schools] to economic development, to transportation, to providing utilities for development, such as water and sewer."

At its inception, the new sewer plant treated eighteen million gallons per day (MGD) of wastewater; subsequent expansion programs increased its sewage treatment capacity to thirty-six MGD in 1978, fifty-four MGD in 1995, and sixty-seven MGD in 2005. Dewberry & Davis was involved in the design and engineering of the plant's expansion. "Wherever there was excess sewage, other than in the extreme western part of the county, it could now be pumped over to the Lower Potomac Plant for treatment," says Ruck. New developments were also able to dispatch their wastewater to the Lower Potomac Treatment Plant. The plant played a critical role in developing the Pohick watershed, and was later renamed in honor of Noman Cole, thanks in large part to Til Hazel's and Sid Dewberry's persistent lobbying, personal financial contributions, and fund-raising efforts.

At the July 4, 1976, bicentennial celebration in Washington, an armada of pleasure boats the likes of which the Potomac had not seen in years jammed the river. "No one aboard those boats who'd been on the river before could fail to notice that the raw sewage and other filth were gone," Noman wrote in 1980 for *The Washington Post Magazine*.[132] "In 1978 the members of the Harley family of Mason Neck, who have fished the Potomac commercially for five generations, told me that the lower river was in better shape than they had seen it in more than 40 years."

He added, "You give a river half a chance, and it will come back."

Battle for Burling

Having failed in its attempt to stymie growth through sewerage, the Fairfax County Board of Supervisors now turned to other means of halting development: selectively processing zonings and delaying the approval of site and subdivision plans. "The 1968 to 1972 Board of Supervisors did not fully perceive the changing nature of the land use conflict, and they responded with an ad hoc slow growth program [implementing] a wide assortment of devices and techniques designed to impede, delay, hinder and otherwise interfere with the development process," Til wrote.[133]

Various supervisors, for instance, mandated that approval on rezoning applications they deemed "sensitive" be deferred indefinitely. As a result, from May 1966 to October 1967, there grew a steep backlog of zoning applications—from 149 to 290 unheard applications. And the

Pictured, left to right, are Warren Cikins, Marie Travesky, James Scott, Martha Pennino, Alan Magazine, Jack Herrity, Audrey Moore, Joseph Alexander, and John Shaconis—members of the Fairfax County Board of Supervisors, 1977.

numbers kept growing. When faced with requests for action, the Board came up with a variety of excuses. Eventually, a procedure was created for requesting early action, which included a public hearing before the supervisors. But this, too, failed to trim the backlog, as applicants were often told to return to a subsequent hearing. Moreover, the order of the hearings was determined by the supervisors' preference and the amount of citizen opposition the zoning was anticipated to generate—not the typical first-come-first-served procedure.[134]

So once again Til returned to court, this time to challenge the Board to hear the backlog of cases. "We told the court that due process required hearing these cases, and we [wanted] an order to the Supervisors to hear these cases," he said in 1987. "It broke the logjam."[135]

The 1968 to 1972 Board of Supervisors wasn't strictly anti-growth . . . allegedly. Rather, it was seeking to slow development to provide enough time to address the comprehensive plans put forth by Rosser Payne and his planning staff. Unfortunately, populism had penetrated the Board's thinking, and despite the sincere and prolonged efforts of county executive Carlton Massey, the Board lacked both the commitment and competence to provide the necessary systems, facilities, and services to support Fairfax County's Master Plan. While the Board of Supervisors

Harriet F. Bradley speaks at a meeting of the Fairfax County Board of Supervisors, 1968.

had little difficulty funding politically popular infrastructures like parks and hospitals, it resisted endorsing other vital proposed infrastructure improvements such as highways.

The growing environmental movement was one factor in the Board's swing toward populism. For instance, the Board of Supervisors did not initially stand in the way when Miller and Smith Associates bought 336 acres north of the Beltway along the Potomac River in the Burling Tract and announced plans to build a 309-home subdivision. But organized citizen's groups did, and ultimately the Board was compelled to change its position.

"We went through the zoning and approval process, and then the first Earth Day [in 1969] happened," remembers Gordon Smith, CEO-emeritus of Miller and Smith, a real estate development company started by Smith, Dave Miller, and Otis "Skip" Coston, three MBAs from Harvard University who met at school and founded the firm. "Fairfax citizens were screaming that the property should be developed into a park," Smith adds. "[But] since we already had the zoning, the county would have to condemn the land, and it didn't have the money to do that."[136]

To prevent Miller and Smith from performing construction work at the site, a Fairfax County Circuit Court judge ruled that the county would have to put up a hefty $300,000 bond. The Board of Supervisors was in a bind: it didn't have that kind of cash, but it also needed to support the county's Master Plan of managed growth in the county. As Supervisor Happy Bradley put it to *The Washington Post*, "If the citizens expect to be able to rely on master plans, [then] the landowners and the prospective developers in the county have the same right. This land has never been planned or zoned for any other use than that to which the developers propose to put it."[137]

The "Burling Tract Fight" was daily fodder for area newspapers, which seemed to favor the conservationists. Photos of earnest students and Fairfax matrons picketing the Board of Supervisors ran alongside stories about the "struggle between nature lovers who want a natural park and a developer who wants to build a . . . subdivision." That Miller and Smith planned to leave 52 percent of the tract open as green space was rarely mentioned. In several articles, *The Washington Post* called the

FAIRFAX COUNTY
VIRGINIA

SCALE IN MILES

LEGEND

FREEWAYS (200-300 FT. R.O.W.)
━━━ EXISTING OR PROGRAMED
     FOR CONSTRUCTION
╍╍╍ PROPOSED ROUTES
  ⟡ PROPOSED INTERCHANGE

PARKWAYS (110 FT. VARIABLE R.O.W.)
━━━ EXISTING ROUTES
╍╍╍ PROPOSED ROUTES
  ⬥ PROPOSED INTERCHANGE

ARTERIAL HIGHWAYS (110-160FT. R.O.W.)
━━━ EXISTING ROUTES
╍╍╍ PROPOSED NEW ALIGNMENTS
  ⬥ PROPOSED GRADE SEPARATED
     INTERSECTION

MAJOR THOROUGHFARES (80-110 FT. R.O.W.)
━━━ EXISTING ROUTES
╍╍╍ PROPOSED ROUTES
─○─ AREAS REQUIRING REALIGNMENT
     FOR PURPOSES OF CURVE REDUCTION

EXISTING LOCAL THOROUGHFARES
     MINIMUM 60 FT. R.O.W. OR GREATER AS ESTABLISHED
     BY THE PLANNING ENGINEER, EXCEPT ON LOCAL SUBDIVISION
     STREETS WHERE MINIMUM REQUIRED R.O.W. IS 50 FT.

MAJOR STREETS AND
HIGHWAYS PLAN

NORTH

FAIRFAX COUNTY PLANNING DIVISION   1965

Above and opposite page: A 1965 Major Streets and Highways Plan, prepared by the Fairfax County Virginia Planning Office, proposed new roads and improvements to existing roads.

Burling parcel "one of the last great wild places on Washington's outskirts . . . cherished by wildlife, the songbirds and people."[138] The newspaper even stated that lawyer Edward Burling, from whom Miller and Smith had bought the land, had chopped wood outside his log cabin on the property until his ninetieth birthday a decade earlier.

Gordon Smith didn't have a chance. Still, he had the law on his side: his money had been spent fairly and the zoning had been approved. So he hired Til Hazel to represent his legal interests and Bill Hazel to begin clearing the woods and grading the roads. By the end of July 1970, Bill had cleared four acres from the land, and Smith publicly declared that he was ready to build the first home. His announcement was met with a deafening uproar.

The fight eventually played out on the floor of the U.S. Senate and was reported in the Congressional Record.[139] Drawing from emergency funds, U.S. Secretary of the Interior Walter Hickel pledged half the land's purchase price, $1.5 million—at the time, the largest contingency grant ever made by the government and one that exceeded the department's annual funding for the entire state of Virginia. Meanwhile, officials held a successful referendum during the state's primary elections to raise taxes to contribute toward the remainder of the purchase price. The ten-month drama finally drew to a close on August 5, 1970, when the Board offered to buy the Burling tract for $3.6 million. Miller and Smith accepted the deal.

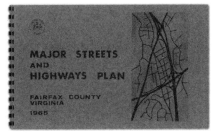

The die had been cast. Although the developers had bought the land in good faith, were supplying an intense demand for housing, and had presented plans to preserve more than half the property as open space, "development" had become a pejorative word in Fairfax County. Meanwhile, the suburbs of other major U.S. cities, unhampered by growth control governments, grew like weeds. For example, in Bellevue, across Lake Washington from the city of Seattle, 61,196 people called the suburb home in 1970, up from fewer than six thousand inhabitants in 1953.[140]

Much of the responsibility for the beginning of this slow-growth movement in Fairfax County rested with its populist Board. The Board of Supervisors may have thought it was simply preservation-minded, but its efforts created development problems and housing shortages that would take many years to resolve. "As a result, Fairfax County experienced an acute increase in the cost of carrying and developing land, which in turn imposed an artificial inflationary factor on housing costs and availability that alarmed responsible community leaders, the building industry and the business community," Til wrote.[141]

And yet as slow-growth as the 1968 to 1972 Board of Supervisors was, it was no match for the next Board.

Further Inroads to Expansion

The mid- to late-sixties brought intense political and cultural upheaval to the United States. The protracted war in Vietnam, ongoing racial discrimination and related strife, and the assassinations of popular leaders stirred the younger generation. New forms of music and art, and more relaxed attitudes about work and intimacy surfaced. Young people migrated geographically toward the country's coasts, while older Americans fled the inner cities torn by racial turmoil for the perceived safety of the suburbs.

This period of change fueled the development of federal programs that would have a profound effect on the expansion of Fairfax County, despite the local government's efforts to control growth. Both the Vietnam War and President Lyndon Johnson's "Great Society" program—predicated on the elimination of poverty and racial discrimination—resulted in a buildup of federal employees. The Johnson administration also introduced new federal spending programs on a scale that almost rivaled Roosevelt's New Deal agenda to address education, medical care, urban problems, and transportation.

These programs helped Fairfax solidify its position as the bedroom community of Washington. As Washington's employment numbers grew, newcomers flocked to Fairfax for housing. Between 1960 and 1970, the number of civilians employed in the executive branch grew by twenty-two percent to 2.2 million.[142]

Several studies were subsequently conducted on how to deal with the Greater Washington Metropolitan Region's mushrooming population. In 1968, the Virginia Department of Transportation (VDOT) commissioned the Highway Urban Needs Study, which assessed transportation requirements for the year 1985. The study, prepared by the consultant firm Hayes, Seay, Mattern & Mattern, Inc., called for two additional Beltways as well as three major highways: the Monticello Freeway, the Northern Virginia Expressway, and the Potomac Expressway. The

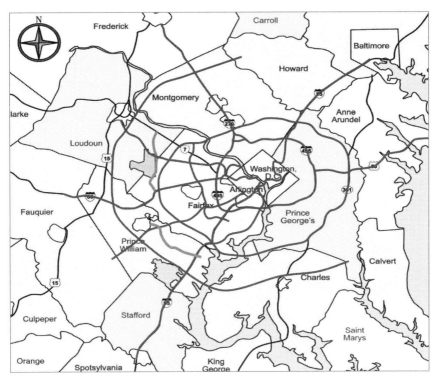

A 1966 Northern Virginia Economic Development Commission map details road and bridge plans proposed in the Year 2000 Plan.

Monticello Freeway and the Potomac Expressway would be radial highways, while the Northern Virginia Expressway would be a circumferential road that, unlike the Beltway, did not cross into Maryland. Instead, the Northern Virginia Expressway was to be located between the Beltway and the proposed Outer Beltway, with its northwestern terminus at the Outer Beltway north of Route 7 and its southeastern terminus at U.S. Route 1 north of Fort Belvoir. The Outer Beltway would cross the Potomac River into Maryland near Great Falls in the northern part of Fairfax County, and across Mason's Neck in the southern portion of the county.

Many other studies picked up ideas from the Metropolitan Washington Council of Government's 1950s-era plan, which posited a dire need for improved transportation. For example, in 1964 the Maryland-National Capital Planning Commission adopted the Year 2000

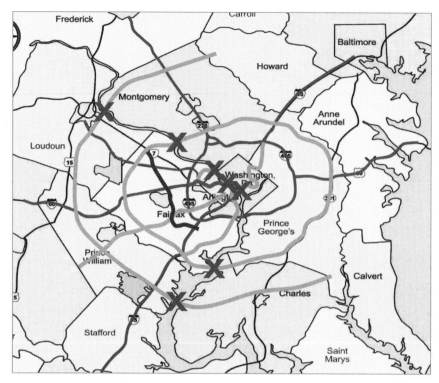

Year 2000 Plan road projects deleted to control growth, such as the Monticello Freeway, among others, are shown as light gray routes in this contemporary map.

"Wedges and Corridors" Plan, which called for the construction of two outer Beltways circumnavigating the District of Columbia and the states of Virginia and Maryland. Two years later, the National Capital Regional Planning Council proposed four circumferential highways and seven radial growth corridors that would crisscross them like a spider's web. The council noted that "extensive portions of right-of-way" for a second Beltway were "already purchased or reserved by government agencies," and "should be open to accommodate the projected traffic in the early 1980s." It further proposed opening a third Beltway by the year 2000.[143]

The Northern Virginia Regional Plan for the Year 2000—endorsed by the Fairfax County Planning Staff as urgent—was presented to the public on February 25, 1965, and similarly expressed the need for more transportation. Authored by the Northern Virginia Planning and Economic Development Commission, the plan called for two additional

Beltways "wide enough to accommodate rail or bus transit," as well as the building of additional bridges crossing the Potomac River. Only two major Potomac crossings were available to commuters within Fairfax County—the Woodrow Wilson Bridge south of Alexandria and the American Legion Bridge linking Montgomery County in Maryland with

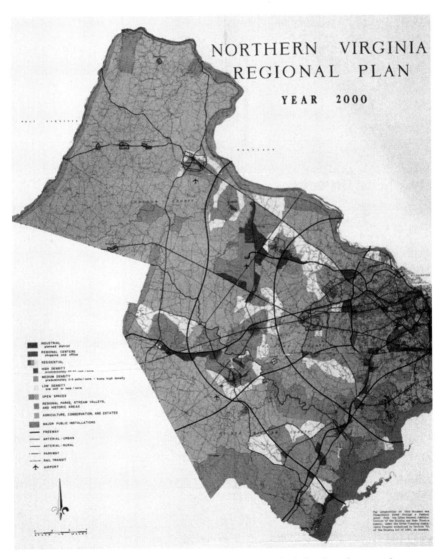

The Northern Virginia Regional Plan for the Year 2000 provided a land use framework as color-keyed cells within a network of transportation in this original 1965 map.

Dulles Airport and Tysons Corner. (Other bridges linked the District to Arlington County, including Chain Bridge, Key Bridge, Arlington Memorial Bridge, and the 14th Street Bridge.)

The plan predicted that eight hundred thousand people would work in northern Virginia in the year 2000, but that only two hundred thousand of them would be commuting to jobs in Washington. "Many workers should be able to go from one Virginia town to another in a circumferential movement," the authors stated. "For these reasons the plan calls for two more beltways . . . With this new concept, lesser roads will not grow larger and become overrun with thru-traffic . . . Virginia depends on the motor car and forecasts indicate this will still be true when the Year 2000 arrives." As the director of the commission Walter Schilling said wryly, "Yes, Virginia, there is a regional plan."

Dead End Indecision

The county's Board of Supervisors studied the various transportation plans, but it made no effort to implement them. Neither the Monticello or Potomac roads recommended by the Highway Urban Needs Study were ever constructed, although some segments of the Northern Virginia Expressway would be built in the 1980s as part of the Fairfax County Parkway. And "Fairfax County did not find it feasible to implement its own version of the National Capital Planning Commission 'Wedges and Corridors' plan," wrote Harvard researchers Lucille Harrigan and Alexander von Hoffman in the study "Happy to Grow: Development and Planning in Fairfax County, Virginia." "There were no real attempts—other than the notable exception of the new town of Reston—to implement the development of the 'satellite' cities that would provide shopping and employment within walking distance of many residents." The researchers concluded, "The Board of Supervisors [simply] gave lip service to the philosophy of the Year 2000 plan."[144]

Doug Fahl, who ran the transportation planning branch of the Fairfax County Planning Department from 1966 to 1970, seems to concur. "We would put together these plans and put [them] in front of the Board and the planning commission, and some were adopted and some weren't," Fahl says. "In cases where they were adopted, roads would later be deleted. For example, the Bull Run plan in 1969 called for building an Outer Beltway, but that was later taken off the map."[145]

Like Fahl, Dave Edwards was a member of the planning department under Rosser Payne in the mid- to late-1960s. "We were very highway-oriented, but the political folks didn't want it to happen," Edwards says. "After the bribery scandals, the decision was made to bring in more pro-fessional people to the staff. We had the credentials, yet the Board of Supervisors decided that they were the experts on land use and trans-portation, I guess through osmosis."[146]

One factor in the Board's inertia was populism. "When a road is announced, you get people affected by the proposed route showing up at public hearings and making themselves heard," says Bob Chase, president of the Northern Virginia Transportation Alliance. "Obviously, if you have a house next to . . . a projected highway you're not going to be excited about it. That made it extremely difficult for the elected official in the dis-trict to look at the big picture. It's the NIMBY factor—the squeakiest wheel—even though 90 percent of the people may benefit."[147]

The effects of the Board's apathy were far-reaching and resulted in gridlock decades later. Today, many northern Virginians blame traffic congestion on a lack of planning for future highway needs, but the truth is that planners fully appreciated the anticipated population growth and made a great effort to devise a system of roads addressing it. County politicians simply failed to heed their advice.

Derailing Plans for New Roads

The region's various transportation plans also called attention to the need for a rapid rail transit that would service the District of Columbia through its outlying suburbs. In many plans, the proposed rail system intersected with the proposed circumferential highways. Unlike most of the roads, though, the rail system was actually completed. On March 1, 1968, the Washington Metropolitan Area Transit Authority—which had been created by executive order the previous November—approved the building of a 97.2-mile Metropolitan Rail transit system comprising 38.4 miles of track in the District, 29.7 in Maryland, and 29.1 in Virginia. Officials broke ground on December 9, 1969, although the rail system did not open in Fairfax County until the early 1980s.

Since rail service was considered less environmentally contentious than highways and cars, politicians and the public soon embraced it as the solution to the county's transportation needs. This was a shortsighted conclusion. The problem with relying on a rail system that radiated from Washington was that it was predicated on the expectation that people would be working primarily in the District (and to a lesser extent in Alexandria and Arlington counties). Planners predicted, however, that most people in the county would someday work not in the District but in Fairfax—hence the need for circumferential highways.

As developers feared, rail service only took the pressure off politicians to build highways and ultimately did very little to solve the county's tightening gridlock.

Due to the nascent environmental movement and the emphasis on rail service, many carefully considered highway plans that had been on the map for decades were either deleted or deferred. For example, Interstate 66, which was slated to be built inside the Beltway, had been on the drawing board since 1938 but was postponed to allow planning for Metrorail right-of-way in the highway corridor. It wasn't until 1958, two decades after I-66 was first proposed, that the Arlington and Fairfax County boards voted in favor of an eight-lane route along the soon-to-be-abandoned Washington and Old Dominion Railroad line. But organized citizens groups in Arlington County later leveraged the 1969 National Environmental Protection Act (NEPA), further derailing plans for the road.

The opposition argued that Arlington citizens would never use the road because there was no reason for them to go to Fairfax—an absurd contention since numerous studies predicted substantial employment growth in the county. Ironically, the failure to build I-66 as proposed and designed in 1958 spawned devastating consequences for both Arlington and Fairfax counties. In news accounts of the 1960s, "I-66 inside the Beltway" was frequently referred to as the "missing link."

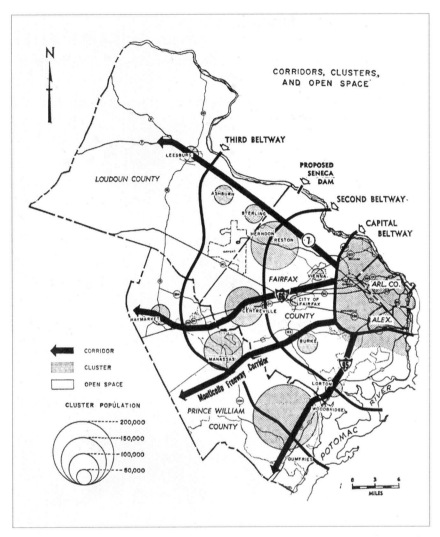

Corridors and population clusters are illustrated in this Northern Virginia Regional Plan Year 2000 map of transportation and residential development.

The political and public opposition to the highway marked the beginning of populist control of highways in Fairfax. "The furor led then-commissioner Doug Fugate of the Virginia Department of Highways to refuse to support the building of additional highways in northern Virginia," Bill Wrench says. By the 1970s, even more "missing links" would disappear.

GMU's Academic Evolution

Though the Board sought to stunt the expansion of the county's transportation and sewerage systems, other planks in Fairfax's infrastructure grew solidly—education in particular. In 1966, the Virginia General Assembly authorized the expansion of George Mason College into a four-year institution that could award baccalaureate degrees. George Mason—still an extension of the University of Virginia at this time—graduated its first senior class of fifty-eight students two years later. The same year, Harvard University graduated 1,128 undergraduate and 2,889 graduate students.[148]

Around this time, Til was appointed by northern Virginia's Board of Control to represent it in acquiring more land to expand the George Mason campus. The Board of Control, established in 1965 by the eleven jurisdictions of northern Virginia, recognized Til's success as an eminent domain/land condemnation attorney. The board members had passed bond issues in each jurisdiction to raise a total of $3.5 million to purchase land for George Mason, in addition to the 150 acres previously gifted by the City of Fairfax. "We recognized that 150 acres was insufficient for what we wanted to develop—a major, quality institution, which we felt was necessary and vital to the future of northern Virginia," Til says. "There were some who still thought it should remain a four-year commuter college, but the majority felt otherwise, and we began to lay the foundation for a more significant institution."

The Board of Control successfully acquired 422 acres of land in 1969, 415 of which were conveyed to the college by a deed signed by Governor Mills E. Godwin Jr. The following year, George Mason began offering courses at the master's level, and in 1972, the school was finally cleaved from UVA as a separate institution and its name was changed to George Mason University.

By 1973, the institution's original four baccalaureate programs—biology, business and public administration, English, and history—were augmented to include chemistry, mathematics, elementary education, French, Spanish, economics, psychology, physics, business, secondary education, German, government and politics, law enforcement, philosophy, music, social welfare, and business administration. Master's degrees were also available in history, biology, elementary and secondary education, mathematics, psychology, and business administration. New buildings included a lecture hall, student union, and Fenwick Library, and separate structures for health and physical education and arts and sciences.

In addition to providing legal support to the Board of Control, Til was appointed by Virginia Governor A. Linwood Holton Jr. to George Mason's newly formed Board of Visitors when the college became an independent university. One fellow board member was A. George Cook III, who had graduated from George Washington University in 1957, attended law school, and then went to work for Colonial Parking, building it with two partners into the eighth largest parking company in the country.

"Til and I were on the same wavelength about what kind of institution we felt Mason needed to become," Cook says. But it was, as Cook says, "an uphill climb all the way."[149] For example, the new board wanted GMU to be able to provide living facilities to students, but the State Council on Higher Education in Richmond wanted to preserve the institution as a commuter college. "A student, even from northern Virginia, should not be relegated to living at home to attend George Mason," Til said in 1987. Cook remembers: "We . . . knew we would never attract the kind of students we wanted from outside the area without having dormitories to offer them. The kids wanted housing, and the board voted 8 to 7 for it. We flexed our muscles and wings and eventually got the General Assembly to support us."[150]

Cook adds that another struggle was "acquiring funds from Richmond to hire faculty that [weren't] all second career folks . . . We wanted a first-class faculty with higher-level degrees to educate the students. We also wanted funds to build more buildings. Whenever the State Council on Higher Education turned us down, we went to the General Assembly. They got so tired of seeing us, they started giving us [what we needed], sometimes at the displeasure of UVA, which wanted to remain the number one institution in the state and keep us a commuter college. Ultimately, the private sector, led by people like Til, became the dominant force in the university's evolution—not the legislature, state senators, or various governors, although they were helpful."

The City of Fairfax's visionary mayor Jack Wood, who'd had the prescience to acquire land and gift it to GMU, was the university's first rector. Til, who served eleven years on the Board of Visitors, was its second. He ultimately served two terms. In this capacity, Til set his sights on bringing more effective leadership to the university. "We needed someone," says Til, "who would work to make GMU the most it could be."

NOVA: Educating the Community at Large

G MU wasn't the only institution of higher learning expanding in the 1960s. Around this time, Fairfax County's Northern Virginia Community College (NOVA) also took flight. Established as Northern Virginia Technical College in 1964, the college opened for classes in a single building at Bailey's Crossroads in the fall of 1965. The enrollment was 761 students, served by a faculty and staff of forty-six. Robert W. McKee, formerly with the U.S. Office of Education, was the first president.

The school's name was changed in 1966 to reflect recent legislation sponsored and signed by Governor Godwin to create a statewide system of twenty-three two-year community colleges. Although Godwin recognized the importance of Virginia's scattered technical colleges, he believed in the democratization of higher education. Community colleges could offer not only post-secondary technical classes, but also academic programs. "If we look at the numbers of potential students, and if we also look at the relative costs involved, the implication is clear that a community college system is the quickest . . . most efficient [and] most economical . . . way the future of our young people can be met," Godwin said.

Following its metamorphosis from technical to community college, college-transfer curricula were added to NOVA's existing occupational and technical curricula for a more comprehensive program. In 1966, NOVA bought seventy-eight acres in Annandale, which became the first of six permanent campus sites. One-hundred-acre sites were acquired the following year to create campuses in Sterling, part of northern Fairfax

County, and Manassas and Woodbridge in Prince William County. Another tract was purchased for a fifth campus in Alexandria in 1969. These new campuses were located at least an hour's drive from the original site, allowing NOVA to reach the widest range of students in the area. (A small campus for medical education was later built in the 1990s in Springfield.)

The first building at the Annandale campus was dedicated in 1968, and that year, Dr. Richard J. Ernst succeeded McKee as president, a role he held for the next three decades. By 1970, NOVA served ten thousand students and offered a plethora of study options, including courses in electronics, mechanical, and architectural engineering and/or architectural technology, and business management, merchandising and distribution, and data processing.

John W. Ryan, who in 1966 worked for the U.S. Office of Education in Washington, D.C., which awarded fellowships to institutions of higher learning, recalls that in the early days, "[NOVA's] primary purpose was to prepare students to transfer to a four-year institution or to take up some kind of career with an associate degree."[151]

NOVA's mission is still just that—although in recent decades, the school has evolved into the second largest community college in the nation after Miami-Dade in Florida, and one with the largest diversified group of students. With more than sixty thousand students, NOVA "is a place where first-generation Americans can come, learn English as a second language, take a range of classes and further their education," says Ryan. "These are very smart people just not used to a U.S. culture. NOVA helps them pursue the American dream."

Washington's Economic Exodus

The emphasis on higher education in Fairfax was predicated in part on enticing more companies to the county to do business. At the time, most companies were there to service the population, not employ it. To encourage desirable business and industrial development, the advisory Fairfax County Economic Development Authority became a standalone organization in 1964. Its primary job was to sell the county to the right kinds of companies: for the most part, non-smokestack firms that supplied products and services to the U.S. government.

"We began to think of ways to get more firms like Atlantic Research and Melpar to come here," says Dave Edwards, who joined the authority in 1970 as deputy to its executive director, Russell G. Hanson. Hanson worked closely with John Tydings at the Greater Washington Board of Trade to tout Fairfax County's economic virtues. He also ran herd on the development of the county's first industrial zoning map and its first directory of business and industry. "With Tydings," says Edwards, "we hosted tours of the county for senior executives of companies looking at relocating their operations. We also had people on our board like Jerry Halpin, a savvy businessman and solid person willing to talk up the county's plusses."

Tydings says a driving force in Washington-based companies "looking over the river at Fairfax" was the so-called "white flight" to the suburbs following the murder of Dr. Martin Luther King Jr. in 1968. The term described the trend of white city dwellers relocating to the suburbs and beyond, a migration attributed to inner-city violence, tight housing stock, and racism. Washington wasn't alone in experiencing this historic exodus. Other cities losing significant portions of their white populations at the time included Atlanta, Baltimore, Boston, Philadelphia, Detroit, Los Angeles, Memphis, Houston, Cleveland, St. Louis, Milwaukee, Newark, and New Orleans.[152]

"Downtown Washington was being ravaged by race riots, and more affluent citizens and businesses like retailers began to look elsewhere," explains Tydings, who was chief administrative officer of the Greater Washington Board of Trade from 1969 until 1971, when he became the board's chief economic development officer. He eventually climbed the ladder to become the board's CEO.[153]

Many retailers found a home at Tysons Corner Center, a $50 million complex on ninety acres of former apple orchards and cow pastures. The brainchild of developer Theodore N. Lerner, Tysons Corner Center was one of the largest enclosed, single-level shopping malls in America when its doors opened in July 1968, near Jerry Halpin's burgeoning West*Gate Research Park. The 1.5-million-square-foot mall was anchored by a

Woodward & Lothrop department store at one end and the Hecht Company store at the other. Between them were movie theatres, banks, a town hall, spacious courtyards with fountains, and the traditional array of shops and restaurants. "I knew the Beltway was coming and thought it would be a great location for a mall," Lerner says. "Leasing was tough the first few years because of the location, but by 1972 we were in high gear and it was a tremendous success."[154] Lerner later purchased another one hundred acres across the way for future development. The second tract included some farmland, but was "mostly an old gravel pit originally developed by Marcus Bles," says Til.

Washington-based companies also began looking to northern Virginia because the State of Maryland was rapidly and deliberately closing its borders to new development. Another factor was Virginia's passage in 1968 of the so-called "Liquor by the Drink" law, which allowed restaurants, taverns, and bars to serve hard liquor. Prior to the 1969 implementation of this law, customers had to join a private "bottle club" and bring their own liquor to a restaurant in a brown paper bag—not exactly enticing for high-level executives entertaining important clients.

Federal government decentralization was another factor. By 1970, northern Virginia was home to the U.S. Department of Defense at the Pentagon, the Central Intelligence Agency at Langley, the U.S. Geological Survey in Reston, and the National Technical Information Service in Springfield—and the private companies servicing these agencies were seeking closer proximity. Washington also had severe restrictions on the height of new buildings, and its older structures did not fit the design aesthetics of most upstart technology firms selling their wares to Uncle Sam. "There were a lot of reasons," says Fahl, "not to be in the District anymore."

A Surge in Office Space

And so they came, although slowly at first. From 1960 to 1967, Fairfax captured 47.2 percent of all the industrial employment growth in the Greater Washington Metropolitan Region. During the same period, land zoned "industrial" nearly doubled, from 1,754 acres to

3,334 acres. In 1969, the county added seventy-five new firms employing more than 1,700 people to its corporate roster, capping a five-year period during which more than three hundred companies settled in Fairfax. Nearly half the county's industrial employment was provided by research and technical manufacturing firms that paid substantial salaries, and Fairfax boasted the second highest median income per household in the U.S. that year, with 29 percent of its citizens earning more than $15,000 annually.[155]

One survey of companies relocating to the county indicated that 60 percent had chosen Fairfax because of its proximity to the federal government.[156] Among these newcomers were Dynalectron and TRW, which moved to the county in 1969 and 1970, respectively. Dynalectron provided facilities management services to the government, including the operation and maintenance of technical systems for the White Sands Missile Range. TRW developed highly sophisticated computerized systems and software for the U.S. Navy and various government agencies.

Back in 1955, there had been only one office building—which consisted of less than six thousand square feet of floor space—in all of Fairfax County. Five years later, there were twenty buildings offering a total of 350,000 square feet. By September 1971, more than 148 office buildings with over 4.8 million square feet of floor space dotted the county, with seventy-eight buildings containing 3.4 million square feet of space constructed in the previous five years alone.

The West*Gate and newer West*Park complexes developed in Tysons Corner by Jerry Halpin and his colleagues boasted the lion's share of the development—twenty-eight office buildings with nearly 1.7 million square feet of floor space.[157] West*Park was an agglomeration of office buildings and a few residential homes built on 152 acres of the Ulfelder family's former Maplewood Farm and property purchased from other landowners outside the Beltway in Tysons Corner. It was also adjacent to the one hundred acres of farmland purchased by Ted Lerner. After Tysons Corner, the remainder of development in the Fairfax County was geographically concentrated in Reston-Herndon, Seven Corners, Springfield, Merrifield, Vienna, and Bailey's Crossroads, where construction was underway on the Skyline Towers, a one-hundred-acre office, apartment, and condominium complex.

As more companies moved to the county, the housing crunch worsened. More than 454,000 people lived in Fairfax as the 1970s dawned, an 83 percent increase over the past decade—a rate double that of the entire Washington Metropolitan region. Many were lured by high-paying jobs and the increasing quality of life, from lush parkland to improved higher education. The quality of housing in Fairfax was another factor: in 1970, the median value of owner-occupied housing climbed to $35,400 per unit, among the highest in the nation.

For people with modest incomes, however, affordable housing became a problem. In a last ditch attempt to control land use decisions before the 1971 election that would unseat nearly all of them, the Board of Supervisors mandated that 15 percent of all projects over fifty units be devoted to low and moderate income housing. Once again, Til Hazel stood up for the rule of the law. "It was another desperate effort by the Board to be all things to all people and, obviously, was without any authority in the state zoning enabling legislation," he says. "I could not allow the failure of the Board to provide adequate housing to be offloaded onto the development community. Neither I nor the building community was opposed to affordable housing. Unfortunately, what the county couldn't do in an orderly and legal fashion they tried to do illegally, putting a public problem on the backs of the private sector." Til won the case for the developers, which was hardly a contest. The county's insistence on an appeal, says Til, "only memorialized the illegality" of the Board's efforts.

The Development of Hazel/Peterson

Having represented private enterprise in a landmark series of "land use by litigation strategies," as he calls them, Til emerged the most prominent zoning attorney in the Commonwealth of Virginia. Yet he was not content to simply react to Board decisions on land use matters. He next turned his sights outside the law to pursue another enterprise, one that would promise roofs over the heads of the hordes of newcomers.

In 1971, Til formed a real estate development company with developer Milton V. Peterson called Hazel/Peterson Companies. A native of Worcester, Massachusetts, and the son of a builder, Peterson stands 6-feet, 3-inches and is built like a linebacker, a position he played in high school and college. Like Jerry Halpin, who served in the U.S. Navy Sea Bees, Peterson served in the U.S. Army Corps of Engineers, in his case at Fort Belvoir, where he was taught the essentials of construction. In 1959, he cut his teeth selling houses for the Yeonas family, making it into the prestigious "Million Dollar Club"—which honors salespeople with more than $1 million in annual sales—his first year. After his stint with Yeonas, he set out on his own. Few developers rose to his level: Peterson was once described by colleagues as a man "genetically wired to strike deals, to find the profitable edge in any situation, to see infinite possibility in what to most eyes looks like just another clump of trees or open field."[158]

Til Hazel was captivated by Milt Peterson's salesmanship and negotiating skills as much as his unbridled confidence, energy, and charisma. They were an incongruous pair—the soft-spoken, deliberate, Harvard-educated attorney and the hard-driving, intuitive salesman with a voice so gravelly you could drive on it.

Everyone needs an anchor to windward, and Milt and Til were each other's. With the establishment of their firm in 1971, they set sail on a remarkable course destined to provide profound opportunities to Fairfax and its denizens.

CHAPTER 4

Land Use By
Litigation

DM International, Inc. was among the firms relocating to Fairfax County to be near Uncle Sam's purse strings. For most of the 1960s, the company had leased a one-person office on Connecticut Avenue in Washington to be closer to its main customer, the Department of Defense. In 1970, it moved its headquarters from El Paso, Texas, to Tysons Corner. A defense consultancy, BDM provided the Pentagon with research and advice on military weapon systems analysis and testing. "In this business, you have to be close to where the decisions are being made, and El Paso was a long way from Washington," says Stan Harrison, who joined BDM in 1968 and rose through the ranks to become chief operating officer.[159]

BDM was named for its founders, Joseph Braddock, Bernard Dunn, and Daniel McDonald. The scientists, who each had a PhD in physics, incorporated the firm in 1959. The following year, the company received its first contract: to provide analytical support to the U.S. Army at the White Sands Missile Range in south-central New Mexico, analyzing the flight paths of missiles and their required fuel capacity. Shortly thereafter, the firm set up shop in El Paso, the largest city near the missile range.

In 1962, Earle Williams joined BDM as its seventeenth employee. Williams had graduated from college with a degree in engineering and was also an ROTC graduate. After a three-month stint in the army at Fort Monmouth in New Jersey, Williams was relocated to Albuquerque to finish his service as a U.S. Army Special Weapons Electronics Officer. He subsequently ventured east for a short while and then returned to Albuquerque, where Sandia Corporation hired him as an engineer and put him to work on the design, development, and testing of nuclear weapon systems. Meanwhile, he studied for an MBA at the University of New Mexico.

After six years with Sandia, Williams learned that BDM was looking for a senior engineer. "I took the job with the proviso that I'd eventually be [able] to go into management," says Williams. He didn't want to be a "detail-oriented engineer" for the rest of his career. "As it turned out," he continues, "the three founders, all of them exceptionally bright people doing very important things, didn't want to be executives. It was a good fit."[160]

As the number of its government contracts increased and more federal work grew in the offing, BDM put down stakes in Fairfax County, leasing several offices in a building on Gallows Road and Route 7. The building was flanked by a bank on one side and a vacant lot fenced with barbed wire on the other. A big oak tree in the lot shaded the cows grazing within.

The firm had considered locating in Washington, but was turned off by the District's extreme deterioration. "We felt it would harm our recruiting efforts," Williams explains. "The public schools, for example, had fallen on bad times, whereas Fairfax County, by contrast, had very good schools."

BDM quickly discovered just how vital it was to be headquartered close to the Department of Defense. "When we relocated, a fellow at the Pentagon whom we'd worked for before called me and said he had this 'crash problem' in Air Defense and needed immediate help," says Williams, who was director of operations at the time. "He said, 'When can you get down here?' It was nine in the morning, and I told him that normally it would take me thirty minutes, but the traffic was bad and it might take me fifty. Had we still been in El Paso, he wouldn't have called."

In 1972, Williams became president and CEO of BDM. The company had just won a major contract for weapon systems testing and evaluation from the government—with the stipulation that someone with business skills would take over the organization. "The army didn't like our organizational chart," Williams explains. "If there was a problem, they said they didn't want to negotiate contract issues with a scientist; they wanted to negotiate with me." When Williams informed the founders that the firm stood to lose a major contract unless he was named president, they quickly agreed.

That year, the firm posted $7.7 million in sales and tallied 430 employees. Under Williams's leadership, BDM gradually evolved from assisting the government with "guns and butter" analytical services during the Vietnam War to providing high-level research to support policy-related decisions in the ongoing Cold War with the Soviet Union. As the company grew, it leased office space in other buildings, "picking up floors here and there," says Harrison. It was finally able to gather all its employees under one roof in 1975, leasing a large office building on Route 7. Three years later, BDM's staff completed a well-publicized study for the Nuclear Regulatory Commission on the dangers terrorists posed to nuclear power reactors.

Banking on BDM

Credit was tight for BDM during the mid-1970s due to the economic recession, which had been spawned by the oil embargo declared by the Organization of Petroleum Exporting Countries. To complicate things, financial institutions were reluctant to fund service companies doing government contracting work. Such business was "not well understood by large banks, and not understood at all by local ones," notes Williams.

This became painfully evident when BDM bid on a major government contract for consulting work overseas. When Williams informed the firm's usual lender, the Bank of Virginia, of what BDM's funding needs would be if it won the contract, he was rebuffed. "The competition had come down to us and one other company," Williams recalls. "On the night before the award was announced, the bank told us they wouldn't finance the contract if we won it."

The next day, he began to search for a new bank in Northern Virginia and was turned down by every one he solicited. Then serendipity intervened. One day while Harrison was eating lunch at a restaurant, he was approached by Milton L. Drewer, president of the local Clarendon Trust. Drewer inquired about BDM's business and asked for a meeting. Harrison called Williams, and they set it up for the next day.

Milton Drewer hailed from Delmar, a small town in Virginia on the eastern shore of Chesapeake Bay. Drewer, who went to college on a sports scholarship, was the ninth person from Delmar to attend college; his parents were two of the others. After he graduated, Drewer took a job as a football coach at a high school in Portsmouth, a historic port city in Virginia. He left a short while later to become the football coach at the College of William & Mary in colonial Williamsburg, the second-oldest institution of higher education in the country. But Drewer gradually became discontented with college politics, and at the age of forty, he took a friend's advice and entered banking. He hired on at Clarendon Trust in March 1964. The following year, he was named the small bank's president.

The meeting between Williams and Drewer became the springboard for a definitive agreement that would make Clarendon Trust the primary source of funding for BDM. After BDM became more bankable in the latter half of the 1970s, other financial institutions approached the firm. Williams says he took great pleasure in turning them down. "I never forgot Milt helping us when no one else would," he adds. "Milt was one of the people to whom BDM and I will forever be indebted."

The tiny Clarendon Trust flourished under Milt Drewer's watch, eventually merging with two local banks, Arlington Trust and Alexandria National Trust. Renamed First American Bank, the institution would play a pivotal role in funding many other important local firms, including developers such as Hazel/Peterson Companies, several home builders, and other pioneering companies that, like BDM, were relocating to Northern Virginia.

With its financing secure, BDM became a top government contractor. From 1972 to 1988, the company's revenues grew nearly 30 percent a year on a compounded basis. During this period, Earle Williams did more than just adroitly guide the firm. He also invested his energy and time into a plentiful array of civic-minded endeavors, becoming one of a dozen or so key individuals dedicated to making Fairfax County a far better place to live and work. During this period, BDM occupied approximately four hundred thousand square feet of office space in West*Park buildings.

Populism and the Packard Board

Change was in the air during the 1971 election year. That March, after nineteen years of highly effective service, Carlton Massey relinquished the reins as Fairfax's first county executive. During his remarkable tenure, the county's population swelled from 131,000 to 469,000 people. One of Massey's first budgets had topped out at $10 million; his last called for $112 million just for schools.

The supervisors accepted Massey's resignation "with regrets" and named Fairfax's twelve-story government office building, only eighteen months old, in his honor.[161] It was a fitting gesture for the Solomon-like Massey, who was able to balance the needs of the fast-growing county while maintaining good relations with the Board of Supervisors. *The Washington Star* wrote that when the board would argue an issue to the point of distress, Massey "would come up with a suggestion that would clear the matter up. . . . He often knew more about Fairfax than the members of the five boards of supervisors he worked for."[162] Ten years later, in 1981, Massey died in an automobile accident in Florida, where he and his wife had relocated the previous year.

Massey's deputy county executive, George J. Kelley Jr., assumed the position on March 15, 1971. Kelley's work as a senior consultant with the firm of Cresap, McCormick, and Paget had brought about changes to the county's magisterial districts and to the composition of the Board of Supervisors in 1967. A firm believer that growth was good for Fairfax, Kelley had at his disposal a budget of $247.2 million, including more than

Rufus Phillips chairs a meeting of the Comprehensive Planning and Land Use Control Task Force, Fairfax County Board of Supervisors, 1973.

$88 million in bond issues for schools, libraries, health facilities, transit, parks, and sewers that had been approved by voters.[163] Unfortunately, Kelley's honeymoon as county executive was short-lived. That November, he learned he would be dealing with a virtually new Board of Supervisors—one that did not share his progressive opinions on growth.

The entire nine-member Board, five Democrats and four Republicans, had been up for reelection that fall of 1971. It was a bruising contest, one that pitted pro-growth and slow-growth incumbents against strict anti-growth challengers. "The principle issue in several key districts was which candidate could most effectively implement a no-growth policy," Til Hazel wrote in 1976. "The incumbent Board of Supervisors did not fully comprehend the populist appeal of the issue and relied on its record."[164]

Roughly 60 percent of all development in the Greater Washington Metropolitan Region was occurring in Fairfax County, which the challengers claimed had resulted in urban sprawl, strip development, air and water pollution, traffic congestion, and higher government costs. Two particularly vocal challengers were Democrats Rufus Phillips and Audrey Moore. Both asserted that, if elected, they would immediately put the brakes on future development. "Rapid growth can only mean higher taxes, congested roads, and higher levels of air and water pollution," Moore said at the time.[165]

Phillips, Moore, and six other Democrats won their respective district elections. Of the incumbents, only Joe Alexander, Martha Pennino, and Herbert Harris remained. John "Jack" Herrity, who represented Springfield, was the lone Republican on the new Board.

The following year, Board chairman Bill Huffnagle retired. Jean Packard, a liberal Democrat and ardent conservationist whose husband Fred had been the first director of the Fairfax County Park Authority, ran for the position in a countywide election against Democrat Bill Wrench and won by a slim margin. Wrench called for a recount, but Packard prevailed.

The daughter of a Cincinnati newspaperman and the niece of a prosecuting attorney, Packard moved to the county with her husband in 1951. She got her toes wet in public affairs as a member of the non-profit Fairfax County Federation of Citizens Associations, working her way up to become president of the organization. Packard vocally opposed the development of the Burling tract along the Potomac River and was instrumental in preserving the area as a park. The victory endowed her with the public persona of an environmentalist.

Needless to say, the new Board and the county executive did not see eye to eye. "Kelley made no secret [that] he, not the Board of Supervisors, would maintain day-to-day control of the County government," wrote Grace Dawson in "No Little Plans: Fairfax County's PLUS Program for Managing Growth."[166] The Board didn't see things that way, however, insisting that Kelley's chief responsibility as the county's highest-ranking administrator was to carry out its agenda to corral growth.

"The Packard Board, many of whom were not native Virginians, wanted the county to stay the way it was, which was a selfish, shortsighted approach," says attorney Grayson Hanes, Til's partner in the firm Hazel and Hanes. "They latched onto sewer, water, zoning, and transportation as the growth control pills. With respect to the latter, their theory was 'no roads, no people.'"[167]

More Roadblocks to Growth

Over the course of the next few years, the new Board continued the work the previous Board had begun, systematically ignoring or erasing most of the highways that had been adopted in the Master Plans for decades, including the two additional beltways and several radial highways. It was a cunning—if ultimately foolhardy—tactic to constrain development. As Packard saw it, "Growth was fueled by new roads. [The proposed highways] were in places where [they] would encourage growth where we didn't want it."[168]

Packard maintains that the Board "didn't object to growth, but the growth was faster than the county's ability to pay for it. As a group we tried to manage growth, not thwart it."[169] Taking planned roads off the map was a start. "We had the power to do it," Packard insists. "We knew VDOT wouldn't build a road if the local jurisdiction was against it. [It] wouldn't spend its money where it wasn't wanted."

But who wouldn't want highways that were designed to make travel much quicker and easier, particularly in a place that was expected to experience a tremendous increase in population? The answer: those who lived close to where the highways would be built. "People said it would mess up their way of life, and the Board listened to them," says Joe Alexander, a supervisor at the time.[170]

For the planners who had invested hours of painstaking, meticulous work laying out the highway grid, the Board's determination to stop growth by making it unpalatable to live in Fairfax was unsettling. "The concept of controlling growth by eliminating necessary modes of transportation [was] not a viable idea," says J Hamilton Lambert, who worked in the county's planning office at the time and later became county executive. "It was naïve to believe that just because you have a two-lane road it won't get more traffic."[171]

"The Board believed that all plans done in the past, such as the Bull Run and Pohick Master Plans, were no longer good," says Doug Fahl, Lambert's colleague in the early 1970s. "They believed roads induced growth and development, even though planners knew otherwise—that highways actually shaped and directed where development occurs."

Other transportation experts concur. "Transportation provides a structure around land use," says Bob Chase, director of the Northern Virginia Transportation Alliance. "Absent that structure, you get development spread throughout the countryside. Planners had recognized that limited access parkways connecting with circumferential highways would provide a way to focus growth and preserve open space."[172]

Fahl says he tried to dissuade the Board from following through with its plans: "I argued that roads didn't fuel population growth; jobs did." But his pleas fell on deaf ears. "They basically took all the rights of way off the map," he says. "No new freeways. None."[173]

"The Outer Beltways, the Monticello Freeway, the river crossings— all were gone, most of them deleted by plan amendments," remembers Shiva Pant, who joined the county's planning office in 1973 and became chief of transportation the following year. "The [Board's] general notion was that Fairfax would remain a bedroom community to the District and the radial rail system would handle commuter traffic to and from Washington, which is why the radial roads were deleted."[174]

Unfortunately, the Board failed to heed anticipated employment patterns. While less than one-third of county workers lived and worked in Fairfax in the 1960s, more than half lived and worked there a decade later. "There was blind reliance on the prospect that rail was going to truly solve current and future transportation needs," says Fahl. In fact, 82.7 percent of area commuters were still driving automobiles to work in 1970, up from 74.2 percent in 1960.[175]

"There was absolutely no evidence that population growth was going to slow down in this county, considering the various government agencies that had been created by Johnson's Great Society program and Nixon's funding of the EPA and Amtrak," Chase says. "Yet Packard somehow thought she could slow the growth or stop it by not building roads, which was preposterous. Developers weren't building homes that sat empty for five years; they were occupied as soon as the paint dried."

Fairfax County's government wasn't alone in trying to curb growth. The San Francisco suburb of Petaluma, for example, made national headlines in 1972 when it limited building permits to five hundred per year. Like Fairfax, Petaluma had grown quickly, ballooning 300 percent

Starting second from the left; Annie Lauler of Annie Lauler Real Estate, McLean; Til Hazel; and Mary Howard, former president of NVAR, Reston; pose with a planning map. The first woman on the left is unidentified.

since 1950.[176] The word "development" was no longer associated with progress. Now a new paradigm called "smart growth" was emerging—and for the regions that espoused it, weak economic growth was often the consequence.

Fairfax County's Master Plans weren't the only studies that had prepared for the expected surge in population and laid the groundwork for the corresponding public services and infrastructure. The Virginia Department of Highway's 1968 Highway Urban Needs Study also called for building additional beltways and radial roads. Pant says the highway department presented "a very comprehensive plan" that the Board "just didn't want to accept. Even though the highway department said we should build these roads, when the county didn't move on the matter, it backed off."

Packard presents a starkly different view of the 1968 Urban Needs Study. "It looked like a mess of spaghetti on the map, almost as though roads were planned for anywhere they weren't existing," she says. "The Board removed some of these proposals as not particularly needed at the time; we felt that much more emphasis should be placed on upgrading and/or widening existing roads."[177]

This strategy, however, did little to reduce future traffic congestion. "When you widen highways, you only serve the demand [that is] oriented in that direction," Pant explains.

Today, anyone stuck battling the traffic on the Beltway or Interstate 66 has the Packard Board to blame. "Planners have been castigated for decades because they didn't plan for growth; well, they planned in great detail for growth, but the politicians didn't have the courage to keep the transportation plans on the map," Til Hazel comments. "If this were Jackson Hole, no one would care. But when it's the world's capital, you can't shut people out when they're coming in droves. Land is a resource people need."

Sitting in his modest home in Warrenton, Virginia, former planning office head Rosser Payne also shakes his head at the county's pervasive gridlock. "We had planned for additional freeways, but they weren't adopted, because of political pressure."[178]

The Packard Board's erasure of roads produced other unfortunate ramifications for the county, too. "By eliminating or downsizing planned road corridors, primarily circumferential highways, the anti-growth crowd and populist politicians essentially eliminated the means by which to support higher density land use," says Chase.

When the energy crisis reared in the late 1970s, the Carter Administration responded by trimming the budget for federal highway spending. Matching federal funds for state highway coffers were cut back drastically, and new environmental impact regulations made it even tougher to get highways built. The times had changed—to the detriment of Fairfax County's mobile residents and visitors.

The effect of the Board's misguided strategy of "no roads, no people" will be felt for many years to come. "While you can always build another school or a fire station, with transportation, once you give it up, it's essentially gone," says Pant. "These opportunities are now lost forever."

Refusal to Rezone

The 1972 Board of Supervisors did more than just shoot down plans to build new highways; the new Board's attempts to devise growth control tactics knew no bounds. One particularly bold strategy was to deny, defer, or simply refuse to hear rezoning applications.

The previous Board of Supervisors had set the stage. In 1971, Roy G. Allman, who owned about three hundred acres with a neighbor near Reston, sought to develop the property and applied for rezoning. The Board turned him down flat. This seemed to make no sense, since Allman had conformed precisely to the higher-density planned housing category (and not conventional quarter-acre development) called for in the county's 1970 Upper Potomac Land Use Plan, the Master Plan addressing the region.

In denying the zoning request, the Board explained that development was premature and that the area lacked public facilities. But this also made no sense, since the property was serviced by the same utilities and other public services used by the burgeoning town of Reston. Meanwhile, adjacent tracts, including the 6,750-acre Reston, had been rezoned to densities equal to or in excess of those requested by Allman.[179]

The Board further contended that the schools in the region were inadequate to absorb the expected increase in population. This, too, seemed to fly in the face of reality. Fairfax school officials pointed out that the anticipated increase in the student population actually conformed to the numbers anticipated in the Master Plan. But Board chair Jean Packard showed little regard for the plans. "The Master Plans from the Office of Planning were a guide—suggestions," she says.

Aggrieved by the Board's failure to permit rezoning, Allman hired Til Hazel to file for a declaratory judgment. Til argued that the action was inconsistent, discriminatory, and illegal. It wasn't the only rezoning case he was handling, though. Til was also representing two other property owners, Tom Williams and Al Van Metre, who together held approximately 414 acres in the Pohick watershed. In 1971, the landowners had filed applications, seeking rezoning to a single-family density of 2.2 to 2.9 units per acre. This time, the Board didn't deny the applications—it simply refused to hear them.

In January 1972, Til brought the Williams and Van Metre case to the Fairfax County Circuit Court and demanded that the applications be heard by the new Board of Supervisors. Two months later, in a decision of great significance, the court determined that a zoning applicant was guaranteed the right to a hearing by the due process sections of both the United States and Virginia constitutions. The Fairfax supervisors were mandated to proceed with the hearings immediately.

Now faced with a backlog of some three hundred zoning cases, the Board was required by the court to hear twenty applications a month, in the chronological order of their filing. It was not uncommon for Board meetings to begin at 9:00 a.m. and end the following day at 3:00 a.m. But the Board of Supervisors interpreted the court's ruling to mean that it did not have to both hear *and* decide the applications simultaneously, so it deferred decision on the applications. Til returned to court to argue that the Board was in contempt of the rule of law. The Board of Supervisors appealed the ruling, however, and the matter stalled.

The Allman case also came to a halt. In 1973, the Fairfax County Circuit Court held that the Board had acted illegally in not granting the rezoning application and directed the supervisors to reconsider their action on or before September 11, 1973. But the Board merely demurred and filed a notice of appeal.

Both the Allman and Williams & Van Metre cases had been tried separately by different judges in the Fairfax County Circuit Court. Both judges held that the Board was arbitrary and capricious in its denial, deferral, and/or refusal to hear rezoning applications. And both concurred that the Board's efforts to suspend the zoning process were not reasonably related to the public's safety, health, and welfare.

The Board was, in effect, practicing exclusionary land use policies. As Til wrote a few years later, "The supervisors who took office in January 1972 were committed to an aggressive and highly publicized no-growth policy designed to change dramatically the course of land use and development in Fairfax County."[180]

In this quest, the Fairfax Board had company. In Boulder, Colorado, officials bowed to pressure from the anti-growth crowd, refusing to extend water and sewer lines to a subdivision just outside the city's limits. Developers sued the city, and the case wound up in Colorado's Supreme Court. The court ruled in favor of the developers in 1976. "As a public utility, the city could not refuse water and sewer services in the area of its jurisdiction merely because the proposed development would be inconsistent with the city's growth policies," *Planning* magazine reported.[181] In Fairfax County, land use and development to provide homes and jobs for people needing them would follow a similar judicial course.

Stall Tactics and Sewer Moratoriums

As Til's cases proceeded through litigation and appeals, the Packard Board revived another tactic to halt development. "We began looking at how we could control [growth]," says former Board chair Jean Packard, "and we came up with the idea that the only control the county had was over sewers."[182] Within the first eighteen months of the new Board's tenure, virtually every watershed in the county was subject to a sewer moratorium imposed by the Board of Supervisors.

The Board claimed that the county's sewer treatment plants were overloaded and insufficient to absorb the effluent created by additional development. The Board needed time to solve this dilemma—hence the moratoriums. One such stall tactic occurred in October 1972, when the Board declared a sewer connection moratorium in the Pohick watershed served by the Lower Potomac Plant, estimating that it would take two years to address the situation. In order to limit residential development in the western two-thirds of the county, the Board simply refused to allocate available sewer capacity on a first-come, first-served basis. Even developers with sewer permits were shown the door.

"I had just finished building my house, and the sewer wasn't hooked up," recalls Gordon Smith, CEO-emeritus of Miller and Smith Associates, which had endured the Burling tract debacle a few years earlier. "The moratorium stopped everything, even though I had the [sewer] permit." He subsequently engaged Til Hazel to represent his interests against the county. Smith recalls, "Til told me to go and hook up the sewer. I said, 'I can't do that; it would be an illegal hook-up.' Til said since I had the permit, I should simply proceed. So I did."[183]

Bill Hazel remembers that Til did a "lot of the heavy lifting" in fighting the sewer moratoriums: "I saw him once in a ditch hooking up sewer lines. The plumbers were afraid they'd get in trouble, so he went down there and tied the lines together himself. He didn't mind getting his hands dirty. He did what he had to do."[184]

Til doesn't recall jumping in a ditch, but he does remember the county sending in policemen to intimidate the plumbers. Soon his firm, Hazel and Hanes, initiated litigation on behalf of a veritable horde of developers. "We represented almost everybody," Grayson Hanes recalls. "We fought for them all." In each case, without exception, the county was either forced to lift the subject moratorium prior to trial, or was ultimately unsuccessful in sustaining it. When a trial did occur, the courts found the county to be acting in a proprietary, rather than governmental, capacity, and required the county to provide sufficient-capacity sewers for all landowners on an equal and nondiscriminatory basis.

Of course, the moratoriums did not—and could not—stop the county's population growth. Instead, the Board's stall tactics helped foster the development of large lots using septic tanks. "The developers set up septic fields in green areas on one-acre lots," says former county planner Dave Edwards. "You can't blame the developers; they were only satisfying market demand."[185] Now, rather than the hoped-for clustered development, the county experienced large lot development. Like the eradication of planned roads, the Board's cure proved worse than its alleged malady.

Still, the supervisors did not give up. They next threatened developers with a moratorium on water permits, recalls Fred Griffith, deputy director of the Fairfax Water Authority at the time. The Board had argued that the county couldn't afford to provide water hookups to the parade of new homeowners and would need time to build new plants and transmission facilities. Otherwise, water rates would have to rise substantially. "We believed that existing residents should have priority over probable newcomers," Packard says.[186]

To persuade supervisors that a water permit moratorium was unnecessary, Griffith developed an innovative rate system "in which growth would pay for growth." He explains, "I told the county that we could build new water and transmission facilities using bonds with low interest rates. I then asked homebuilders that for each new customer we put on-line, they pay us back a share of the [aggregate] expense."[187] Griffith calculated that it would cost about $750 per single-family home to cover the expense of new plants, transmission facilities, and sewer hookups. The homebuilders agreed to pay a percentage of this cost and avoided a moratorium. Griffith says, "We were able to keep rates static and appease the no-growthers at the same time."

A New "Plan" of Attack

Down but not out, the Board imposed yet another moratorium to restrain development, announcing the creation of a Five-Year Plan that would guide development in the county. Such a Five-Year Plan would have been an orderly way to map out growth, but the Board had no such intentions. In its view, the plan would merely provide enough time to prove that growth was too expensive and should be stopped. Since the establishment of the "plan" would require significant attention by the county's planning office—now overwhelmed by a backlog of rezoning applications—the Board declared a six- to twelve-month moratorium on zoning.

Til did not mince words when he was apprised of the situation. "I think your approach is bankrupt—morally, socially and financially," he told the supervisors. "This county has an obligation to provide for the people."[188] Developers reacted harshly and quickly as well, filing lawsuits against the Board to declare the moratorium invalid. The courts ruled in the developers' favor; nevertheless the Five-Year Plan proceeded without the suspension of zoning.

When the contents of the plan were divulged in late 1972, public reaction was negative, because it excluded recommendations on transportation and the environment.[189] The plan also contained disconcerting news for the Board of Supervisors: rather than indicate the need for slower growth, it revealed that the county would be in better shape fiscally over the next five years if growth rates actually *increased*—not what the Board had wanted.[190] *The Washington Post* reported, "The position clashes with the belief in the Washington area suburbs that the tremendous residential growth since World War II has created problems with expensive solutions, thus increasing costs to taxpayers for public services."[191]

Yet not everyone objected to the Five-Year Plan. County executive George Kelley, who favored continued growth, supported its findings. Although he conceded that the county's rapid population increase had pushed up government operating expenses, Kelley maintained that the gap between these costs and tax revenue would be bridged by an increase in population and the tax revenue it would generate. "Many people have the preconceived notion that a jump in the population automatically calls for increases in county government operating expenses," Kelley told *The Post*. "We've found that that isn't necessarily true. Our operating budget seems to grow independently of population growth."[192]

In fact, Kelley opined that real estate development actually had a positive impact on cost, saying, "It costs more to provide new and improved facilities for older communities than it does to add on a new development in the Pohick Valley" (where large development was occurring at the time). Without the additional tax revenues generated by population and employment growth, Kelley believed that the county would have to turn to federal and state sources of funds.[193]

Thus, in Kelley's view, the Five-Year Plan was just what the doctor ordered. "If we can show people where growth should occur, we at least will bring about the acquiescence of the governing body [the Board of Supervisors]," he said.[194]

Kelley's perspective—and the plan's findings—did not sit well with the supervisors. The Board quickly branded the report's conclusions erroneous and invalid. Then in December 1972, after repeated skirmishes with the Board, Kelley angrily resigned during a public session of the Board. A couple of months later, the Board of Supervisors abandoned the Five-Year Plan.[195] As Grace Dawson saw it, the supervisors had "effectively captured control of the government machinery."[196]

Kelley was replaced by his deputy, Robert W. Wilson, who had a close relationship with the Board's liberal majority.[197] At the time of his appointment, Wilson said, "The Board's job is to establish policies, and my job is the proper administration of those policies."[198] In Wilson, the Packard Board had found a valuable ally.

Adding PLUS to the Agenda

By 1973, the Board had attempted several methods of controlling growth: restricting planned road development, instituting sewer moratoria, denying or deferring zoning cases, threatening a water moratorium, declaring a comprehensive zoning moratorium, and instituting the development of the Five-Year Plan. Most had proven fruitless, although the sewer moratoriums and both the Allman and Williams & Van Metre cases had gone to litigation. Nevertheless, the Board continued to search for other means of managing growth.

In early 1973, the Board of Supervisors formed the Task Force on Comprehensive Planning and Land Use Control, which was comprised of Wilson (who was then acting county executive), several supervisors, and various county government agencies. The purpose was to study and outline a strategy "to control growth and achieve a development plan for Fairfax County."[199] The task force's 106-page "Proposal for Implementing an Improved Planning and Land Use Control System in Fairfax County," known colloquially as the "Green Book" because of the color of its cover, suggested revolutionary changes to "improve" the quality of life in Fairfax via land use control and planning.

The conclusions were presented during an all-day public hearing of the Board, which was televised locally. The report argued that the county's current planning, mapping, and zoning systems were outdated, narrow in scope, static, focused on a short-term agenda, and essentially ill-prepared to address the large population increases projected for Fairfax County from the standpoint of land-use development. Instead, the report stated, planning must be "dynamic, responsive and systematic."

Not surprisingly, the task force recommended another moratorium on prospective development, this time to provide for careful reevaluation of "problem areas, procedures to assess environmental impact, and systems to facilitate . . . adequate public facilities in developing areas and to restrict development where public facilities are not programmed."[200] Supervisors dubbed the new moratorium the "Pause for Planning."

In the meantime, the Board approved the task force's recommendation to implement a comprehensive Planning and Land Use Control program, nicknamed "PLUS." It also established a new administrative Office of Comprehensive Planning, replacing the old planning office. Within a year, the staff had been doubled to include more than just professional planners. Among the recruits were retired military officers and clergy members, who were appointed to provide a link to the citizenry. Such appointments supported the program's call for significant citizen participation in the planning process, a concept had been established via several surveys and planning task forces comprised of county citizens.

Only two supervisors voted against authorizing PLUS: Jack Herrity, the sole Republican on the Board, and Audrey Moore. Although she had once referred to the county's astonishing population growth as a "continuing horror,"[201] Moore would later call the PLUS program "that phony effort in the 1970s to 'control' growth."[202]

The mantra of the PLUS program was essentially "out with the old and in with the new." To assist with future planning and land use decisions, PLUS would rely on computerized systems and a quantitative analysis of diverse data as opposed to "past trends and proposed ideal land patterns."[203]

But the most far-reaching recommendations approved by the Board were those that allowed the county to determine the timing of development. In this regard, the Board latched onto the so-called Ramapo system.

Recreating Ramapo

Ramapo, New York, was an eighty-nine-square-mile town located thirty miles northwest of New York City. Like Fairfax County, Ramapo had experienced tremendous postwar population growth. To manage its growth, Robert H. Freilich, the town's attorney in the mid- to late-1960s, devised the Ramapo system.

Freilich believed that Master Plans unjustifiably constrain local governments in managing land use development, and under his watch, the town adopted amendments to its zoning ordinance that required supportive infrastructure to be in place before building and other permits could be issued. The town also created a new type of zoning district called "residential development use," which required developers to obtain a special permit that indicated municipal services like schools, firehouses, and sewers were readily available. Each facility was assigned a point value, and fifteen points were needed to obtain a permit. If a developer didn't want to wait for the infrastructure to be in place, it could install the necessary services on its own. In the meantime, the town unveiled an eighteen-year capital improvement program that indicated when government funding for those public services would likely be in place.

Although several developers filed suit against the constitutionality of the amendments, the Supreme Court of New York State ultimately held that they were within the delegated authority of local government.[204] The case went to the U.S. Supreme Court, but it denied a writ of certiorari. For the first time ever in the United States, a town was legally approved to control its own growth.

In Freilich and his ordinance for "adequate public facilities," the Fairfax County Board of Supervisors had found its messiah. In early 1973, the Board engaged Freilich as a consultant to the PLUS program to do in Fairfax what he had done so well in Ramapo. At the time, he was a law professor at the University of Missouri's School of Law in Kansas City.

Among Freirich's recommendations to the Board was a site plan and zoning moratorium, which would provide time for the new planning office to study land use development issues. So in January 1974, the Board declared that "emergency conditions" existed within the county because of its "unprecedented and rapid growth" and adopted an Interim Development Ordinance (IDO) that prohibited rezoning and the processing of applications for building permits and site plans. The alleged emergency was the anticipated surge in land use applications that would be filed to avoid the impact of the PLUS. The Board stated that the moratorium would continue for up to eighteen months until the PLUS program was completed "to protect the public interest and welfare."[205]

Initially, developers had not stood in the way of PLUS, believing that the program might provide more clarity in the development process—particularly in the way rezonings were handled. The IDO changed their posture. Developers reacted angrily and quickly, threatening litigation.

Above, top: Crowds of picketters protest the Fairfax County building ban. Above: More protesters, wearing buttons that read "No Growth—No Jobs", make their preferences known in no uncertain terms at a Fairfax County Board of Supervisors meeting, 1974.

The country was in a recession, and the Board of Supervisors seemed determined to put the county's building industries out of business. In well-attended public hearings on the IDO, organized representatives of the building industries carried signs that read, "My Kids Need Housing" and "No Growth Means No Jobs." This time, the press seemed to take their side. Articles on the issue implied that the Board was in favor of stopping and not merely managing growth.

A few supervisors later expressed reservations about the "emergency" IDO. Nevertheless, in March 1974, the Board reenacted a revised IDO that bore a striking resemblance to the former ordinance. In effect, the processes for all site and subdivision plans were suspended, as were all zoning hearings, determinations, and the acceptance of new rezoning applications.

Now, when landowners seeking to develop their properties filed site plans with the county, they were rejected on the basis of the new IDO. Their response was to file dozens of lawsuits against the county. Many of these suits were subsequently consolidated for litigation purposes into two cases: one that addressed the site-plan review process and its relation to existing zoning, and another that addressed the rezoning process itself.

Leading the case against the suspension of the site and subdivision process was the law firm of Hazel and Hanes (other respected zoning attorneys representing petitioners included Marc Bettius, Donald Stevens, and Randolph Church). Til argued that the moratorium deprived landowners of lawful use of their property under existing zoning, thereby denying them due process. He also brought forth Rosser Payne, former head of the planning office, as an expert witness on behalf of the petitioners. Payne testified that when he led the department in the 1960s with a much smaller staff, there was no need to impose a moratorium on site plans to provide for planning.[206]

Lee Ruck represented the county. In Ruck's corner was consultant Robert Freilich and key witness Jim Reid, the head of the expanded planning division. But even Reid's testimony couldn't help the county's case. The judge ruled that since he lacked a degree in planning, Reid had to restrict his comments to the management of planners and not the planning process per se.[207]

In the summer of 1974, the Fairfax County Circuit Court ruled in favor of the plaintiffs in *Horne v. Board of Supervisors of Fairfax County*, finding that the moratorium on the site plan process in relation to existing zoning exceeded the Board's power. "We conclude that there was no express or implied authority for the enactment by the Board of ordinances imposing a moratorium on the filing of site plans and preliminary subdivision plats," the court stated. The county later unsuccessfully appealed the ruling.

Ironically, Freilich had helped hammer the last nail in the coffin. Til recalls, "He stood up in front of the Supreme Court and basically told them they didn't understand land use. As soon as he said it, I realized I didn't need to say another word. I just smiled."

The Supreme Court Steps In

The case set a legal precedent that rendered subsequent use of moratoriums ineffective, burying one of the Board's growth control tactics for good. The county could no longer postpone the zoning process to secure time for PLUS to reach a conclusion. As the court specified, the review of pending zoning cases had to resume by July 1, 1975.

The second legal hurdle over the PLUS program's rezoning moratorium was settled out of court in *Presley v. Fairfax County Board of Supervisors*. At the time of the settlement—June 1974—only 160 zoning cases were pending. The settlement order required these to be disposed of no later than the end of 1975, within six months of the scheduled completion of PLUS. Til, who represented the petitioners, explains, "Rather than try a series of cases, I suggested to Lee [Ruck] that we would not contest the one-year moratorium if he would agree that once the year was up and the PLUS program had been completed, zoning and all other land issue decisions would be resumed in the order filed."

Nevertheless, Til believed the county lacked the ability and desire to follow through with the PLUS program by May 1975. "Sure enough, at the end of the year, Ruck and the Board requested an extension," he says. "The court refused it. In one of those unforgettable moments, Judge Sinclair looked down from the Bench and asked Lee [Ruck] if that was his signature on the consent order. Lee nodded his head, and the judge said, 'Sorry, Mr. Ruck, your time is up—the moratorium is over.'"

The consent order had also provided for the filing of new zoning applications during a two-week period in September 1974. Roughly 170 new zoning applications were filed during this window, and by the end of 1975, the county's backlog fell to fewer than one hundred cases. Now, as in much of the rest of the country, when a zoning application was filed, the Board was required to hear and dispose of it on a timely basis, in the order it was filed. As the IDO breathed its last in Fairfax County, Freilich was sent home hat in hand.

Meanwhile, the Allman and Williams & Van Metre cases progressed to the Virginia Supreme Court, which upheld both trial court decisions. In the Allman case, the court sustained the trial court's findings that the landowners had been discriminated against and the alleged inadequacies of public facilities either did not exist or would be corrected by the time development routinely occurred.

Bowed but not broken, the Board made an unsuccessful attempt to obtain writs of certiorari from the U.S. Supreme Court. Once again, the rule of law had reaffirmed fundamental land use and the due process considerations of landowners. The entire rezoning and development process was finally in rational perspective, and at long last, the exclusionary approach to land use was over. Future Boards would attempt other means to control growth, but the die had been cast.

When the Board of Supervisors came up for election at the end of 1975, their populism had lost popular appeal. The recession and the long lines at gas stations caused by the oil crisis had wearied the public. Citizens were now eager for an economic resurgence. Mills E. Godwin, Virginia's former Democratic governor, had just been reelected to his old job as a Republican. As he told four hundred cheering members of the Northern Virginia Builders Association, "I know your counties and cities here cannot stand still. I know that babies are going to continue to be born. I know that people are going to continue to move in. And I know you can't declare a moratorium on [growth in] any locality anywhere in this state. . . . Growth is inevitable. We don't stand still. We don't maintain the status quo. Once we try to maintain the status quo, we slide backward."

Godwin won the election. On the other hand, Packard and many of her liberal allies on the Board of Supervisors were ousted. The throngs of new citizens coming to the county could now relocate with confidence that they would find homes for their families.

Washington's Bedroom Community

Although the Board of Supervisors attempted to keep newcomers away from Fairfax County, they came anyway—in droves. By mid-1972, the county's population reached 515,000, approximately sixty thousand more than recorded in the 1970 census. The growth rate was so strong that Virginia Electric and Power Company, the utility serving Northern Virginia, built two additional offices in Springfield and Reston to service customers, each with an array of meter readers, line crews, and office personnel. "We were adding 150,000 homes and businesses a year in the state of Virginia, with Fairfax County accounting for half the additional demand," recalls William Berry, former chairman and CEO of Dominion Resources, Inc., the holding company created for VEPCO in 1983.[208]

And who could blame people for coming? Fairfax was still Washington's bedroom community, "a nice place that was friendly to newcomers," says Bill Hazel.[209] Moreover, jobs were beginning to materialize. Jerry Halpin's aptly named West*Park complex was the scene of much of the commercial activity. On 152 acres of the old Maplewood tract and an additional several hundred acres of West*Park, dozens of office buildings sprouted, many of them leased by government agencies like the CIA and the Department of Defense, and the private sector companies serving them. "We sort of saw our market as being defense contractors," says Chuck Ewing, cofounder of West*Group.[210]

The architects designed these buildings away from the street by a considerable margin and in most cases, buried the parking lots beneath the structures. "Jerry built five buildings for Freddie Mac at West*Park in parklike settings, and not only took care to put the parking underneath, he [also] didn't take down a single tree . . . [In fact, he] planted many more," recalls Alice Starr, former vice president of marketing at West*Group. "He was so conscious of the environment."[211] Through the years, there were buildings added for Gannett Company (*USA Today*), Hilton Hotel, Honeywell, Chicago Title, Boeing, Mitre, Verizon, MCI, Planning Systems, and Sunrise Senior Living.

Even Jean Packard had kind words for Jerry's environmental objectives. "He was the first developer at that time that had a concept of open space," she says. "Nature and greenery were big in his eyes. He took me through West*Park once and pointed out all the plants that he'd brought in. He was justifiably proud."[212]

The new buildings were substantially larger and more modern than the one- and two-story edifices that comprised the old West*Gate complex. One such building, the headquarters of the National Machine Tool Builders' Association, encompassed sixteen thousand square feet of office space and featured a geometric design suggesting a giant automated machine. Dedicated in 1971, it resided on two acres of sloping, highly landscaped property that today virtually obscures the structure.

The National Machine Tool Builders' Association had moved to Fairfax to be closer to the District of Columbia. Three other trade groups relocated to the county for the same purpose in the early 1970s: the American Automobile Association, the National Education Association, and the American Newspaper Publishers Association. By the end of the decade, an astonishing 125 trade and professional associations had made the move, and collectively, they employed more than three thousand people. Most of them were headquartered in Tysons Corner or Reston.

Other measures were undertaken early in the decade to draw more commercial activity to Fairfax. Washington Dulles International Airport became the first airport in the country—and one of only eight locales in the entire United States at the time—to have a Foreign Trade Zone (FTZ). The FTZ allowed the entry of goods and their storage, assemblage, packaging, manufacture, and subsequent re-export without having duties levied.

Also abetting the county's commercial interests was the work by the Fairfax County Economic Development Authority to expand the

Washington Commercial Truck Zone, which doubled the area allowed for truck deliveries. The new zone was a boon to the commercial and industrial development of Merrifield. Just ten years earlier, the suburban community had comprised a dilapidated assortment of rundown dwellings and businesses, and unused land. By 1972, Merrifield had evolved into a fast-growing, unified industrial and business complex, with more than 130 firms employing over three thousand people. Located south of McLean, Merrifield's proximity to the District of Columbia, Interstate 66, the Beltway, and a planned Metrorail station on Gallows Road further encouraged commercial and industrial development. The American Automobile Association built its 210,000-square-foot national headquarters there, as did the U.S. Postal Service's Northern Virginia Sectional Center, which employed more than 1,500 people in a 625,000-square-foot building.

Burgeoning Communities—and Challenges Ahead

Jobs weren't the only thing luring people to the county. The quality of homes was a factor, too, as was Fairfax's growing list of lifestyle amenities. The first residential community developed by Hazel/Peterson in 1972 consisted of single-family colonial, traditional, and contemporary homes in western Fairfax near Herndon. Called Fox Mill Estates, the community was built in phases. By the time it was completed in 1985, it boasted 1,144 homes on quarter-acre to half-acre lots with amenities that included two swim-and-tennis clubs, an elementary school, and a shopping center. In contrast, a builder in Santa Clara County, California, sold two thousand inexpensively built single-level homes with the same modern design on tiny, five-thousand-square-foot lots in 1971. Houses were packed in tightly in the "Valley of Heart's Delight," as it was called before earning its Silicon Valley moniker.[213]

The new homeowners at Fox Mill Estates in Fairfax, however, found burgeoning higher education at George Mason University and Northern Virginia Community College, improved health care following the 1974 completion of a 250-bed addition to Fairfax Hospital, and ample land set aside for recreational activities and key public infrastructure. From 1964 to 1974, half the vacant land absorbed by development was given to public use, including parks, private open space, schools, and fire stations.[214] Fox Mill Estates, for example, offered prospective homeowners fifty-seven acres of open space intersected by a pond and a creek. Residents today say they still see the occasional fox in the woods, along with woodchucks, rabbits, and deer.

The suburbs were thriving in Fairfax County in the early 1970s. "Dreamers found green space, clean air, shiny new housing and relatively low-cost housing," *The Washington Post* stated. "New roads carried them to work and the shopping centers. . . . Home building [became] the biggest private industry in the area."[215]

Yet the people and companies coming to Fairfax faced a host of obstacles that ranged from the Packard Board's stiff posture against growth to the lack of an effective plan that would lure more corporations to Northern Virginia. For instance, Dulles Airport, a veritable mausoleum in the early 1970s, required significant marketing. The airport was so empty that Dave Edwards recalls ticket booth personnel of competing airlines using the public address system to play pranks on each other, since few people were there to hear the bogus announcements anyway.

While the county had come a long way, there was still much work to be done. Fairfax desperately needed more private enterprise to take the burden of public services off the backs of homeowners. Both George Mason University and Northern Virginia Community College required better leadership and more funds to pursue their ambitious agendas. Fairfax Hospital Association was still a long way from providing modern health care that would be on par with major cities. Sewage treatment still needed significant upgrading. And despite the opening of the Wolf Trap National Park for the Performing Arts (on land donated by Catherine Filene Shouse), cultural life in the county remained primitive.

In January 1976, a pro-growth Board of Supervisors came into office. With the new Board's support, such barriers to residential and commercial development would finally be overcome by a small group of private citizens. These very people would carefully and unstintingly lay the foundation for economic prosperity that Fairfax County rests on today.

Past to Present
to Future Vision

**A VISUAL PRESENTATION OF THE CHARGED GROWTH
FROM RURAL LANDSCAPE TO MEGALOPOLIS
TO FUTURE VISIONS OF FAIRFAX COUNTY**

Crossroads Market, Tysons Corner, c. 1955.

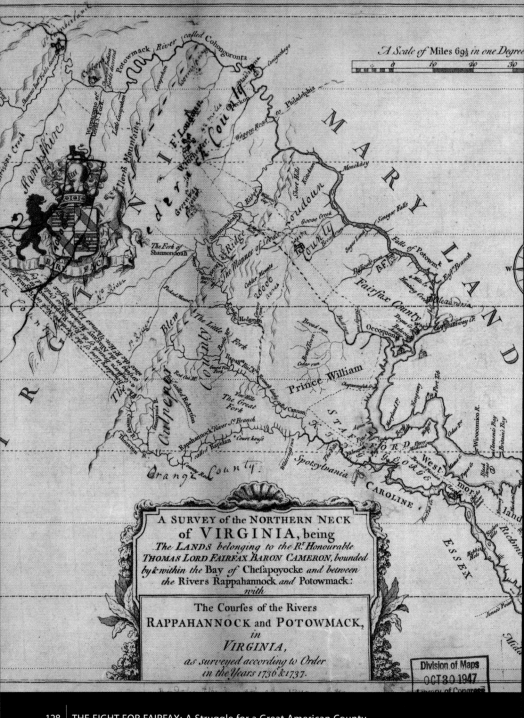

A dirt road, typical of the day, runs alongside a dairy farm in Fairfax County, c. 1940.

Opposite page: C. 1742, this old Fairfax County map shows Arlington and Alexandria were then part of Fairfax County.

Above: Viewed from the west, this unpaved street is the major intersection of Braddock Road and Warrenton Turnpike in Centreville, Virginia, c. 1904.

Right: The Maplewood estate, pictured here in 1969, will soon be completely enveloped by office building construction near Tysons Corner.

Opposite page: A Fairfax City of the past—the county seat of Fairfax—can be seen in this early aerial.

Right: Two men are readying a horse team to pull out an auto stuck in a muddy road, a common problem in those days. The driver in need of rescue is ankle-deep in the mire.

Below: Progress is pictured in the act of erecting a telephone pole, 1950, along a still-unpaved road.

Above: A sign of commerce to come arrives in the form of the Fairfax Car Wash, Annandale Road at Route 50, 1956.

Below: Under construction in 1948, Shirley Highway will become a major artery from the Pentagon to Fairfax County.

An aircraft from Dulles seen overhead at Sully Plantation, 1972, contrasts the present with the past.

Inset: Terminal and tower at Washington Dulles International Airport, 1960

Above, top: President John F. Kennedy and former President Dwight D. Eisenhower attended the opening of Washington Dulles International Airport.

Above: Award-winning architecture aside, it will take another two decades to attract passengers to Dulles Airport, as its relatively empty interior in the 1960s indicates.

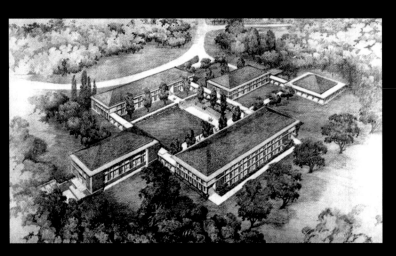

Above: An architectural rendering, Stage I construction, c. 1960, of George Mason College of the University of Virginia (now George Mason University) provides for just a small college.

Left: Present at the groundbreaking of George Mason University, Fairfax Campus, August 1, 1963, were (left to right) Fairfax Mayor John C. Wood, Clarence Steele of the Advisory Council, State Senator Charles R. Fenwick, Director of George Mason College J.N.G. Finley, and Virginia Delegate C. Harrison Mann Jr. of Arlington.

Right: George Johnson, GMU President, c. 1980, accelerated the university's growth.

Opposite: Donald L. Wilkins, Fairfax County Hospital and Health Center Commission chairman, and Franklin P. Iams, Fairfax Hospital administrator, preview a Fairfax Hospital sign in 1958. Aspirations were for a large, extensive complex.

URE FAIRFAX HOSPITAL

...IAM FRANCIS SCHORN
...ARCHITECT

...UBARD MASSEY
...SITE ENGINEER

Opposite page, top: Gerald T. "Jerry" Halpin, president and CEO of West*Group

Opposite page, bottom: Jerry Halpin strategized relocating the Atlantic Research headquarters to Fairfax County, c. 1958—one of the first technology companies to do so.

Top right to bottom right: The U.S. Geological Survey, General Technologies Corporation, and Motorola all occupied these buildings during the early period of the county's development in the 1960s and 1970s.

Right: Harriet F. Bradley, a long-term member of the Fairfax County Board of Supervisors

Below: John Tilghman "Til" Hazel Jr. and Milton V. Peterson, founders of the Hazel/Peterson Companies

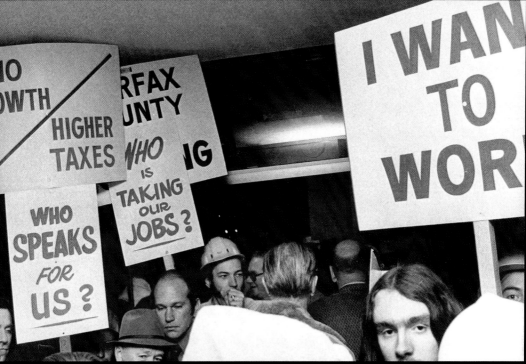

Clockwise from top, this page: Picketers protesting restrictive zoning jammed the lobby of the County Office Building during a hearing, 1974.

The anti-growth Fairfax County Board of Supervisors appointed a Task Force on Comprehensive Planning and Land Use Control, filmed during a work session in the studios of Channel 53 WNVT, c.1972–73.

Earle Williams, president and CEO of BDM International, Inc.

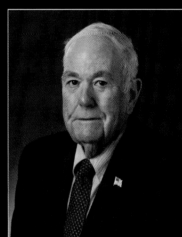

Top: Yates Village, Springfield, 1955, was an early residential subdivision.

Above, left: By 1975 traffic was heavy in Tysons Corner.

Above, right: William A. "Bill" Hazel, chairman of the Directors of the Board, William A. Hazel, Inc.

Opposite page, bottom: The magnitude of planning continued to spiral upward, with construction underway on major projects like Tysons Corner Center, 1967.

Above: Fairfax County zoning administrator Phil Yates visited Burke Centre, c. 1970s, with planning map in hand.

Opposite page: (left to right) Sid Dewberry, Jim Nealon, and Dick Davis of Dewberry, Nealon & Davis. c. 1969. Inset: Sidney O. "Sid" Dewberry, chairman of the Board of Directors, Dewberry

Above: By 1973 Shirley Highway remained a key thoroughfare but had to be greatly expanded with elevated ramps in this area known as the "Mixing Bowl."

Above: A rendering of one complex in the planned community of Reston

Right: Dwight Schar, president and CEO of Northern Virginia Homes (NVR)

Opposite page: Lake Anne was the first village center developed in Reston, c. 1968.

Right: Advertisements were designed to draw businesses to Fairfax County, 1979.

Below: 2008 Techtopia—a fanciful map poster—was designed to show the concentration of technology and other companies in and around Fairfax County.

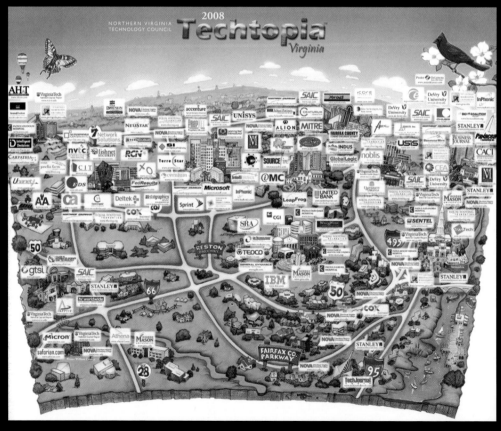

Above: The Dulles Greenway Toll Road pushed economic development west of Fairfax County.

Left: The CIT building, built c. 1985 and home of the Center for Innovative Technology in Herndon, Virginia, is still one of the most futuristic buildings in Fairfax County.

Tysons Corner Center (interior shown above), the largest shopping center in the Metropolitan Washington, D.C. area, was greatly expanded from its initial plans over time. It is now surrounded by an enormous business and residential community, representing one of the largest concentrations of jobs in the U.S.

Bottom left: The shopping mall can be seen center-photo in this aerial of Tysons Corner, mid 70s–early 80s.

Above: George Mason University's architectural imprint in Fairfax exploded in size from its earlier plans into this immense campus of nearly 100 buildings. In addition, there are campuses in Arlington, Prince William County, and Loudoun County.

Opposite page: Northern Virginia Community College is one of the largest such institutions in the nation.

Left: John Toups, former President of PRC, a high tech defense contractor and engineering company

Left: Washington Dulles International Airport's main terminal was recently expanded.

Below: The National Air and Space Museum's Steven F. Udvar-Hazy Center, opened in 2003 and located near Dulles Airport, displays thousands of aviation and space artifacts.

Reston Town Center is one of many recent urban concentrations of residences and businesses in Fairfax County.

march of dimes
march for babies
Reston Town Center • Sunday, April 13, 2009 • 3:30 p.m.

Sprint

Surrounding the initial red brick structure on the Inova Fairfax Hospital campus are a series of modern buildings housing cutting-edge medical technology, 2008.

A Blue Ribbon
Resolution

E arle Williams was working in his office in mid-1975 when one of BDM's vice presidents walked in and asked him to come down to the Fairfax County Chamber of Commerce. "He said, 'We've got a problem in this county,'" Williams recalls.[216]

The "problem" was the county's Board of Supervisors. Several supervisors were up for reelection that November, including Jean Packard, the Board's chair. Packard's failed policies to impede growth and development in the county had been repeatedly repudiated by Virginia's courts and the General Assembly, and had left a sour taste in the mouths of the local citizenry. Challenging Packard for her seat was Jack Herrity, the only Republican on the Board and a pro-business advocate.

When Williams arrived at the chamber, he was asked to become involved in Herrity's campaign. Williams was consumed with building a company and had little interest in politics at the time, but he agreed to meet Herrity for lunch later that week. "I was so disgusted with Packard and her people," Williams recalls. "I became convinced that Jack would be a good thing for Fairfax County, so I got involved in his campaign and stuck with him through the election."

As Earle and other local businesspeople were happy to discover, John F. "Jack" Herrity was Packard's polar opposite. Herrity believed growth was inevitable, as "uncontrollable as the weather."[217] Instead of fighting it, he argued that the government should encourage the rapid expansion of commercial and industrial construction. Doing so would shift a greater percentage of the tax burden from homeowners to businesses, thereby providing additional revenues for schools, libraries, parks, police officers, and firefighters. With a county tax base that was 92 percent residential and 8 percent commercial, Herrity had a point, and he fully believed a 75 to 25 percent ratio was both appropriate and achievable.[218]

"Jack's position on growth rubbed off on me, even though it meant I would bring [BDM's] competitors here," Williams concedes. "But I believed him when he said that people in the county needed services, and we had to increase the business-industrial portion of real estate taxes to provide them. Otherwise, we'd remain a bedroom community."

Herrity had a strong platform, but unlike Packard, he was a virtual nonentity. So Fairfax's business community, which by and large supported Herrity's election, decided to take matters into its own hands. "Jack was running around knocking on doors saying, 'I'm Jack Herrity,' but no one knew who he was," recalls developer Chuck Veatch. "The brother of my business partner was the team doctor for the Washington Redskins, and he allowed us to put up a giant banner in burgundy and gold Redskins colors below the scoreboard at RFK Stadium saying, 'Jack Herrity Loves Those Redskins.' Every time they cut to the scoreboard on Monday Night Football, everyone saw the banner. [From] then on, when Jack knocked on doors and introduced himself, people knew who he was."[219]

Herrity won the election. What really aided his victory, however, was a noticeable change in electoral perspective. As opposed to the strident anti-growth sentiments of the past, this new point of view saw the growth of business and the accommodation of new citizens as a common good. The new Board of Supervisors largely shared these pro-business views, and they gave Herrity a mandate to practice what he preached: that is, capitalism is good as long as it furthers the welfare of citizens.

As Board chairman, Herrity's personality seemed right out of central casting. He was a colorful character whose profanity, bluster, and occasional buffoonery were complemented by a quick mind, iron clad will, and extraordinary charisma and tenacity. "Jack had a knack for attracting people to his way of thinking and bigger ideas," says Jim Wordsworth, CEO and president of JR Goodtimes, Inc., a restaurant and catering company in Tysons Corner. "He firmly believed in what he was doing, which was to make the county a better place for all of us to live."[220]

To accomplish those ends, Herrity had a pivotal ally: J Hamilton Lambert, who had become acting county executive after Robert Wilson's resignation in 1976, and won the post on a full-time basis four years later. Although Lambert had only a high school education, he had worked in Rosser Payne's planning department and was blessed with a brilliant mind and keen organizational skills. "Jack had the big ideas and then J came behind him to pick up the pieces and put together the plans," Wordsworth explains. "They were 'Mutt and Jeff.' . . . Jack couldn't have done what he did without J."

A Real Business Plan

Herrity's first action as chairman was to hammer the final nail into the maligned PLUS program, which was on its last legs anyway. His next, and some would say most pivotal decision, was to organize the Committee to Study the Means of Encouraging Industrial Development in Fairfax County. Herrity charged the committee with studying ways to bring new tax-paying businesses and industry into Fairfax, thus delivering on his campaign pledge to relieve residents of rising property taxes. Sixteen leading members of the business and development communities joined the Blue Ribbon Committee, as it was popularly known, including Til Hazel, Jerry Halpin, and Earle Williams. Noman Cole served as its chair.

In its published findings, the committee noted that the growth in the county's residential tax base was much larger than the assessed value of its commercial and industrial real estate. For example, in 1972 the share of the total assessable tax base represented by commercial and industrial development had been 16.8 percent. By 1976, it had fallen to 14.8 percent. The committee maintained that "in an overall assessable base of nearly $4 billion," the two percent drop represented "a tremendous shift in tax burden to the residential sector." The Blue Ribbon Committee concluded: "If this trend is not abated and, in fact, if the trend is not completely reversed, residents of Fairfax County can expect to shoulder an increasingly heavy tax burden."[221]

As Williams later told a reporter, "[The county] had an inadequate tax base to support the services our population needed and wanted. We had to promote development, not just let it happen, so that we could control the type of business that came into the area, broaden the tax base, and provide employment within the community."[222]

Not promoting development would have made Fairfax another Scarsdale, New York—a city that derives just 6 percent of its tax base

Noman M. Cole Jr., a nuclear engineer, fought both to control water pollution and to improve Northern Virginia's water supply to the highest quality.

from industry. In 2006, Scarsdale residents paid an average of $20,282 in property taxes.[223] Williams and his peers on the committee realized they needed to quickly and substantially increase business and industry within Fairfax County. Yet as the committee acknowledged, this would be a significant challenge. Because of the previous Board's no-growth agenda, Fairfax was perceived both nationally and locally as anti-business. Persuading the commercial sector that Fairfax County would now encourage business development required accepting the fact that the county had a negative image. Fairfax needed to take "some positive and aggressive steps to overcome it," the committee urged.

One step in that direction would be the Board's formal adoption of a "clear statement of policy" that would "take all positive steps necessary to encourage appropriate business and industry to locate in Fairfax County." The committee stated, "The message should be clear that Fairfax County sincerely welcomes financially beneficial and environmentally sound business development." It added that sewer and building moratoriums must no longer be used as growth-control devices, and planning, zoning, and ordinance amendments "must not unnecessarily jeopardize [the county's] ability to attract desirable business development."

Fairfax County: Finally Open for Business

To publicize the county's new pro-business stance, the committee recommended a substantial increase in the staff and budget of the Economic Development Authority (EDA), which would "assist [in] an aggressive marketing and sales campaign." The committee urged, "The Authority must now be given the resources, the responsibility, and the unequivocal mandate to get the job done." It also recommended empowering the county executive to make the development approval process more efficient, thus speeding up the time spent reviewing and approving proposals in compliance with planning and zoning procedures.

To help fund the improvement of schools, utilities, and transportation, the committee suggested revisions in the county's general tax structure to make it comparable with other regions of the country. With respect to the latter, it proposed constructing Interstate 66 within the Beltway and developing the dormant right-of-way lanes that ran parallel to the Dulles Access Road. In all, the report was an important blueprint for the county's economic future—"a milestone document and an attitude adjuster," says J Hamilton Lambert. "The public couldn't find fault with [it], and virtually all the recommendations were acted upon."[224]

The first order of business was improving the county's reputation—job number one for the Economic Development Authority. Herrity had appointed Earle Williams as a commissioner of the EDA. Williams agreed, but only if he could make a difference. Herrity replied that he expected Earle to do so. Williams served for two years before being elected chairman of the Authority by the other commissioners.[225]

At Earle's urging, Herrity announced significant staff and budgetary hikes at the Authority. "Earle is the one who built the budget, plainly and simply," Dave Edwards acknowledges. "He has the oratory zeal of a Baptist minister saving you from hell and damnation. He could eloquently convince you of anything, and he convinced the Board of Supervisors, with Jack's prodding, to raise the budget dramatically to over $750,000."[226]

It was a huge hike. The Blue Ribbon Committee had advised a budget of just $350,000. Some of the funds went toward the marketing and advertising of the Authority. One of the board members, Lee Schur, "was incredibly clever and knew the routines of advertising, marketing, and promotion," Edwards says. With Schur's help, the Authority hired a PR firm to run an ad campaign. Edwards continues, "The authority's advertising went from nickel and dime stuff to double-truck ads in *The Wall Street Journal* and *BusinessWeek* extolling the county's plusses as a corporate headquarters. [The team] came up with some very dramatic ads for the times, and they got us attention."

Jim Todd, who volunteered as the Authority's marketing chairman, recalls a particular advertisement: "It had nothing about Fairfax County in the headline. There was a picture of the Capitol, and superimposed on it were the words, 'Locate your company next to the highest concentration of power in the free world.' At the bottom in small [type] it said, 'Fairfax County.'"[227]

The county's marketing efforts had significant impact. Prior to printing the ads, the Authority's marketing staff had gauged the county's recognition factor by surveying straphangers riding the New York to Washington shuttle train. "It was a disappointing twelve percent," Todd recalls. "After the ads ran, we went through the same exercise a few years later and eighty percent recognized the county. Of course, it wasn't just the ads that did the trick. We'd do things like rent out a ballroom in New York and invite every businessman there to meet with us and whoever was governor of Virginia at the time."

Meanwhile, other organizations began extolling the virtues of Fairfax County. John Tydings, who became CEO of the Greater Washington Board of Trade in 1978, remembers, "The county was looking to attract the not-for-profit community, given its proximity to Washington. It also sought clean industries that wanted access to the federal government and the area's bright workforce, [as well as] trade associations and professional societies, the retail market, and investment and real estate firms. We'd bring executives in from the major markets as part of our marketing missions to show them what Fairfax had to offer. We even coined a term for the practice—'exec-u-tours.'"[228]

The Washington Post reported on the region's efforts, noting that Jack Herrity himself was traveling "across the country to court industrial America." The newspaper added that the revitalized Economic Development Authority led by Williams had effectively established Fairfax's reputation "as one of the East Coast's premier corporate locales."[229] The timing was critical, as the rest of the nation was still suffering from the protracted recession. Seattle, for example, was reeling from massive layoffs at Boeing Corporation, one of the region's main employers. To diversify the area's economy, local government and business leaders attracted the then-unknown Microsoft Corporation from Albuquerque in 1978.[230]

Paving the way for those firms hoping to locate or expand their operations in Fairfax, the Board of Supervisors approved five new measures in 1977 to help streamline procedures for processing building and zoning plans. The measures would eliminate as much as one year's time from the development process.[231]

In succeeding years, the county's private citizens would give companies other reasons to move to Fairfax by putting their energies into improving secondary and higher education, health care, cultural attractions, and transportation, particularly air travel. As new companies planted stakes, the county became a region of bedrooms *and* boardrooms. Twenty years earlier, 13,509 of its 204,000 citizens worked in Fairfax. In 1976, the two hundredth birthday of the United States, nearly 109,000 of its 554,500 citizens had jobs there.[232] By the 1990s, tens of thousands of people would commute to Fairfax every day, serving the county much in the same way that Fairfax served Washington, D.C.

At long last, the private sector had an ally in the Board of Supervisors. Now citizens like Earle Williams, Til Hazel, Sid Dewberry, and Jerry Halpin, could work with the Board to help transform the county—at least while Jack Herrity was chairman. Future attempts by local government to control growth and development would have little impact. Fairfax County was on its way.

The Problem with "Pump and Dump"

Afew years before he had been asked to chair the Blue Ribbon Committee that would guide Fairfax County's economic future, Noman Cole had set his brilliant mind to creating one of the most important infrastructures in the county's history: the Upper Occoquan Sewage Treatment Plant. Had this highly innovative plant not been constructed, the quality and quantity of drinking water in Fairfax would not be what it is today.

In the late 1960s, the 1,700-acre Occoquan Reservoir, a major source of drinking water in Northern Virginia, was under severe duress. The reservoir was adversely affected by sewage discharges from eleven small, outdated wastewater treatment plants. These facilities released high concentrations of nitrogen and phosphorus into the reservoir, causing blue-green blooms of cyanobacteria algae that produced serious water quality problems.[233]

In January 1968, the Virginia General Assembly funded a study to determine the cause of the reservoir's deterioration and related water quality problems, and to outline technical solutions and other approaches to improve these conditions. The study confirmed that the effluent from the existing sewage plants was indeed the primary reason for the water quality problems. To remedy the situation, the study recommended building two new secondary plants to replace the existing ones. The secondary effluent from the new plants would then be pumped out of the basin and piped to the headwaters of Neabsco Creek, which flows into the Potomac River.

But this solution was a costly one, and would create additional problems for the already-polluted Potomac. The plan was also certain to cause political division. The citizens of Prince William County, where Neabsco Creek is located, would not want effluent from Fairfax County coursing through their backyard.

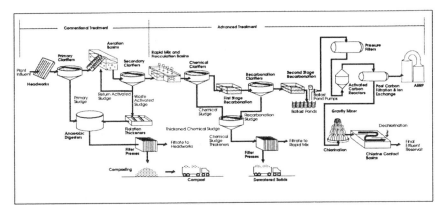

An old schematic describes the water treatment process at the regional water reclamation plant, the Upper Occoquan Sewage Authority Water Reclamation Facility. The plant was later renamed the Millard H. Robbins Jr. Water Reclamation Facility.

Another plan suggested in the study was to export the secondary effluent from western Fairfax, Manassas and Manassas Park, and western Prince William County via a twenty-five-mile trunk sewer to the Lower Potomac Treatment Plant in the Pohick watershed. But this plan also lacked support for the same financial and political reasons. Not surprisingly, voters soundly defeated a $9 million sewer bond referendum for the export system. "We called it the 'pump and dump on somebody else' solution," recalls Millard Robbins, at the time a member of the State Water Control Board, a government agency regulating water quality standards.[234] As time passed, it became increasingly apparent that a less expensive—and less troublesome—approach to handling sewage waste from the Occoquan watershed would need to be developed so Northern Virginia could protect its water supply.

In 1970, Virginia Governor A. Linwood Holton, Jr., appointed Cole to be the volunteer chairman of the State Water Control Board, and Noman promptly found himself in the middle of the highly contentious issue. A dedicated conservationist, he had already made a name for himself as a nuclear engineer (he would later work on remediating the Three Mile Island incident). He had also been the designer and primary advocate of the Lower Potomac Treatment Plant, later named in his honor. He was a highly publicized opponent of the waste export strategy, a concept he almost single-handedly quashed, and that had given Holton pause.

"I was a bit nervous about [appointing] Noman because he was a brash individual who didn't mind stepping on toes," the former governor says. "He had been trained as a nuclear engineer by Admiral [Hyman G.] Rickover, who was just as brash. I figured that before this guy destroys the whole system throughout the state I better get him up here and [have] a talk with him."[235]

Holton recalls that he planned to initially reprimand Cole "as a way of calming him down." But, as he remembers, "Noman came prepared with all these charts with different colors indicating the levels of water pollution [in the drinking water] and how it could be cured. I came out of that conference realizing my job was to back that boy as strongly as I could. And I did."

State-of-the-Art Sewerage

Cole's solution to the problem was to treat the sewage where it originated via a new, state-of-the-art treatment facility. The sewage would be treated at this new plant, located just a few miles upstream from the Occoquan Reservoir, and then be released into the Occoquan River. Of course, the notion of drinking treated wastewater didn't sit well with many people. But Noman insisted his advanced waste treatment facility would turn the effluent into potable drinking water of the highest quality. Unlike the export solution, this so-called "in-basin treatment" borrowed safeguard design features and philosophies developed in the aerospace and nuclear power fields.

Cole presented his ideas—including his design for the new plant—to Northern Virginia policymakers in a report titled "Tahoe East for the Occoquan." The title referred to an innovative, advanced wastewater treatment plant built in South Lake Tahoe in 1965 to treat sewage to drinking water standards. The report was favorably received and approved unanimously by the Board of Supervisors in 1971. The governing bodies in the towns of Manassas and Manassas Park, and Prince William County soon followed suit, and those three jurisdictions then

The Upper Occoquan Sewage Authority Water Reclamation Facility, a state-of-the-art treatment facility, was located just a few miles upstream from the Occoquan Reservoir.

joined hands with Fairfax to form the Upper Occoquan Sewage Authority, the organization entrusted with implementing the plan.

The only roadblock was funding. "[Initially, I] tried to double the cigarette tax from two and one-half cents to a nickel and, at the same time, put a ten percent tax on the sale of whiskey, with all this money to go to the municipal treatment facility," remembers Holton. "It hit the fan as soon as it was announced."

Holton's bill passed in the state's Senate but was defeated in the House by the finance committee, which had a tobacco farmer as its chair. But the action in the Senate "scared [tobacco manufacturer] Phillip Morris," he notes. "They came to me and said, 'We know you're going to try to get this passed again. Instead of tacking on excise tax on our product, we'll support you if you suggest an increase in the income tax.' They did just that and got the state Chamber of Commerce to back them."

With funding now secure, Millard Robbins took a temporary leave from the State Water Control Board to build the Upper Occoquan

Sewage Authority Water Reclamation Facility, as the plant was originally called. When the $80 million facility came online near Route 28 at the Fairfax–Prince William border in 1978, the eleven overloaded secondary treatment plants were decommissioned. Both Cole and Governor Holton were on hand at the plant's dedication. "I had the great pleasure of drinking the first glass of reclaimed water," Holton recalls. "It tasted just fine."

The reclaimed water from the facility flows into a fifty-five-acre, manmade reservoir adjoining the plant before moving twenty miles downstream to a tributary of Bull Run, a creek that flows into the Occoquan Reservoir. There, nature stores the principal source of Northern Virginia's potable water supply.

At its inception, the plant treated five million gallons of sewage each day. Today, it treats thirty-five million gallons daily, with the capacity to treat up to fifty-four million gallons each day. Thanks to Cole's brilliance and resolve, Northern Virginia's water supply is among the highest quality in the country. "You could go out in a boat [at the manmade reservoir] and look down through the clear water forever," says Robbins, who retired in 2000 as the executive director of the Upper Occoquan Sewage Authority. The plant was renamed in Robbins's honor; today it is called the Millard H. Robbins, Jr. Water Reclamation Facility.

As for the facility's designer, Noman, of course, already had a plant named for him: the Noman Cole, Jr., Pollution Control Plant (previously the Lower Potomac Treatment Plant). He remained volunteer chairman of the State Water Control Board until 1974, his humble work benefiting all who live along the Potomac River and Chesapeake Bay. Of the arduous effort, he simply said, "God help those who propose and advocate a solution to a problem."[236]

A Landmark Community Centre

With two state-of-the art waste treatment plants, Fairfax County had taken care of its sewerage and water needs for the foreseeable future. Just in time, too. As more newcomers crossed the threshold into Fairfax County, homebuilders worked overtime to satisfy demand. Soon

numerous mixed-use real estate developments sprouted on land formerly used for cattle or dairy farming.

One such community was Burke Centre. The community had been
built on property previously set aside for the county's second international airport and developed by Hazel/Peterson and Giuseppe Cecchi, who
had built the Watergate complex in Washington. In 1974, the partners
assembled 1,250 acres of rolling wooded hills west of Springfield bought
from Ed Lynch, Bill Downey, and Homer Hoyt, who had all acquired the
property at auction from the federal government. Three years later,
ground was broken for the community's first 228 houses. The homes—
built by a total of nine homebuilders—ranged in price from $44,000
to $70,000.

Altogether 1,054 single-family homes, 2,835 townhouses, 828 garden
apartments, and three hundred high-rise apartment units were planned
at Burke Centre, enough housing for 15,500 people. Several tracts
screened by the woods were earmarked for light industry. Other parcels
were set aside for business and commercial activity, including a forty-
acre town center and a seven-acre village center. The developers even
gave the county several large lots to create subsidized housing for low-
and moderate-income families. Burke Centre would rival the "new town"
concept established in Reston, but without the radical stigma.

The first several years of planning were difficult. Peterson recalls
haggling with Board supervisors who didn't want highways built in the
lightly developed Pohick watershed, even though the roads had been on
the Master Plan for some time.[237] Some county officials protested that the
project would generate more costs for public facilities and services than
it would create in tax revenues. Worries mounted over a possible show-
down with the Board. But unlike Til Hazel's other rezoning cases, Burke
Centre proved to be a "love affair" with the supervisors, as Til told *The
Washington Post.*[238]

In September 1975, Til and his partners successfully petitioned the
Board to permit the new Residential Planning Community rezoning,
which allowed for denser development. It was only the third time
the Board had given its approval for the rezoning, the first being for
Reston in the early 1960s. Burke Centre would be the largest Fairfax

rezoning since then. "We have now [passed] the 'great thoughts' department," Peterson said when apprised of the ruling. "It's no longer a 'might be' project."[239]

People flocked to the new community, from 441 residents in 1977 to 3,823 in 1979. It was an astounding population increase of 900 percent in two years, and one that *The Post* called "phenomenal, the most dramatic in Northern Virginia."[240] Although the circumferential and radial highways on the Master Plan never materialized, the developers built connecting roads to Route 123 on the west, Pohick Road on the south, Burke Lake Road on the east, and the Southern railway line on the north, which would provide for the Burke Centre train station.

Burke Centre ultimately became home to more than eighteen thousand residents whose houses spread over more than 1,700 acres. The high-rise apartment buildings were never built due to the demand for town homes. Nevertheless, the community still provided the broadest mix of housing in the county, and its amenities were unrivalled. More than four hundred acres of woods and meadows were preserved as open space for residents. These residents, who spanned five neighborhoods, also had access to sixty playgrounds, five swimming pools, eighteen tennis courts, six ponds stocked with fish and ornamented with gazebos, decks and docks, and a band shell on a pier. The community even included a train station on the Virginia Railway Express system, a major train stop today. Burke Centre, *The Washington Post* enthused, was "meticulous" and "park-like."[241]

For Hazel/Peterson, taking on a development the size of Burke Centre had been daunting. Otis "Skip" Coston, the project's general manager, remembers, "There weren't that many people wanting to dive into this huge piece of ground . . . and take that risk. Unlike the typical subdivisions going up, this was truly a planned environment, which in those days wasn't common. We tried very hard not to harm the land . . . to preserve it as best we could with parks and open spaces. At the time, the [real estate] market was going up and down, but we were very successful. The project came at the right time and was economically viable."[242]

While there is little to compare to Burke Centre, Foster City outside of Silicon Valley, which was incorporated in 1971, is considered the West

Coast's first planned community. Today, it is home to nearly thirty thousand people.[243]

Burke Centre was Hazel/Peterson's second and largest real estate development. It would not be their last. As Til told a local magazine, "We moved more and more into the land business until the first thing I knew I was more in the land business than the law business."[244]

The Cornerstone of Employment

Just north of Burke Centre, Tysons Corner had become a booming metropolis. The days of wrestling gorillas for fifty bucks a pop were now part of a bygone era. By 1977, Tysons Corner, which had a workforce of fourteen thousand, had become a major economic hub of Fairfax County and one of the largest centers of employment in the Greater Metropolitan Washington Region.

The high-rise office buildings and apartment houses in Tysons Corner had dramatically altered the skyline. These office buildings housed every kind of white-collar enterprise: major corporations, trade associations, research and development firms, technology companies, systems planning firms, and financial investment boutiques. "Everywhere were signs of the specialized business of a new age," *The Washington Post* reported.[245] Other than a few car dealerships, pizza parlors, and the old stump removal company on Leesburg Pike still owned by Marcus Bles, few remnants of the past remained.

As *The Post* opined, Tysons Corner offered "an increasingly popular lifestyle—suburbia that isn't just a bedroom community. It isn't downtown, but it isn't country. It's trying to be the best of both worlds, to generate a lot of money without cutting down too many trees."

Most of the people who worked in Tysons Corner lived in Northern Virginia, although many trickled in from Washington, Maryland, and elsewhere in the county, which accounted for the one hundred thousand cars that passed through the area each business day.[246] For those workers weary of commuting, a luxury condominium complex of five ten-story buildings dotting forty-two acres was planned. The project, The Rotonda, was developed and built by Giuseppe Cecchi.

The elected Fairfax County Board of Supervisors were sworn in at the Old Courthouse in Fairfax, December 1971. Members included Rufus Phillips, James Scott, Alan Magazine, Martha Pennino, Audrey Moore, John Herrity, Joseph Alexander, Herbert Harris II, and Dr. William Hoofnagle, chairman.

Tysons Corner boasted the second and third most valuable pieces of property in the nation in 1976: the land on which Ted Lerner built his shopping mall, and the space where Jerry Halpin had erected the West*Gate industrial complex. These were assessed at $19.6 million and $16.6 million, respectively. Roughly half of the county's 7.5 million square feet of office space was in Tysons Corner.

Lerner's Tysons Corner Shopping Center had more than two hundred thousand people a week trafficking through its stores, which included Bloomingdale's, New York City's high-end department store. "They don't all come from Fairfax, they come from all over—as far away as Richmond, two hours to the south, not to mention the District, Maryland and tourists from all over," *The Post* stated about the shoppers.[247]

Lerner had high hopes to build another, larger mall on 107 acres opposite his original shopping center. He retained Til Hazel to represent him in requesting rezoning from the Board of Supervisors. But the Board stalled. By 1977, the supervisors had put off a decision to rezone the acreage for a fourth time, waiting to craft a plan to ease the area's traffic congestion. Although Lerner offered to provide $1 million toward the building of new roads, another eleven years would pass before Tysons II Galleria, his planned $1 billion office, retail, and hotel complex, opened to the public. It wasn't until Til masterminded a $14 million road network funded by Lerner that the supervisors were finally appeased.

PRC and the Beltway Bandits

With such office buildings, retailers, and housing in place, hundreds of companies flocked to Tysons Corner. One such firm was PRC. A high-technology defense contracting and engineering firm, PRC was founded in 1954 by three scientists from the Rand Corporation. In the 1960s, PRC began acquiring several technical companies to broaden its menu of services, among them a consulting business run by civil engineer John Toups. By the time PRC bought his firm in 1970, Toups had grown his small consultancy to a staff of 250. For the next three years, he continued to head the firm as a unit of PRC. In 1976, when one of PRC's three founders, Bob Kruger, retired, Toups succeeded him as president and then CEO the following year.

Toups was born into a peripatetic family in Texas in 1929. During his childhood, he moved from Texas to Chicago before finally landing in Southern California's Orange County in 1940. John served in the military during World War II and won a Purple Heart for a gunshot wound to the leg, an injury that caused him pain until a successful hip operation in 2005. His time in the hospital during and after the war left a dramatic impression, inspiring him to volunteer on many occasions to help improve the quality of health care. After the war, Toups moved to northern California and enrolled at the University of California at Berkley; he received his engineering degree in 1949. His first job was as a civil engineer with the California Division of Highways. He became the city engineer for Fullerton, California, in 1955.

As with BDM, the lion's share of PRC's work was with the federal government. The firm initially leased a small office to be close to its employer in Washington. When the company outgrew its space, Toups began to look for larger quarters. He had never heard of Fairfax County before, but he decided to lease a new 131,000-square-foot building from Jerry Halpin on Jones Branch Drive in the West*Park complex. "We had more people working here handling federal government contracts than anywhere else," he says. "We were doing about $200 million a year back then [and] were a significant player. Our engineers were scattered all over the world in Iran, Kuwait, Saudi Arabia, and Spain. We had an office in England and did a lot of work for oil companies in the North Sea."

When the building on Jones Branch Drive became too confining, Toups again looked for suitable accommodations. "I had met Milt Peterson and Til Hazel, and they sold me on northern Virginia as the site of our new headquarters," he says. "In 1978, I cut a deal with them to build the PRC Building in Tysons [Corner]." The four-hundred-thousand-square-foot office structure opened in 1980.

PRC's story is similar to BDM's. Both firms were founded by three scientists and had a core competency in high technology systems. Both had moved their headquarters to Tysons Corner to be close to the federal government in Washington. And both inspired a mass migration of other technology businesses to the county.

By the beginning of the 1980s, the county's myriad government consulting and contracting firms in Fairfax were the talk of the nation. No longer a bedroom community, Fairfax County was swarming with what the press humorously called "Beltway Bandits"—a seemingly endless string of private companies eager to share in Uncle Sam's munificence.

Building Up Northern Virginia Homes

The "Beltway Bandits" brought thousands of people to the county who needed suitable places to live. Dwight Schar was more than happy to oblige them. Schar headed up Northern Virginia Homes, one of the nine homebuilders at Burke Centre. Resourceful and hardworking, he had left home for Ohio when he was just thirteen years old to work on his ailing uncle's farm. Schar had a knack for academics, studying hard in high school and paying for his tuition at Ashland University with the money he earned working the graveyard shift at a factory. The only people he knew were schoolteachers and farmers, so he decided on the former as a career, teaching at the local high school in Stow, Ohio.

But with a wife and young family to support, Dwight's salary as a teacher barely covered the monthly rent. So he got his real estate license and started selling houses on the weekends. He was a natural. "Houses weren't selling at the time, so when the sales manager quit, I took over and stuck furniture in the houses, fertilized the lawn, put up more eye-catching 'for sale' signs, and stuck ads in the paper," he recalls. "We started selling houses."[248]

When his boss became president of Ohio Home Building, Schar gave up teaching and took a full-time job with the company in Cincinnati. He was twenty-six years old. "I was put in charge of their largest operation, and I didn't know the difference between a sewer line and a water line," he laughs. "But I was good at organizing things."

He soon left the company for Pittsburgh-based Ryan Homes, which sent him to Fairfax County to take over its floundering Metropolitan Washington-area business. Ryan Homes was one of the smaller home-builders around, but Dwight believed it had great potential. The real estate market was ripe for the plucking. "I hired a single engine plane and flew over the region, and everywhere I saw equipment moving dirt I circled it on a map," he says. "I'd then find out who owned the land and go talk to them. Gradually we got more business."

Within a short time, Schar took Ryan Homes from a middling player to the top homebuilder in the Metropolitan Washington market. In 1977, he left Ryan Homes following a dispute with its new CEO and set out on his own, incorporating Northern Virginia Homes. While he waited out his non-compete agreement with his former employer, he eventually leased an office from Jerry Halpin right down the hall from the West*Group founder. Jerry soon employed Dwight to develop "Alamos," a community in Scottsdale, Arizona, featuring townhouses, condos, a large hotel, and a shopping center. They became close friends, despite a generation's difference in their ages, and they often traveled to Arizona together to oversee the project and buy Western art at auctions. "We really went for the free entrees and appetizers," Jerry laughs. "We used to fall asleep in the lobby at the Phoenix airport waiting for the red eye home."

Once he was ready to secure financing for his upstart company, Dwight contacted Milt Drewer at First American Bank. "I had about $55,000 to my name and figured I had about a year to get something working," he says. "But it was tough getting lots because of the sewer moratorium. I asked [Drewer] who was the most important guy around here, and he said, 'Til Hazel.'"

Dwight called Til and told him he was a young fellow just getting his feet wet and needed advice. "Til agreed to meet me and spent hours explaining everything going on in the county, even though he and Milt [Peterson] were ostensibly [my] competitors," he says. "They were developing Burke Centre at the time [and] I was able to get some business. To this day I don't know why they invited me in. Both of them are very special human beings."

Northern Virginia Homes hit the ground running, benefiting from the area's real estate boom. In 1986, Schar took the company public as NVR. Just weeks later he mounted a hostile takeover of Ryan Homes, which was eight times NVR's size and sales. He quickly fired the CEO he'd clashed with earlier.

By then, Dwight Schar was a force to be reckoned with. And with powerful friends in the real estate community like Til Hazel, Milt Peterson and Jerry Halpin, his future—and that of Fairfax County's—was star bright.

Proffering Only the Best

Thanks to the recommendations of the Blue Ribbon Committee and the speed in which Jack Herrity and Earle Williams implemented them, more companies were now considering moving their headquarters to Fairfax County. Once again, developers began to petition the Board of Supervisors for rezoning to accommodate the county's growing housing

Doug Fahl, former head of the transportation planning branch at the Fairfax County Planning Department

needs. But this time, when developers came before the Board, they had a new tool at their disposal.

The tool was a proffer system developed by Til and county attorney Lee Ruck and designed to ease potential zoning application issues. Under state legislation approved in 1974, the system afforded the county the opportunity to accept the developers' voluntary "proffering" of property and other amenities in return for rezoning a parcel of property. Amenities included the building of roads, road improvements, and the dedication of sites for parks and schools. Cash payments were frowned upon.

For example, if the Board of Supervisors had concerns about the potential traffic that might stem from a new corporate headquarters, the developer could voluntarily donate land and build the roads, effectively solving the dilemma. Or if residents were upset by a proposal for rezoning that would affect the natural splendor of their neighborhood, the developer could present an easement that protected the grass and trees. Although many developers had committed to such improvements in the past, there had been no clear method for enforcing them, and some developers failed to carry out their promises. "I recall representing developers who promised to not cut down a particular tree in the rezoning request, only to cut it down after the approval," Til says. "The Board would never blame the client; they'd blame me. The problem [was] there was no way to enforce the developer's promises. It was a weak link."

Til and his frequent courtroom adversary, Lee Ruck, collaboratively developed the concept of a proffer system and coauthored the legislation (other early and key players in the development of proffers were

Arlington land use attorney Barnes Lawson and Doug Fahl). Ruck asked Til to lobby the bill through the Virginia General Assembly on his own. "Back then no county representative was welcomed in Richmond," Til explains. "Had the county sponsored it alone, it would have gone nowhere. I was determined that a better system should be available, as long as it was voluntary [for the developer] and did not include cash payments, which are nothing more than a bribe."

Proffers were—and still are—rather unique to Northern Virginia. While impact fees in other jurisdictions can sometimes include land or be designated for specific public use, Fairfax is unique in its successful use of this tool. The system has since become controversial.[249] It unraveled in the mid-1990s, as Til feared it might, when dollars rather than infrastructure improvements and amenities became the bartering currency. But from the late-1970s to the early 1990s, proffers allowed for equitable, orderly development of the county and worked in the best interest of all constituents. As historians Ross and Nan Netherton wrote: "Proffers . . . have been used to bring project plans in compliance with various environmental protection standards or residents' concerns about impacts of development. Enhancement of neighborhood amenities and preservation of natural or historic landmarks also have benefited from the use of proffers."[250]

By putting millions of developer dollars into the coffers for highway construction, the proffer system helped developers do what the county had fought against for many years: build roads. The system also provided developers greater assurance that the capital invested in planning a project was not ill-spent. "Before the proffer system, it was an all-out battle who could get what and from whom, with no rules and much chaos," says Skip Coston, general manager of the Burke Centre project. "We never knew where a situation stood or how to deal with the county. Once the proffer system was adopted, there were procedures for negotiating improvements in zoning cases."

Ruck concurs, "[The proffer system was] phenomenally successful. What it did was [provide] legal enforceability to protect the community [by holding the developer] to the promises that the developer was willing to make and traditionally has always made. It brought regularity. And it became the single most important device and philosophy that got us out of the land use wars of the 1970s into the relatively stable, business-oriented growth cycles of the 1980s and 1990s."

The new system also helped dispose of the hundreds of rezoning applications that had made life miserable for the Board of Supervisors. "We went from one thousand pending zoning cases in front of the planning commission and the Board," says Ruck, "and more than one hundred cases pending in the courts, to five or ten cases on land use issues [by 1980]. It was a huge relief."

He chuckles, "Til should get a gold star, as should I."[251]

George Johnson's Educational Crusade

By the late 1970s, many impediments to luring commercial and industrial firms to the county had been overcome, but several still remained. For instance, Fairfax County's quality of health care, education, cultural entertainments, and transportation continued to lag behind comparable areas. Once again, a small group of private businesspeople worked to turn these detractions around. They had a stake in the county's future, but more important, they believed they were building a metropolis where all would thrive.

Til Hazel was unequaled in this capacity. He had committed his time, professional abilities, money, and connections to George Mason University virtually since its beginnings. In 1978, the same year he joined the Board of Governors at St. Stephen's, a private secondary school in Alexandria, Til took it upon himself to find the university new leadership. He sought someone who could skillfully manage the growth of GMU's enrollment, buildings, qualified teachers, academic programs, and advanced degrees.

Til found all this and more in George Johnson, the dean of arts and sciences at Temple University. Johnson not only directed GMU toward extraordinary growth and progress, he also leveraged his role with the university to catalyze commercial business growth in Fairfax. With Til Hazel by his side and Earle Williams at the Economic Development

Authority, Johnson ignited a boom at GMU that reverberated economically throughout the county.

Ironically, when GMU's board of visitors wrote to Johnson to inquire about his interest in becoming president, he admitted he had never heard of the institution. Apparently many others hadn't, either. Johnson, an ex-English professor, would become intent on changing that. Still, he initially wasn't sure he wanted the job until Til convinced him otherwise over a pitcher of martinis. "George was flying in and out on a commuter airline during his visits, and I would meet him at Crystal City when he was waiting to fly home," Til recalls. "One day we had an after-lunch martini that went on well into the evening. I kept up with George. We talked and talked, and then came to find we shared a mutual enthusiasm for the future. He had wanted to rebuild Temple [University], but when he saw the opportunities here, he knew this was the place for him."

Johnson's crusade to remake GMU was not without its challenges. He soon encountered Richmond's so-called Main Street power bloc of influential businesspeople and Virginia legislators, which wanted to suppress the university in order to secure better funding and students for the state's other advanced institutions, such as Virginia Tech and the University of Virginia. For years, these downstate interests resisted parity on salaries for teachers at GMU with their counterparts. As Virgil Dykstra, Johnson's predecessor at GMU, stated, "[Richmond's] attitude was basically one of condescension toward the upstart."[252]

It didn't take long for Johnson to size up the situation. "I learned my first week here that things were rigged below the Occoquan River to keep GMU from becoming a serious institute of higher learning," he says. "It was practically open warfare. I was brought in to make something happen."[253]

Unfortunately, with few GMU alumni, little money, and a hostile political environment, it was not going to be easy. But the North-Dakota-born Johnson enjoyed a good fight. Like many Americans reared in the heartland, Johnson had what Alexis De Tocqueville called an "apocalyptic imagination." As he once told a reporter, "I tend to see developments not so much in terms of social institutions incrementally moving in an institutionalized society. I see things as great collisions of abstract forces of light and dark."[254] In Virginia, the forces of light and dark were starkly evident.

Johnson, who stands six feet six inches tall, shook things up on his very first day. He didn't simply meet with the Fairfax County Chamber of Commerce; he joined it, becoming its secretary and eventually a director. Johnson was bent on working with everyone and anyone that had a stake in the county's future, from local officials and members of the General Assembly to the real estate developers, homebuilders, construction companies, and engineers changing the landscape. He also sought relationships with the CEOs of many technology companies that, like PRC and BDM, were headquartered in Fairfax.

As Johnson saw it, in order to make GMU a world-class institution of higher learning, he needed to position the university as a neutral convener that could create strategies to grow the county's business base. In this pursuit, the benefits were mutual: a first-rate university would draw more companies to Fairfax County, which would then provide high-paying jobs to its undergraduate and graduate students.

His background as an English professor—with a penchant for the writings of Nathaniel Hawthorne—helped him to eloquently describe his plans. He described Fairfax County as lying "in the shadow of the Paris of the 21st century"—Paris being Washington, D.C. The county, he said, was "at the epicenter of global change," a "golden, fertile crescent on the Potomac,"[255] and a "Wild West frontier where pioneering companies and other enterprises were sure to grow along with the territory."

George wanted to hitch the university to Beltway Bandits like PRC, BDM, and the other expanding businesses and industries of the New Age—including telecommunications, high technology, computer science, bioengineering, applied physics, information services, and consulting firms. "Earle Williams had helped turn the tax situation around, and that brought in the first technology companies," Johnson says. "I wanted to bring in more of them and figure out ways to hold them together. Fairfax was a new frontier with no focal point. The people running companies didn't know each other."

A Hot Spot for "Highway Helpers"

Johnson knew that if these "bandits" could band together, they could help combat the anti-contractor bias that was rampant in many Washington circles. "Burt Lance [of the Carter administration] tried to make a career out of bashing the government contracting community," Earle Williams remembers. "We countered by describing ourselves as 'Parkway Patriots' or 'Highway Helpers.'"

Clustering these Highway Helpers in a specific geographic location was also good for business. "Proximity breeds greater competition, more ideas and, thus, more business," George says. In 1978, he concocted a strategy to fuel such cooperative competition among technology firms, leveraging the university as the organizing center. "There were no watering holes or other places to meet," jokes Johnson.

He called his organization the George Mason Institute of Science and Technology. Its mission was to serve as a liaison between the university and area high technology firms, much in the way that Stanford Research Institute helped connect companies in what became Silicon Valley. "I entreated the principals of six high-tech firms to meet with me in the boardroom at GMU to craft a plan to grow the university and the county as a commercial nexus," he says. "Among this group were Earle Williams, John Toups, Dan Bannister from Dynacorp, and the local CEOs of TRW and Unisys. I then asked each of them to recruit one or two more people."

By the 1980s, the Institute's roster included its original members as well as the national or local heads of Tandem Computers, Flow General, Cerberonics, Xerox, IBM, Comsat, AT&T Long Lines, Mobil Oil, Boeing Computers, GTE, Honeywell, and American Management Systems. Soon developers, homebuilders, and diverse other businesspeople joined the Institute. Other early members included Til Hazel, Sid Dewberry, Bill Hazel, and Dwight Schar.

These corporate leaders were able to work in ways that would have been impossible without the cover of the university, and soon the Institute became one of the most important organizations in Northern Virginia. "I got involved because I wanted to build a community with the other players," Toups says. "Government contracting is a unique business: someone you compete with today could be a partner on a project tomorrow."

The Institute gathered the discrete economic forces spread throughout the county and coalesced them into a unified whole similar to Silicon Valley and other technology corridors. "To create an economic hotspot you need first of all an entrepreneurial environment, an adequate system of interstate highways, a major airport, sophisticated telecommunications, and a nice place to live," says Johnson. "All this was being followed in the county without any conscious formula, with the driver being the economy and the key to the economy being the high tech industry. The exponential growth in information technology drove everything here."

George Mason Institute provided just the right infrastructure and mix of businesspeople for the technology industry to flourish. "We started with about eighteen high tech firms . . . When the Northern Virginia Technology Council superseded us [in 1993] it had three hundred members, and then twenty minutes later had eight hundred members," Johnson says. Today, the Northern Virginia Technology Council boasts more than 1,100 members.

Legacy of Leadership and Change

When George formed the Institute back in the late 1970s, few people even realized that Fairfax was home to so many technology firms. "Fairfax had a hole, and the university began to fill that void, serving as a convener of business and educational leadership," says John Tydings, then-CEO of the Greater Washington Board of Trade. "George Johnson and Til Hazel made [the Institute] a clubhouse for the private sector, and as it began to recognize the changing economy, it became a promoter and participant."

Earle Williams says the county's high tech boom had gone as far as it could before the Institute stepped in. "A high technology center cannot survive for long and grow without a respectable university at its core," the BDM CEO told *Regardie's* magazine. "The kind of people we have to recruit and want to retain are people who come from an academic environment, and they want to continue to be a part of an academic environment even if they're not employed by the university. They want the opportunity to go back in and deal with the university professors, deal with people who are doing research [and have] access to faculty for consulting purposes."[256]

When George Johnson arrived at GMU in 1978, he counted twenty-six buildings, and that included "every chicken coop, outhouse, and shack on campus," he jokes. When he left the university in 1996, there were too many structures to count: more than 120 buildings in all, including the ten-thousand-seat Patriot Center athletic and entertainment arena. The faculty was among the country's best, recruited from elite colleges and universities. As *The Washington Post* reported, "Johnson has been successful at luring faculty stars with high salaries, paid in part by the many high tech local industries [within] the George Mason Institute."[257]

The newspaper also cited the university's wholesale import of the Center for the Study of Public Choice in 1983 from rival Virginia Polytechnic Institute. Corporate donations funded the salaries for the noted economists who staffed the Center. In 1986, one of those economists, James Buchanan, was awarded the Nobel Prize in Economic Science.

New curriculum burst onto the scene as well, with Masters of Science degrees in geographic and cartographic sciences, computer and electronics engineering, operations research and systems management, and applied physics; and Bachelors of Science degrees in accounting, finance, geology, management, marketing, and computer and electronics engineering. There were Bachelors of Arts degrees in anthropology, speech communication, and theatre; and Masters of Arts degrees in music and sociology. Technology became part of the core curriculum, too, with three departments—Computer and Information Sciences, Electrical and Computer Engineering, and Systems Engineering—established in 1984.

Incredibly, most of this growth took place within the first five years of Johnson's tenure. No wonder that when a reporter once asked Johnson to describe himself he said, "Energetic and impatient."[258]

Lobbying for a Law School

Til Hazel was awarded the first George Mason Medal in 1987 in recognition of his efforts, which resulted in both a law school and doctoral status for the university.

Thanks to the efforts of its visionary president, GMU's reputation was soaring. But the university's most important academic development of the time came through the work of Til Hazel. Til believed that for a university to be considered world class it must have professional schools like a law school. Such schools would be reasonably affordable to create and would appeal to residents in the Greater Washington area seeking higher education. So from his first day on GMU's board, he made the creation of a law school his number one goal. "It would give professional status to the university and raise it above the community college status it otherwise always would have," Til once explained to a reporter. "[GMU] needed a professional school, and the law school was the doable way to achieve that because it was not capital intensive. And, besides, though I share the view that lawyers have proliferated to a nuisance factor, I don't think that should stop people from studying the law as a part of their education."

Every year beginning in 1973, Til petitioned the General Assembly in Richmond to approve a law school at GMU. Every year he was rebuffed. Til's opportunity finally came when a private law school, the International School of Law, moved from Washington, D.C., to an abandoned department store one block from his father's former medical practice in Arlington. On the advice of Arlington Circuit Court Judge Charles Russell, Til and Russell met with the school's dean, Ralph Norvell. The three men had lunch and agreed on the concept of an alliance. "The only problem was the law school had an option on the land that had to be exercised before the General Assembly could meet and approve the merger, and the land cost $3 million," Til recalls. "George Mason had about thirty cents at the time. [But] we worked it out." Russell later became a Justice of the Virginia Supreme Court.

Milt Drewer at First American Bank funded the acquisition. "It was a gamble," remembers Drewer, who had backed many of Hazel/Peterson's real estate developments, "but I trusted Til completely."[259]

Still, the state legislature opposed the measure, blocking it twice. As Johnson explained at the time, "A law school was the mark of a real university. For that reason, if not for others, it was fiercely resisted [by the state educational system]."[260]

In 1979, Til drove to Richmond once again to solicit the General Assembly's approval of the law school. "I was down there lobbying every way I knew how, but the real lobbyists, the effective ones, were the law students," he says. "They went down there and talked quietly and behaved and got the job done. The legislators saw they weren't a bunch of student radicals but were serious people who wanted a good law school."

The law school was approved the next day. The General Assembly also voted unanimously to approve GMU for doctoral status. "Til had connections in Richmond," says former Fairfax County supervisor Happy Bradley, "[and] without [Richmond] you cannot accomplish anything. He is a very canny person who understands people very well, and he just knew where to push the right buttons. He was indispensable in my opinion in [GMU] getting the law school, which was his vision from very early on when we both sat on the Board. Back then, no one but Til could imagine it happening, but with George Johnson sharing his views, they accomplished the seemingly impossible. It's a remarkable story."[261]

As important as the law school was, doctoral status for the university was even more critical. In Virginia, funding from the state is related to academic status and increases markedly when a program affords a doctorate degree. In 1980, the university won permission from the Virginia Council on Higher Education to offer a doctoral degree in public administration. A Doctor of Arts degree in education and others in environmental biology, information technology, and nursing soon followed.

The Filene Center at the Wolf Trap National Park for the Performing Arts in Vienna, Virginia, was redesigned by Dewberry & Davis after a fire in 1982.

For his efforts on behalf of GMU, Til was awarded the first George Mason Medal in 1987. The prize honors "individuals who have a record of service to their community, state, or nation consistent with the level and quality of the historical George Mason's public service in his own time." In 2005, an Arlington campus building constructed for the George Mason University School of Law was named John T. Hazel Jr. Hall. As Sid Dewberry, then-rector of the university's Board of Visitors, states, "Til fought hard for the acquisition and the accreditation of the law school in the face of considerable opposition throughout the state."

"The most embarrassing thing in the world for Til is when somebody wants to honor him," says his close friend L. B. "Bud" Doggett, former president of the Greater Washington Board of Trade and a successful parking magnate in Washington. "But the truth is he built that university. Others helped, but he led the way, getting millions of dollars pumped into it over the years and, of course, building that law school. He always enjoyed a good fight. And he deserved every damn penny he got for GMU."[262]

Long Life and the Pursuit of Happiness

As the university and the technology corridor it inspired grew at lightning speed, Til Hazel, Jerry Halpin, and other private citizens worked to improve Fairfax County's other public services. In the mid-1970s, Til chaired the county's Hospital and Health Services

Commission, a private, non-governmental entity that received federal dollars for medical care. In Northern Virginia, the funds went toward the construction of an addition to Fairfax Hospital and the new Mount Vernon Hospital, both owned and managed by the Fairfax Hospital Association. The latter was located close to the Potomac River and opened in 1976 with seventy-six beds, seventy doctors, and thirty-two staff members. As the commission's chairman, Til oversaw the construction of the addition and the planning and architecture at the new hospital. "With the population growing and companies eyeing Fairfax as a place for their business," Til remembers, "we needed to greatly enhance the quality and size of our health care facilities."

Two years later, Fairfax Hospital Association bought the ten-year-old Commonwealth Doctors Hospital in the City of Fairfax. The facility was converted into an emergency room and nursing home when a new 160-bed hospital was built in Fair Oaks in 1983. The hospital association also expanded the laboratory facilities and emergency room at Fairfax's main hospital in the late 1970s. Meanwhile, Til got involved in other health care initiatives, including fund-raising for the Northern Virginia Hospice and the Second Genesis drug treatment program, and serving as a director of the Potomac Tuberculosis and Respiratory Disease Association and Northern Virginia Mental Health Association.

To further the quality of life in Fairfax, many private citizens labored to create a major center for the performing arts at Wolf Trap, near Vienna as well. (The name "Wolf Trap" derives from the traps set to capture wolves in the 1630s. Wolves were a menace in the area, and the Commonwealth offered rewards of tobacco for each wolf's head that was delivered to authorities.)

The Wolf Trap National Park for the Performing Arts was established in the late 1960s through the generous donation of local landowner and philanthropist Catherine Filene Shouse, who gave one hundred acres of farmland to the U.S. government. As the first national park for the performing arts, the venue is managed through a unique collaboration between the government's U.S. National Park Service, and the privately held Wolf Trap Foundation. Some of Wolf Trap's earliest performances included traveling ballet troupes, Broadway musicals, and local opera productions.

The Wolf Trap Foundation's first finance chairman was Jerry Halpin. In this role, Jerry helped raise the funds to build the seven-thousand-seat, indoor/outdoor Filene Center in 1971. He also purchased an old log cabin off Route 7 east of Tysons Corner and donated it to the venue. "We took it apart log by log and then rebuilt it log by log," he recalls. "It's still there."

In later years, Wolf Trap would endure several setbacks, including two fires, in 1971 and 1982.

Sid Dewberry remembers, "The [1982] fire occurred on a Sunday night. I happened to be on vacation. Monday morning I was on my boat off the coast of Florida fishing when Jack Herrity called. He said, 'Sid, can you be in my office today at 5:00 p.m.?' I told him, 'It's going to be hard for me to do that as I'm at sea. What's going on?' Jack replied, 'Don't you read the papers, dummy? There was a big fire that burned down Wolf Trap last night. I want to rebuild it for the summer performance, and I know you can get it done.'"

Sid knew there was no way he'd be able to get there by 5:00, so he sent business partner Dick Davis in his place. They got a temporary tent, courtesy of Saudi Arabia, for the summer's performance. The tent didn't work out for that season or the following one, but the new facility was completed by the next year.

Just as it had after the 1971 fire, the private sector pitched in. Sid Dewberry's engineering firm provided the Filene Center with architectural and engineering design and supervised the contractor for construction. And Dwight Schar erected several pavilions at no cost.

Meanwhile, other institutions blossomed to the benefit of Fairfax citizens. Since the creation of the Fairfax County Park Authority in 1950, great pains had been taken to balance the housing needs of newcomers with the county's natural splendor. From 1959 to 1970, the Authority spent more than $20 million on park acquisitions, a track record that continues today. (Approximately 2.3 acres of parkland per one hundred county residents have been preserved, an extraordinary ratio.) In 1979, the National Park Service selected Fairfax as the location of a major state park: at Mason Neck near Gunston Hall, the ancestral home of George Mason. Mason Neck Park opened in 1981 on 1,800 acres, the largest state park in the county. Picnic areas and nature trails dot the park today, which is home to several pairs of nesting bald eagles.

Another park, Turkey Run, became available to the public in the early 1970s, although for a different purpose. Located in McLean next to the headquarters of the Central Intelligence Agency, the land at Turkey Run was originally owned by the Bureau of Public Roads, which decommissioned it for public use. Unlike Mason Neck Park, this park was built to teach visitors about the life and work of Virginia tenant farmers in the 1770s. Back then, the farmers rented the land on which they lived and farmed, paying for their rent with the tobacco they grew. (For example, 530 pounds of tobacco could equal free rent for a year on 150 acres.) The park contrasts with colonial Williamsburg in Virginia, which depicts the lives of more affluent merchant and landowning classes.

The park fell on hard times in 1981 following the loss of its federal funding. Once again, a Fairfax citizen jumped in to help. Alice Starr lived near the park and was the vice president of marketing at West*Group. She rallied her boss, Jerry Halpin, to corral his fellow developers and corporate tenants to fund the park's resurrection. The money came flowing in. The biggest donation came from developer Claude Moore, but there was a catch: his monetary bequest at the time of his death required matching funds. "The private business community led by Jerry and Til decided it didn't want to lose this beautiful one-hundred-acre park in McLean and have it developed into a subdivision," says Starr. "They tapped everyone else to raise the money to match the grant from Claude." [263]

Among those cutting checks were Jerry, John Toups, Milt Peterson, and Til Hazel. Dwight Schar offered to erect several pavilions at the park for free, while Bill Hazel offered the services of his construction company. Now called the Claude Moore Colonial Park, the park has the distinction of being the only privately run park in the U.S. National Park Service today.

Collective Soul and Civic Duty

From creating Fairfax's vital public infrastructures to rescuing its treasured parkland, one core group of private citizens continually gave of themselves. They battled the liberal, anti-business crowd that wanted prosperity to locate elsewhere and joined forces to create a blueprint for the county's systematic development. They built world-class office buildings of architectural merit and constructed a mix of housing options with superlative amenities for the newly arrived. They constructed roads, schools, parks, and cultural venues and entreated their friends and colleagues to follow suit. They combined their efforts to develop a major university and an unparalleled health care delivery system. And they built the foundations of a major national technology corridor, bringing much-needed tax relief to homeowners and permanently making northern Virginia a vital employment center.

In the 1980s, following the election of President Ronald Reagan, the county's position as a robust economic center would become the talk of the nation. Reagan's historic buildup of the military, dubbed "Star Wars," encouraged hundreds of defense contractors, technology firms, and supporting companies to plant stakes in Fairfax, following pioneering firms like BDM and PRC. In 1982, U.S. Department of Defense contracts for Fairfax County firms alone would exceed $900 million.

Still, much more needed to be done, including transforming Washington Dulles into a bona fide international airport, enhancing the county's secondary schools, and enlarging Northern Virginia Community College. The right-of-way for Dulles Access Road's parallel lanes would require action, as would other modes of transportation. Zoning and plan review procedures had to be upgraded, and more office buildings and homes had to be built.

In these and other quests, the men who fought for Fairfax would tackle the trials and opportunities both individually and collectively. To do so, they would form a unique and powerful organization to channel their concerted efforts—the 123 Club.

The 123 Club, an alliance of businesspeople dedicated to Fairfax County's growth, prosperity, and quality of life, took inspiration from Route 123 for its name.

CHAPTER 6

Uniting for
Change

The 123 Club sprang from George Johnson's fertile imagination. Cognizant of the influence downstate Richmond and the "Main Street" power bloc had over Fairfax County, Johnson formed an alliance of businesspeople with sharp elbows to ensure that Northern Virginia received its fair share of state resources. "George is a can-do guy," says Earle Williams of the George Mason University president.[264]

The club's name was a wry play on Richmond's Main Street, as Route 123, which runs through Tysons Corner, was essentially the county's main drag. Early members included Earle, Til Hazel, Milt Peterson, John Toups, Dwight Schar, Sid Dewberry, Milt Drewer, Bill Hazel, and later, Jerry Halpin. "We were honest men of integrity and character that came to a place, shared a vision, and made it happen," says Til. "And we all felt a keen sense of civic duty."[265]

Club meetings were held at the president's mansion near GMU, a house that Til, Earle, and others had helped secure. George's wife, Joanne, served dinner while the members jawed over how to best secure money from the state for the county's needs, from education to roads. Gatherings were not limited to members. Depending on the club's agenda, a Virginia congressman, senator, or governor could be present. Or if improving local schools were the subject matter, the school superintendent might be asked to join the group. As George saw it, his role was to be a convener. "I'm the guy driving the truck hauling the bulldozer, who is Til, who knew everyone down in Richmond and had their respect," he explains.[266]

The club's principal goal was simply to make the county the best it could be. "We all began to realize that quality of life was the key to creating a worthwhile region," Dwight Schar explains. "That meant education, health care, parks, and high quality, high paying jobs. We were and remain a close-knit group, and we were always concerned about doing the right thing. To succeed you have to have a culture of doing the right thing."[267]

The "right thing" for club members was to heal the old animosities dividing Virginians on either side of the Rappahannock River—what some historians call the "grits line." Given its proximity to Washington and its large population of newcomers, people above the river are generally more liberal, transient, and hectic. Below the river, the politics, dialect, and pace diverge. "Many downstaters regard the denizens of Fairfax somewhat suspiciously, as if they were an alien race—strange, threatening and armed with advanced technologies—[while] Northern Virginians suspect that many of their downstate brethren still are fighting the Civil War," *Virginia Business* magazine stated only partly in jest.[268]

Northern Virginia was expanding rapidly in population, commerce, and influence in the early 1980s, but state politics were still controlled by leaders south of the river. Often, when Northern Virginia knocked on Richmond's door for funding, legislators were tightfisted. J. Wade Gilley, senior vice president of George Mason University at the time and Virginia's former Secretary of Education, recalls, "The information technology revolution was taking off and economic growth in Northern Virginia was exploding. But the region had lost key leaders in the Virginia General Assembly, which was largely controlled by senior legislators from Richmond, Tidewater, and rural Virginia." *Virginia Business* magazine concurred: "Northern Virginia's uniquely regional agenda, such as money for its Metrorail lines, often encountered resistance in a General Assembly dominated by rural legislators."[269]

As the 123 Club understood and appreciated, if Fairfax County wanted to attain the highest possible quality of life, it would need to build rapprochement with downstate Virginia. So Til, Earle, and Carrington Williams (no relation), a lawyer and former delegate to the Virginia Assembly, turned to J. Wade Gilley for assistance. Gilley's experience as Secretary of Education made him personally familiar with the state legislature, and he helped the men conceive a strategy that would benefit all Virginians, not just those living north of the Rappahannock. They called it the Virginia Initiative.

A New State of Initiative

The Virginia Initiative was predicated on creating opportunities for the state's political and corporate leaders to discuss mutually beneficial issues that would increase the Commonwealth's economic prosperity. "Northern Virginia business and governmental leaders were recruited to go to Richmond to get to know the downstate leaders better," says Gilley. "[We] also [brought] state legislative leaders up to Fairfax to get them more familiar with the economic revolution that was underway here and the need to sustain it through legislative action—such as help for roads, schools, and for the university. We wanted them to understand our potential and what needed to be done to advance it."

As the two sides got to know each other, they created several programs. One initiative eased high unemployment in Southern Virginia by finding southerners jobs in the north. Several county businesses also extended their reach to the state's southern region. For instance, Dewberry & Davis—by now Virginia's largest architectural, engineering, and planning firm and a principal contractor to the Federal Emergency Management Agency—opened an office in Roanoke, its ninth in Virginia.

Meanwhile, several other forces converged to improve every aspect of life and work in Fairfax. The county's Economic Development Authority, led by chairman Earle Williams, continued to promote the area's lifestyle and commercial advantages. The local Chamber of Commerce and the Greater Washington Board of Trade also extolled its virtues. And thanks to Johnson's other brainchild, the George Mason Institute, the technology sector was exploding: by 1981, one out of every four firms in Fairfax listed itself as "high-tech."[270] In all these organizations, the same altruistic businessmen were involved, dedicated to the belief that the private sector could better the lives of people through concerted action, investment, and leadership. "I have asked each of these guys at one time or another to participate in something that had a civic component to it and don't remember any one of them [turning me] down," says former Virginia governor Charles S. "Chuck" Robb.

Few jurisdictions in America could boast such spirited allegiance to a single cause. "There is no other region or county in the country that has benefited from an extraordinary combination of private sector leaders who had a civic perspective [and] a huge hand in shaping the flavor of the county," says John Tydings, CEO of the Greater Washington Board of Trade. "This is unequalled."

The county had much to commend it to the corporate sector. Fifty percent of its residents over the age of twenty-five had completed four or more years of college, and more than 75 percent of the workforce was considered white collar. Eighty percent of high school graduates had gone on to some form of post-secondary education, 60 percent of them to a four-year college or university. "Fairfax County had a very talented gene pool to draw from," says Robb, "a critical mass of really talented people, many with terminal degrees in their fields."[271]

This highly educated workforce found jobs in the businesses of the new age, from high technology to telecommunications. By the middle of the decade, the county boasted more engineers and scientists per one hundred thousand people than any other comparable region in the country.[272] As author Joel Garreau said when he sized up Fairfax in the 1980s: "It was the new Dominion, with an economy and a power to make the rest of the state and the District of Columbia quake."[273]

Redefining Dulles

After the brief recession of 1980 to 1981, Fairfax entered a period of unprecedented expansion. The county's population reached six hundred thousand residents in 1980, up from 454,000 a decade earlier.[274] The surge of people put Fairfax nearly on par with San Jose, which numbered 628,000 people in 1980, an increase from two hundred thousand in 1960.[275] More people were on their way, too, making the District of Columbia's old bedroom community bigger than Washington itself. But work still needed to be done to put Fairfax County on level ground with the other fast-growing commercial sectors of the country, such as California's Silicon Valley and Boston's technology corridor Route 128, the partial beltway the press had dubbed the "Magic Circle."

For one, the so-called Washington Dulles International Airport straddling Fairfax and Loudoun counties was a misnomer. Few direct flights to places "international" were available, and only one international carrier, British Airways, served the airport—a glaring impediment to companies considering a location in the county. "You always had to fly to New York or Atlanta to catch a plane out of the country," recalls Stan Harrison, now chair of the Washington Airports Task Force.[276]

The overall volume of passengers at Dulles was also tiny when compared to other U.S. airports, increasing from just 2.1 million travelers in 1970 to 2.6 million a decade later. As *Virginia Business* magazine recalled, the airport had a "mere handful of passengers trickling through the metal detectors."[277] In contrast, Boston's Logan Airport in 1980 handled 15.1 million passengers, while San Francisco International Airport handled 22.6 million.

Part of the problem for Dulles was the stiff competition being provided by National Airport and Baltimore Airport, with the latter aggressively building up and marketing its air services. "Other airports were gobbling up passengers while Dulles sat there with nobody," says Alice Star, vice president of marketing at West*Group at the time.

Things only deteriorated for Dulles when the industry was deregulated in 1978. "Airlines were now free to make their own market decisions and didn't want to serve Washington through two airports, so they concentrated [their] service at National, which led to declines at Dulles," explains Leo Schefer, a former British Aerospace executive.[278]

To dramatize Dulles's barren ticket counters, Governor Robb, son-in-law of former president Lyndon Baines Johnson, chartered eight buses and brought the entire General Assembly up from Richmond to peruse the airport. "We could park on the runway," Robb recalls. "It was a white elephant out there."[279] County business leaders quickly grasped the importance that the airport represented to Fairfax County. "When you combine Dulles on the west with the U.S. Capital on the east," Til said at the time, "it's like a big economic development engine that's anchored on each end by a major drive force."[280]

Dulles Finds Its Wings

Gradually, important steps were taken to improve conditions at the airport. In 1980, the Dulles Policy Task Force was formed to urge lawmakers to create a policy that was more equitable to the two airports. Two years later, under the direction of Carrington Williams, the public/private organization changed its name to the Washington Dulles Task Force. "Carrington was a brilliant policymaker who absolutely understood the role transportation played in society," says Schefer. "He had played a major role at the General Assembly in the creation of the Virginia Port Authority, and after he retired, he came back to Northern Virginia and saw Dulles as a wasting asset. National [Airport] was over-crowded and he clearly realized that if National was the problem, Dulles was the solution."

To fund the task force, Williams knocked on the doors of Fairfax companies like BDM, West*Group, and PRC. Each donated ten thousand dollars to get the organization going.[281] He also entreated Schefer to join the task force as its de facto air services expert. In this role, Schefer essentially did what Earle Williams had done at the Economic Development Authority—the difference being that Schefer squired executives of air carriers around Fairfax while Williams hosted corporate CEOs. "I'd drive them down the Dulles Access Road (on the way to the District of Columbia)," Schefer remembers, "and they'd be impressed at the dedicated access to downtown Washington."

Schefer later succeeded Carrington Williams as president of the renamed Washington Airports Task Force, with Stan Harrison as the organization's chair. Both men still hold these positions today. "When

Leo and Stan took over, there was no looking back," says Alice Starr, who joined the task force around that time. "Those guys lit a fire."

Soon more carriers pitched their tents at Dulles, many lured by Fairfax County's expanding technology sector and the air travel those companies required. The number of passengers the airport handled doubled from 2.6 million in 1980 to 5.2 million five years later, and in 1986 and 1987, the volume skyrocketed to 9.1 million and 10.9 million, respectively. Cargo volumes also soared from 53,000 pounds in 1981 to 288,000 pounds in 1988. Best of all, Dulles finally became a bona fide international airport. The number of international flights went from sixty a week in 1982 to more than 160 a week in 1988, while international nonstop fights jumped from six to nineteen over the same period.[282] These figures would continue their stratospheric ascent in succeeding years.

In June 1987, both Dulles and National airports were transferred from federal to local control when the FAA released them to the newly created Metropolitan Washington Airports Authority. Prior to the transfer, Dulles and National had been the only major commercial airports in the U.S. owned and operated by the federal government. U.S. Secretary of Transportation Elizabeth Dole appointed former Virginia governor Linwood Holton to handle the transition to the quasi-independent authority. The move was considered imperative to the growth of Dulles and the future of the region.

That year also saw the formation of the Dulles Area Transportation Association. The organization coordinated the efforts of the numerous agencies and jurisdictions involved in the region's transportation agenda. The agencies ran the gamut from the airport authority and Metrorail to the Virginia Department of Transportation. Fairfax, Prince William, and Loudoun counties, as well as the cities and towns of Manassas, Manassas Park, Herndon, and Leesburg, also had a stake. "We were trying to bring new commercial development to the Dulles area," says Sid Steele, the association's executive director.[283] "We wanted a forum in which all these different constituencies could come together, identify transportation issues, and work toward solutions, which we've been very effective doing through the years."

In 2006, twenty-three million passengers passed through Washington Dulles International Airport. On a typical day, 1,800 to 2,000 flights are handled at Dulles, up from 1,000 to 1,200 daily flights in 2003. Following substantial upgrades and the acquisition of more than nine hundred adjacent acres, Dulles is poised to reach forty million passengers by 2010. Boston's Logan Airport, on the other hand, is expected to reach 37.5 million passengers by 2015. "Private businesspeople in Fairfax," says Til, "made Dulles what it is today."

Opening Up the Road Less Traveled

As the private sector labored to increase domestic and international air traffic at Dulles, the public sector finally did something about the restricted Dulles Access Road. The road sent traffic without interruption from the airport to the Capital Beltway and then on to Washington. In the 1960s, officials had set aside right-of-way alongside the existing access road to address the future needs of commuters—and for years, both private businesses and the general public had urged the Federal Aviation Administration to approve its use.

The groups held that parallel lanes not only would address local access needs, they would also spur development along the road. Jack Herrity, chairman of the Board of Supervisors, agreed, stating that the roads were "the last step in a long trail" toward developing the industrially zoned property between Tysons Corner and Dulles Airport—a stretch of land referred to today as the Dulles Corridor.[284] *The Washington Post* also endorsed the construction, stating that the parallel lanes would create a "lifeline for all development west of Tysons Corner," including the rapidly growing town of Reston, now largely owned by Mobil Oil.[285]

Yet despite these fervent pleas, the FAA remained reluctant. The agency was equally opposed to the idea of opening Dulles Access Road to local traffic. For instance, when the FAA learned that the Fairfax Board of Supervisors had voted in March 1979 to open the road to local traffic until the parallel roads were built, an agency official tersely commented, "Our position has been no." He added that this would not likely change.[286]

The following month, the ice broke. Both houses of the Virginia General Assembly approved a bill, signed by governor John Dalton, to provide a $57 million bond issue that would fund the building of Route 267, a four-lane highway that would run parallel to the access road. The bonds would be paid back by charging drivers a fifty-cent toll. Toll proceeds also would fund maintenance of the thirteen-mile highway as well as future enhancements (in coming years, the thoroughfare would be widened twice to four lanes each way). The road was officially named the Omer L. Hirst–Adelard L. Brault Expressway after the two Virginia state legislators who authored the bill, but it is more commonly known as the Dulles Toll Road.

Ground was broken on the toll road in January 1983. Later that year, Virginia legislators gave motorists another gift: the December opening of a 2.5-mile extension of the Dulles Access Highway to Interstate 66. Finally, after decades of failed attempts, I-66 would course through Arlington. The new thoroughfare would cut driving time from Washington, D.C., to the airport in half.

Dulles Toll Road officially opened on October 1, 1984. The highway featured ten interchanges, plus a special ramp to the Wolf Trap performing arts venue. Putting the first quarters in the tollbooth during opening ceremonies was Governor Robb. Sitting in the passenger seat as Robb drove the car through a blue ribbon stretched across the road was Sid Dewberry. Sid's firm, Dewberry & Davis, had provided the highway's design and engineering services. Shortly thereafter, the firm hired transportation expert John Fowler, who made highway design and engineering a core competency of the company.

Sid had always been confident the toll road would be built. "Having right-of-way for any road is 75 percent of the battle," he explains. "Once you have it, you can figure out a way to build."[287]

By February 1985, more than forty thousand cars traversed Dulles Toll Road, testifying to its acute importance.[288] As hoped for, development along the Dulles Corridor—the strips of land along either side of the highway—began in earnest. Plans on the drawing board included ten business parks that would provide more than seven million square feet of office and industrial space. The corridor quickly exploded with a startling array of companies, most of them high technology and telecommunications, and a fair sprinkling of banks, corporate headquarters, trade associations, and research and development firms.

The efforts waged by the private sector on behalf of the area cannot be overstated. Bill Hazel's long service on the Metropolitan Washington Airports Authority is but one example of this leadership. In succeeding years, Dulles Corridor became what business leaders had always predicted: "an economic engine for surrounding communities." This statement was the consensus of a 2004 study of development and planning in Fairfax County, conducted by the Joint Center for Housing Studies at Harvard University. The study noted that the corridor had provided more than fifteen thousand direct jobs and billions of dollars in business revenue.[289]

Silicon Valley, long the premier technology center in the country, now had stiff competition for entrepreneurial startup businesses and technology know-how. The number of high technology businesses in the Santa Clara Valley had soared to more than 2,600 in 1985, up from just 905 high tech companies in 1977. By 1990, approximately 150,000 jobs would be provided by these enterprises.[290]

In succeeding years, Fairfax County would close in on these numbers—in part because of Washington Dulles International Airport. Dulles was "probably the single most phenomenal development in Northern Virginia [over] the course of a decade," said Hugh D. Keogh, director of the Virginia Department of Economic Development. "It made Virginia identifiable to business individuals all over the world."[291]

A High-Tech Haven

Although Dulles Corridor itself was just beginning to thrive, the two primary stops along it—Reston and Tysons Corner—had already become major centers of industry and commerce. By 1988, 463 companies occupying 16.6 million square feet of office space and more than five million square feet of retail, hotel, and other commercial space employed close to eighty thousand people in Tysons Corner.[292] And Reston was home to major divisions, business units, and headquarters of a broad spectrum of companies, including Tandem Computer, Sperry Systems, and GTE. Over the decade, these two corporate galaxies attracted tenants that occupied more than two million square feet of office space each year, the lion's share of them high technology firms.

Fairfax County was now a high tech mecca, thanks in large part to the efforts of the George Mason Institute and the pioneering example set by BDM, PRC, and other Beltway Bandits. Not only was America Online born in Northern Virginia, so was the Internet itself. The Internet had been conceived by two Arlington residents, computer scientists Vinton Cerf and Robert Kahn, in the 1970s. A decade later, marketing whiz kid Steve Case began building America Online into a leading provider of Internet services. Case had moved to Virginia in 1983 to work for Control Video Corporation (CVC), an online game company that changed its name to Quantum Computer Services in 1985. Quantum morphed into America Online in 1989. Two years later, Case became its CEO and subsequently ran herd on the firm's merger with Time Warner.

The Reagan administration lured its share of high tech firms to Fairfax County as well. In 1982, the Department of Defense provided $900 million of business to county firms alone.[293] Defense funding further rocketed when the president, in an arm's race with the Soviet Union, announced his Strategic Defense Initiative the following year. Dubbed "Star Wars" by the press, SDI called for building ground-based and space-based systems to protect the country from nuclear attack. "Washington was looking to spend the Soviet Union into oblivion with technology," says April Young, who became the director of the Economic Development Authority in 1982. "There was an explosion of telecom and information technology companies [here] around Star Wars."[294] *Regardie's* magazine concurred: "One would need the Hoover Dam to stop the flood of defense-related federal contracts that continue to flow into Fairfax County."

Altogether, the United States spent about $158 billion on private sector contracts in 1983.[295] In succeeding years, this figure would increase markedly, as would the percentage of money going to Fairfax-based companies.

In effect, government contractors were literally compelled to plant stakes in the county. "It was becoming increasingly clear to most major industries that they needed to have a seat . . . at the heart of government," says Chuck Robb. "Advertisements would show a picture of the Capitol and then the words 'Fairfax County.' That was our pitch."

Engineering a New Center of Growth

Of course, sometimes the pitch fell on deaf ears. One such case was Microelectronics and Computer Technology Corporation, a large technology firm the county had failed to lure. Determined not to let that happen again, Robb formed a task force on science and technology to study ways to attract more high technology firms to the region. One of the task force's forty-four recommendations was the establishment of the $30 million Center for Innovative Technology. An administrative and coordinating bureau, CIT would entice firms to Virginia and serve as a liaison between the research talent from the state's academic institutions and the area's private sector technology companies. Robb endorsed the idea, noting in a speech that Virginia had given the country its first industry, glassmaking. Now CIT would give it "a new business for the future."

The challenge then became where to locate the bureau. Til, Earle, and George Johnson lobbied hard to establish the center in Fairfax, on land adjacent to GMU. But while Main Street Richmond was not necessarily opposed to locating CIT in Fairfax, it did have stiff reservations about putting the bureau so close to GMU, since the university competed with downstate institutions like Virginia Tech and the University of Virginia.

"We had a terrible fight in the General Assembly," recalls Robb, "and [the CIT] had to be shepherded along." George Johnson also remembers the contentious period well. "It was a real 'hurly burly,'" he says. "I was a thorn in everyone's flesh."[296]

The wrangling marked a setback in the more cordial relations between downstate and upstate, and for a while it appeared CIT was headed for the dustbin, a "dead hen on the tiller," says Robb. Finally in 1983, the governor brokered a compromise, locating the center on a thirty-five-acre site overlooking Dulles Airport, on the boundary separating Fairfax and Loudoun counties. The site was within twenty miles of more than eight hundred technology companies, and 525 of those companies—employing more than forty-two thousand people—were located in Fairfax County.

Robb situated one of CIT's five on-campus research institutes at GMU, and earmarked $20 million in state funds toward creating a separate information technology program there. The funds only covered the salaries of twenty-five people, but Johnson and others were able to help augment the state's offerings. "We bolstered it through a state program for eminent scholars, whereby the state would match the salary [for hiring] an eminent scholar," George says. "It turned out there were a lot of restive and eminent information technology professors out there in the hinterlands." GMU recruited academicians whose qualifications were unquestioned, "and everyone we went after we got," he adds. "Practically overnight we had a PhD in information engineering—one of the first in the country—and we got a pretty substantial student base. Away we went."

Gilley, Johnson's right hand man at GMU, says the new School of Information Technology and Engineering "forever changed the character of GMU and Virginia higher education." He elaborates, "Not only did the university get a greatly-needed school, a new form of engineering education emerged [as traditional engineering and information technology were combined]."

The school was the first in the nation to offer a PhD in information technology. Following a $10 million donation by Dr. Ernst Volgenau—chairman of SRA International, Inc. and the current rector of GMU—and his wife, Sara, the school was renamed the Volgenau School of Information Technology and Engineering. That year, in 2007, ground was broken on a new 180,000-square-foot building to house the engineering school. The engineering school is, says Til, "a tremendous accomplishment for GMU and continues to change the entire landscape of academe in Northern Virginia."

CIT chalked up an impressive track record. By the end of 1994, it had co-funded more than 830 research and innovative technology projects—

involving approximately 785 companies—at Virginia's public universities. The bureau also helped raise Virginia's ranking in the number of patents issued to universities and non-profit institutions nationwide, from twenty-eighth to sixth in its first ten years. Finally, and perhaps most important, the center established thirteen technology institutes at the state's universities, increasing the research and development capabilities in leading-edge technologies like fiber optics, biotechnology, and wireless communications. Such industries would become fundamentally important to the county's continuing economic growth and outstanding high tech reputation.

The Best-Laid Plans: Fairfax Station and Fair Lakes

The growth in high technology and the resulting flood of new companies coming to Fairfax sent real estate developers in Northern Virginia into overdrive. Among the most active was Hazel/Peterson Companies.

After completing Burke Centre, the firm built the adjacent Fairfax Station in the late 1970s, named for the county's last operating railroad station, which had closed in 1973. The affluent planned community is nestled amid rolling hills and a dense forest, but is in close proximity to major shopping hubs, national monuments, museums, parks, fine dining, and popular cultural attractions. The community has the highest home

A sign at the Fairfax County Parkway marks the entrance to Fair Lakes, a large commercial and residential community near the intersection of I-66 and Route 50.

values in all of Fairfax, and the nineteen thousand residents of its zip code, 22039, earn the second-highest incomes in the nation. Completely residential, Fairfax Station is often recognized by the press in such categories as the "Best Places to Live" and the "Highest Quality of Living."

Meanwhile, Hazel/Peterson had other developments underway. In the 1970s, the firm had purchased several large parcels of remote forest land and stream beds in the western-central part of the county. It planned to develop 657 acres of the property into a large commercial-residential community called Fair Lakes. Situated near the intersection of I-66 and Route 50, the development would comprise a thirty-five-building office complex with more than five million square feet of commercial, office, hotel, and retail space, and over 1,300 houses, town homes, and condominiums—all intersected by parkland and ponds. The press took to calling it an "urban village" and the "next Tysons Corner."

William A. Hazel, Inc., which had grown to more than 1,200 employees by the 1980s, did much of the earth-moving work. Dewberry & Davis provided the design and engineering. "Sid's engineering company was just so reputable," says Milt Peterson, "it felt like an extension of our company." Now widely considered one of Hazel/Peterson's finest planned communities, Fair Lakes accommodates both residential and business needs in a leafy, park-like environment that boasts more than seven miles of nature trails; basketball, tennis, and volleyball courts; and several neighborhood programs. The community is near the Fair Oaks regional shopping mall at the intersection of I-66 and Route 50, the 120-acre campus of TRW, and a new county government complex.

A Wrench in Highway Development

At the same time that Fair Lakes was on the drawing board, so was a thirty-five-mile, $200 million cross-county highway that would intersect I-66. The road would relieve traffic on the beltway and the snarled Route 50, providing access to motorists driving through the county's outer suburbs and employment areas in Fair Lakes, Reston, and Herndon. Called the Springfield Bypass/Dranesville Connection, the thoroughfare combined remnants of the outer beltway and the

Northern Virginia Expressway that had been put on hold by the Board of Supervisors a decade before.

The name of the partially circumferential road had some history behind it. Fearful that citizens would object to another beltway, transportation-planning official Shiva Pant had masked the new highway with language, never calling it a "beltway" even though it would use vestiges of right-of-way that had been secured for the two outer beltways (minus the section crossing the Potomac River).

The transportation department thus avoided public furor—but the road nonetheless became enmeshed in controversy. In September 1981, Bill Wrench, Northern Virginia's representative on the state's highway commission, proposed that ten miles of the highway be diverted, based on advice he received from the state's transportation planners. As he stated, the original route approved by the Fairfax Board of Supervisors was circuitous and costly. It would put north and south traffic on an east and west road, causing gridlock, and would not properly serve residents of the Fair Lakes development.

The Virginia Highway and Transportation Commission understood the logic and voted 10 to 0 in favor of the rerouting.[297] But when the media learned that the new route was near two tracts of property Wrench owned and would potentially provide a valuable I-66 cloverleaf on land owned by Hazel/Peterson, reporters pounced. The media argued that the proposed cloverleaf could potentially triple the value of the Hazel/Peterson tract. What the stories buried, however, was that the new route made far more sense than the previous one.

Hazel/Peterson was gratified by the commission's vote, but it resented the media's implications of impropriety. The firm had in fact purchased the tract of land prior to any knowledge of a future highway. Til says, "While Fair Lakes and the Springfield Bypass coincided and complemented one another, we did not at the time of the acquisition recognize a clear connection." He adds that the firm had anticipated an I-66 interchange and had lobbied for it well before the original route was disclosed.

Wrench felt similarly maligned. His land holdings—two small warehouses and 3.8 acres of vacant, essentially unbuildable property—were

This map details a signalized ramp plan for the Fairfax County Parkway near Fair Lakes. The cross-county highway caused much controversy during its planning.

meager and would not benefit from the rerouting. Moreover, he had written a letter to the state's top highway official, Harold King, prior to voting, in which he disclosed that he owned parcels along the proposed new route. A man of unimpeachable character with a record of distinguished public service, Wrench had led the early Economic Development Authority and chaired the Fairfax School Board. As he informed *The Washington Post,* "If you think I'm going to let a road affect my reputation, you're talking to the wrong man."

Nevertheless, Wrench was dogged by conflict of interest allegations. The county's Board of Supervisors were split on the merits of the new route, with Chairman Herrity and Supervisor Marie Travesky strongly opposing it, and supervisors Martha Pennino and Joseph Alexander and former Supervisor Anne Wilkins in favor.

Wilkins, a lifelong Democrat, opined to *The Washington Post* that its report was misleading and inaccurate. Wrench, she wrote, had been treated unfairly. "To imply that Bill Wrench 'moved' the Springfield bypass to increase the value of his fully rented mini-warehouses and his 3.8 acres of undeveloped industrial land is ridiculous," she argued. "The 3.8 vacant acres are vacant because they are unbuildable in the present state, being almost entirely in the Field Lark Branch flood plain, not because of lack of good access. . . . Bill Wrench worked hard and successfully to get the Springfield bypass approved, but certainly not to benefit his holdings. They do not need the road, but Fairfax County does."

With respect to the Fair Lakes development, Wilkins added, "To say or imply that the state highway commission 'changed' the route in west ern Fairfax so as to put an interchange on Hazel's land to his benefit is just not true. There was nothing to 'change.' Several routes had been studied by consultants, [and] the state Department of Highways and Transportation, which is the agency responsible for construction, approved a route that its staff believes to be less costly and better from a traffic safety standpoint."[298]

Supervisor James Scott framed the issue differently. He blamed Wrench for unnecessarily creating the perception that his vote was made for private gain.[299] To clear the air, Herrity successfully urged Virginia governor John N. Dalton to force Wrench from the Highway Commission. Tossed to the political wolves despite having done nothing illegal, Wrench resigned "with deepest regret" on September 19, 1981.[300] One week later, the Highway Commission voted unanimously to uphold the route that it, and now-former Commissioner Wrench, had endorsed.

The issue did not end there. Eviscerated by the scandal and doubtful the Springfield bypass would ever be built, the state declined to participate. For a time the whole project was in jeopardy; even Herrity retracted his support. It was past history as prologue: county officials constraining much-needed transportation. And once again, the private sector tipped the scales. Til Hazel and Milt Peterson dipped into their own pockets to build a one-and-a-half-mile segment of the parkway from Route 50 to I-66, including half of the interchange at I-66 that had caused the ruckus.

Although this proffer was levied as a condition to rezoning the Fair Lakes development, it provided much-needed momentum to the stalled highway plans. After the firm had constructed a critical segment of the road, County Executive J Lambert was able to persuade the Board to finance another segment north of Route 50 and a second segment to the south, thereby creating the highway's arc through the county's suburbs. The additional segments of the parkway were constructed via the sale of county bonds.

By now the road had a new, shorter, and more graceful name: the Fairfax County Parkway. As Milt Peterson sees it, "Til and I forced the county to build the Fairfax Parkway."[301] Phil Yates, former Fairfax Zoning Administrator, agrees: "Hazel/Peterson essentially got that parkway built with their development of Fair Lakes. Had they not started it, it wouldn't have been built."[302]

Unfortunately, the rest of the parkway would stall. Another fourteen years would pass (from 1981 to 1995) before thirty-three of the parkway's thirty-five planned miles reached completion. The last two miles of the highway, ironically known as the John F. Herrity Parkway, have yet to be finished.

Hazel/Peterson: Fairfax's Headquarters for Growth

Several major developments by Hazel/Peterson followed on the heels of Fair Lakes. One such project was the Tysons McLean Business Park, where Milt Peterson and John Toups negotiated the development of PRC's new headquarters on a 3 x 5 index card and a handshake. Other developments included Virginia Center, on sixty acres north of the Vienna Metro station; Centre Ridge in Centreville; and Franklin Farm, also in Vienna. As the company grew, Jim Todd was recruited from Reston to be Hazel/Peterson's new CEO. His goal was to restructure the company into a more modern organization. "Jim pulled together a much larger, well-organized management group, which kicked off some significant growth for us," says Skip Coston, the firm's general manager.[303]

Franklin Farm was similar to Burke Centre in marketing single-family homes and townhouses to young families with children—people with "a station wagon and a dog," as Milt Peterson puts it.[304] The planned residential community was located on the perimeter of other neighborhoods in Vienna, close to Route 50 and I-66, and near the mushrooming employment centers at Dulles Airport and Fair Oaks Mall.

The property had previously been a dairy farm, the last one left in Fairfax. Spread across more than 850 acres, it had been called Oak Hill Farm since at least the 1800s and possibly earlier (a house on the property dates from the 1700s). The former owner, James Franklin, was in his seventies, weary of rising property taxes, and eager to retire. Hazel/Peterson bought the entire tract from Franklin for $5.5 million, prompting *The Washington Post* to announce, "Third 'New Town' Is Proposed for Fairfax County."[305]

The developers applied for the "new town" zoning that had been awarded to Reston and Burke Centre, but the Board of Supervisors rebuffed them. Not that the denial slowed their plans. In mid-1985, ground was broken on the initial phase of Franklin Farm Village Center, a $15 million, 165,000-square-foot retail, food, and office center near what would become the Fairfax County Parkway. As they had done in Fair Lakes, Til and Milt financed the construction of a segment of the parkway in 1988 running through the property. With additional bond funds approved by voters, motorists could now drive from West Ox Road near Herndon to I-66.

Today, Franklin Farms features twenty-seven distinct neighborhoods comprising 1,777 homes, a commercial shopping center, churches, schools, a community center, ball fields, trails, and other recreation spots spread over 850 acres. In homage to the past, the developers named many streets in the community after owners of the region's early dairy farms. They even retained the old house from the 1700s, as well as an adjacent barn and silo, incorporating them into the community.

By 1987, the volume of Hazel/Peterson projects represented more than fifteen thousand new residential dwellings and 9.5 million square feet of commercial property on 5,500 acres in Fairfax County.[306] No other developer in America had such a profound impact on a community. Even Houston's Gerald Hines and Kenneth Schnitzer, regaled during the oil boom years for painting the city's modern skyscape, could not match Til's and Milt's output. Schnitzer had been responsible for Houston's fifty-acre Greenway Plaza business corridor, as well as the seventy-one-story Wells Fargo Bank Plaza, the fifty-story Enron headquarters, and the Compaq Center sports arena, which opened in 1975. Hines had built the Galleria, a major regional shopping mall, as well as the headquarters of Shell Oil Company and more than four hundred other buildings.

In 1988, *The Washington Post* called Hazel/Peterson developments the "cornerstones of modern-day Northern Virginia."[307] By 1989, an estimated one out of every six Fairfax residents lived on land developed by the firm. Milt and Til were literally building the county from the ground up.

The Downside to Downzoning

Despite such progress, developers still faced a familiar roadblock in the 1980s: the Board of Supervisors. Though still emphatically pro-business, the Board began to employ various strategies to restrict growth in the county's undeveloped regions. The impetus came in large part from the continuing chorus of disapproval over dense traffic congestion. (The irony was that this problem had effectively been created when previous Boards had curtailed planned highways.)

Another factor influencing the Herrity Board to slow development was its purported impact on the environment. One instance occurred in 1982 when the Board downzoned land in the already sparsely residential Occoquan Basin, allegedly to preserve its water resources. Noman Cole, whose hard work on behalf of the county's water and sewerage systems had been heralded by the government and public alike, stated that the Board's action was unnecessary from a water quality standpoint. Nevertheless, in 1985 the Fairfax Circuit Court upheld these severe restrictions on development in the Occoquan Basin. The action baffled developers, who expected that the rights of property owners would win the day, as usual, in the state's courts. Cole later wrote that he believed the downzoning had been predicated on the Board's growth-control agenda.[308]

With this victory in their pockets, the supervisors turned their attention in November 1985 to ten thousand acres of property. The land had been zoned industrial, but preparations were underway to rezone it for residential and commercial development, thereby adding to the county's traffic woes. To discourage these plans, the Board reduced the land's allowable densities by 75 percent and voted to strike the "grandfathering" provisions that were protecting several real estate projects already underway.

These decisions put the development community in an uproar. As developers and other pro-business groups pointed out, the Fairfax County Economic Development Authority had recently released a "feasibility analysis" of corporate marketing targets that identified specific industries that were ripe for relocation, including telecommunications, security, aerospace, medical, and energy. The downzoning would discourage these types of companies from expanding in Fairfax.

"It's vital that all of the Supervisors understand that stopping business development in Fairfax County will not solve the county's transportation problems," the Fairfax County Chamber of Commerce stated.[309] In fact, the chamber blamed the county for creating the area's infuriating traffic problems. "Though growth patterns matched the estimates made by planners decades before, the transportation network, including critical roadways and bridges, never materialized," the chamber reported.

One particularly significant case was the Northern Virginia Major Thoroughfare Plan, a study initiated in 1969 by the Virginia Department of Highways and local governments to address traffic needs by the year 1985. The study called for constructing the Outer Beltway; another circumferential highway known as the Northern Virginia Expressway; and the Monticello Freeway.[310] None would see the light of day as originally conceived.

When the board held a public hearing on the downzoning decision, hundreds of business leaders packed the supervisor's meeting room. Their message was unmistakable: don't muffle the economic boom that is propelling Fairfax into one of the country's most prosperous regions.

They had a point. By the mid-1980s, half of the county's workforce held jobs in Fairfax, and more than seventy-six thousand jobs had been created—most of them white-collar. And additional jobs were on the way. In 1985, a record 242 firms had issued plans for new or expanded facilities in Fairfax.[311] "This is a very desirable place," County Executive J Hamilton Lambert told *The Washington Post*. "The atmosphere, life style, services, relative stability . . . When you stack it up against other places in the country, you see that people are happy here."[312]

The Post seemed to agree, stating that Fairfax offered the middle class "a life style that features a wide selection of traditionally styled houses, most with at least four bedrooms; one-hundred-store malls; public schools that stress scholastics and high college entrance scores; subdivisions complete with community swimming pools; and a growing number of high tech jobs."[313]

As Til told the *Richmond-Times Dispatch* in 1987, "If we can create good new communities in the urban village concept and create jobs and people opportunities in those areas, I don't understand why [one] would not look upon that as a good thing."[314] Milt Peterson shared this view: "We don't create demand by building a house; we satisfy demand by building a house." In short, why get in the way of progress?

The campaign waged by the chamber and the state's private sector ultimately won the day, prompting Supervisor T. Farrell Egge, who was previously undecided on the downzoning proposal, to vote against the restrictive zoning. After the measure's defeat, the chamber worked with six other business groups to create the Northern Virginia Transportation Alliance, which studies how to best reduce traffic congestion and otherwise improve transportation in the area. Together, they created a $1 million public awareness campaign demonstrating the business community's contribution to Fairfax's economy.

And so people continued their steady migration, with more than one thousand making their way to the county each month in 1986. That year, the number of residents in Fairfax not only dwarfed the population of Washington, D.C., it surpassed the population of five states: Alaska, Delaware, Wyoming, North Dakota, and Vermont. The county's annual budget even exceeded the state of Rhode Island's.[315] Economic growth and jobs were protected—at least for the time being.

Reaching New Heights of Influence

Although the Herrity Board's record with respect to zoning generally favored orderly development, the supervisors made some decisions that in retrospect rendered a disservice to the public. For example, as developers sought to erect taller buildings in the already-developed Tysons Corner, thereby preserving more open space at ground level, the Board acquiesced to NIMBY objectors.

Developer James T. Lewis had planned to build Tycon Towers in Tysons Corner, three twenty-to-twenty-four-story buildings designed by the famous Pritzker Architecture Award winner Philip Johnson. When

Lewis petitioned the Board for rezoning, he explained that the tall buildings would permit more green space at their bases. But the Board demurred, arguing that the structures had to conform to current zoning. Derailed in his plans, Lewis instead built one seventeen-story edifice with a barrel-vault skylight across the building's width. Although Johnson's curvilinear design was revered in architectural circles, the public derided the structure as the "Shopping Bag Building" because of its atypical shape. "We tried to add a touch of class to the area, not that it wasn't there before," Lewis says.[316]

The membership-only Tower Club opened on the top floor of Tycon Tower in 1988. Its founding board of governors included James Lewis, Til Hazel, Carrington Williams, Dwight Schar, Milt Peterson, George Johnson, John Toups, and Sid Dewberry. The social club affords extraordinary views of Fairfax from its stylish seventeenth-story perch. According to Leo Schefer, whenever he squired air carrier executives around Fairfax to entice them to move their operations to Dulles, he'd take them to the Tower Club "to explain the region's geography and demographics."

Like Houston's Petroleum Club and San Francisco's Pacific Union Club, the Tower Club filled a distinct void in Fairfax County, providing a place where business and society could come together for the betterment of business and the county itself. (The 123 Club, for instance, meets monthly there.) A few years after the Tower Club opened, *Virginia Business* magazine commented that the county's prosperity had produced a "powerful business elite" who found it more worthwhile to dine with each other than to "hobnob" with Washingtonians absorbed with the federal government. "The Tower Club is emblematic of Fairfax's fission from Washington," the publication stated.[317]

An Age of Industry

In spite of the Herrity Board's few and fleeting swipes at decelerating development, the supervisors provided zoning approval to a great number of projects. One such example was the board's consent in November 1985 to rezone the $2 billion Westfields Office Park. Located near Dulles Airport, Westfields Office Park is situated on more than one thousand acres of what had been cornfields and scrub forest.[318] The office park was completed in 1989, comprising twenty million square feet of space that would house thirty thousand workers by the year 2000.[319] The Westfields International Conference Center is located there. "Contrary to what is so often printed—that developers are adversary to the interests of the public—the development community here has made real, concentrated efforts to make this a better place and, by and large, to preserve and protect it," says Henry Long, chairman of the Long Companies, which developed Westfields.[320]

Til Hazel shares this view. "Everything we have in this county is because of developers," he stated unequivocally to a magazine reporter in 1986. "Industry and prosperity, homes and roads . . . the government has never created anything."[321] Borrowing loosely from the free-market theories of the late Nobel Prize winning economist Milton Friedman, he added, "When the government wants to regulate everything, it takes away the enthusiasm. And then nothing will happen."

Til later sharpened his point. "Nothing constructive happens without business leadership," he said. "[It's] the business leadership that got Northern Virginia together in the 1980s."[322]

The efforts the private and public sector put forth to increase commerce in the county paid off handsomely. Several organizations in particular deserve credit for the economic expansion, including the Economic Development Authority, the Virginia Initiative, the George Mason Institute, the 123 Club, and the Greater Washington Board of Trade. As a result of their efforts, more companies flocked to Fairfax—whipping up unprecedented national awareness for a county that had generated virtually no attention prior to the Second World War.

Changing the Face of Fairfax County

In 1984, Til Hazel was elected president of the Board of Trade, the first person from the Commonwealth of Virginia to hold the title. That year he gave up practicing law, although he retained his partnership interest in what became Hazel, Thomas, Fiske, Beckhorn & Hanes in 1987. With 118 attorneys and offices in Fairfax, Alexandria, Leesburg, Washington, D.C., and Richmond, the law firm was the third largest in Virginia.

Til was persuaded to take the post by L. B. "Bud" Doggett, the parking magnate who helped build the Greater Washington Board of Trade into a major institution, and John Tydings, the organization's CEO. The men wanted the organization to provide greater outreach to the Virginia and Maryland suburbs. As Doggett says, Til was "his own committee [at the Board of Trade]. He always impressed me as a guy who knew a helluva lot more than anybody else in the room, but never let them know. Politically his self-interest was beating the drum for his own county, and he was honest enough to say the potential was unbelievable."

Tall and aristocratic, the gravel-voiced Doggett earned a Silver Star while serving in General George Patton's Third Army during the Second World War. He doesn't mince words, gesturing freely with his hand, finger, or cigar. And though he concedes that he rarely ventures across the Potomac to visit Fairfax, Doggett says, "Til's as solid as a dollar, and is someone who truly cares about [Fairfax] county."[323]

That unstinting support for Fairfax County has made Til Hazel one of its most important figures. In addition to leading drives for education, health care, and other quality of life concerns, Til recognized that the county's suburbs could be transformed into something far greater than mere bedroom communities. In this quest, he rewrote its zoning case by case, hearing by hearing. "When he came before the Board he was never frivolous, and in most cases he was right," commented supervisor Martha Pennino. "It is impossible to overestimate Hazel's role in Fairfax County."[324]

Til had raised money for the American Cancer Society, the Northern Virginia Hospice, and the Second Genesis drug treatment program, and was a director of the Potomac Tuberculosis and Respiratory Disease Association and the Northern Virginia Mental Health Association. Small wonder then that in 1985, *Washingtonian* magazine cited him as one of "Twenty Who Made a Difference" in the Greater Washington area. The same magazine subsequently named Til one of seventeen "Washingtonians of the Year," stating, "That ability to see not what is but what can be has made Til Hazel the man who changed the face of Northern Virginia."

In 1986, Til received the Thomas Jefferson Award for Public Service for his "selfless and significant service to the Commonwealth." The following year he was honored with the first George Mason University Medal, which equates the work of the recipient with the public service record of George Mason himself. As Til said in his acceptance speech, "If people in the private sector don't come forward to serve the public good and propel society towards a better tomorrow, then government has no choice but to fill the void. Each of us must do what we can to lift the world one rung higher."

In 1987, Til and his late wife, Jinx, were presented with the Northern Virginia Community Foundation Founders Award at a black-tie dinner for six hundred people. Jinx in particular was extremely involved in fundraising for the Fairfax Symphony. The tribute recognized the Hazels' outstanding contributions to the community of Northern Virginia and their extensive involvement in charity work, and was just one of many honors Til would receive for his selfless contributions.

Unraveling the Red Tape

Sid Dewberry received the Northern Virginia Community Foundation Founders Award three years later. Like Til, Sid had worked tirelessly to harness the power of the business establishment for the social good. One of his most important efforts was in the creation of the Engineers and Surveyors Institute (ESI), a private sector solution to governmental bureaucracy. The institute was formed to accelerate the lengthy process of reviewing and approving development proposals— required paperwork that would ensure compliance with applicable planning and zoning ordinances. "After zoning was approved, the developer submitted the engineering plans, and it would take at least a year and a half before they were approved," says Hank Hulme, former director of the ESI. "Meanwhile, the demand for housing and office buildings in the county was blistering."[325]

J Hamilton Lambert, then Acting County Executive, presents the Fairfax County budget proposal, 1981.

Such excessive delays had been cited a decade before by the Blue Ribbon Committee, but now the addition of environmental impact assessments and other regulatory requirements had exacerbated the situation. Not only were the myriad rules and regulations mind-numbing for engineers, they also baffled the county government staff. As Sid wryly recalls, "The Public Facilities manual got so thick with so many different regulations you'd have to be a Philadelphia lawyer to understand it."[326]

The approval system prevented the building community from accommodating the intense demand for office space and housing in a timely manner. "One of the builders called me up and said, 'You have the largest and most prestigious firm doing this work in the county. You have to do something,'" says Dewberry.

Sid phoned County Executive J Lambert, who called a press conference. "In front of J on a table were the plans submitted from virtually every engineering and architectural firm practicing in Fairfax," says Sid. "J commented that every one of the firms, including ours, had submitted engineering plans that had been rejected because we failed to understand the complex regulations."

Several firms subsequently joined Lambert and other government officials at a weekend retreat in Williamsburg to determine a solution. ESI was the result. To fund the non-profit organization's startup and ongoing budget, real estate developers agreed to pay higher fees for site and plan reviews. One of its first tactics was to offer an educational program that would help private sector engineers and county staff better understand the county's Byzantine regulatory regime—in effect, teach the content of the brick-sized Public Facilities manual. These courses assisted the county staff in expediting the approval of engineering plans, and the engineers in improving the overall quality of those plans.

Engineers who completed the courses were certified as Design Plans Examiners, which provided a fast-track approval process. "If the engineer certified on the plan that it met the requirements of Fairfax County, he or she would go to the head of the line," Hulme explains. "We needed legislation to do this, and got it." Sid was the first engineer to receive a Design Plans Examiner license (it reads DPE#1). To maintain the license, he and other examiners must take sixteen hours of continuing education courses a year.

Sid's work in founding ESI is just one example of his deep sense of civic duty. In 1991, for instance, he was appointed co-chair of a statewide bond issue on education. He also has been highly instrumental in guiding the development of a civil engineering department at GMU, which currently graduates thirty to forty students each year.

A School of Equal-Opportunity Excellence

ESI ultimately removed the logjam impeding the building process, shortening it from several years to several months. Yet it was not the only organization in which the private sector played a vital role. Many of the area's business leaders also helped develop the Thomas Jefferson High School for Science and Technology.

The background was painted in 1985 when Jack Burkholder, the pragmatic and committed superintendent of the Fairfax County schools, asked Til, Earle, George Johnson, Coleman Raphael (then-dean of GMU's business school), and other academicians and business leaders to discuss with him the business community's involvement in the county's school system. At the meeting, Earle and Til proposed creating a foundation where private sector dollars would be directed toward public schools. Burkholder approved the concept. At a subsequent meeting at BDM headquarters, Burkholder offered a plan to establish a two-year advanced learning program for both college-bound and vocational students.

Intrigued by the idea, Til instead proposed a four-year secondary school for gifted students on their way to higher education. Such a school would be selective and predicated on a highly competitive admissions process. Students smart enough to pass muster would receive an advanced academic and research curriculum emphasizing science, mathematics, and technology. "At Harvard in 1947, I was awed by the fifteen or twenty students in my class who I learned were products of the Brooklyn School of Science and Technology in New York," says Til. "It took me a couple years to realize that their intense preparation was the reason for their excellence."

Burkholder gave his full support to the proposal. The next month, he advocated the creation of the Thomas Jefferson School of Science and Technology. From the get-go, the school was an astounding success, becoming one of the leading secondary schools in the country. In 2005 and 2006, the school produced 153 and 167 National Merit Semifinalists, respectively—more than any other high school in the U.S. And in 2007, it was ranked the number-one high school in the country by *U.S. News and World Report*, ahead of Pacific Collegiate Charter in Santa Cruz, California, at number two, and Seattle's International School at number four. Its students also rank first in the world for Advanced Placement credits. Needless to say, Jefferson graduates are actively recruited by America's top universities; in fact, more Jefferson alumni attend the Massachusetts Institute of Technology than alumni from any other high school. Til takes great pride in Jefferson's success. "The dean of admissions at Harvard," he notes, "has suggested to me on numerous occasions that he views Jefferson as a role model for the country."

As for the foundation itself, it contributed more than $7 million toward county school projects from 1985 to 1994. And the foundation's

"Second Chance PC" program successfully urged numerous Fairfax companies to donate their used computers to Fairfax's public schools.

An Economic Boom Town

By the end of the 1980s, Fairfax County had firmly established itself as a thriving center of commerce, much of it driven by the high technology and telecommunications industries. Of the new commercial construction that had begun in the Greater Metropolitan Washington Region in early 1987, half was claimed by Fairfax—further justifying the widespread view that the county was the economic engine of Northern Virginia. New mixed-use residential and commercial projects included Kingstowne, which sprung up on 1,170 acres southeast of Springfield. Today, the planned community comprises 5,200 residences, which house almost fifteen thousand people.

Between 1980 and 1990, the county generated 28 percent of the state's total job growth, making Fairfax, as one magazine stated, "far and away the most robust locality" in the Commonwealth.[327] With 747,000 residents in 1990, the county would have ranked as the nation's thirteenth largest city—if only it had been an actual city.

As the new decade beckoned, Fairfax had the fastest growing white collar job market in North America, and was a virtual "factory of the Information Age," reported *The Washington Post*.[328] The county's inventory of commercial and industrial space was the fourth largest in America, exceeded only by that of New York, Los Angeles, and Chicago. Even the stock market crash of October 19, 1987, did little to slow its momentum.

Other than the county's irksome highway bottlenecks, quality of life had improved markedly in the past ten years. George Mason University had grown into a major institution of higher learning; Northern Virginia Community College was sprouting new campuses and programs; and Inova Health Systems (formerly the Fairfax Hospital Association) had burgeoned into a world-class provider of medical care. Jobs were plentiful, thanks to the booming Dulles Technology Corridor, which was being touted as the next Silicon Valley. And average income was high: $25,000 per capita, more than $8,000 above the state average. The salaries provided a taxable aggregate income of more than $10 billion, more money by far than any other jurisdiction in the Commonwealth. "Once the bedrock of Virginia's dairy industry, Fairfax has become the cash cow for the entire state," *Virginia Business* magazine stated.[329]

The county had what other regions lacked: "brainpower," declared *Virginia Business*. It cited Fairfax's "rich stew of PhDs, engineers, startup veterans and high tech wizards." *The Washington Post Magazine* echoed these comments, noting that Fairfax's "increasingly private enterprise, high information, high education, post industrial economy [made] it a model of the 21st century."[330]

Employment got another boost following the opening of Tysons II Galleria in 1988, Ted Lerner's long-awaited $1 billion office, retail, and hotel project. Thanks to Til Hazel's legal resourcefulness, Lerner had finally navigated the shoals of the county's rezoning approval process. Lerner's glittering shopping mall, part of the 117-acre complex, was expected to yield more than $150 million in tax revenue for Fairfax over the next ten years. As it did for so many county developments, Dewberry & Davis provided design and engineering services. (Other projects for the firm included the Metro subway system, surveying work for the White House, and the rebuilding of the Filene Center at Wolf Trap.)

In 1987, a new Board of Supervisors was elected when pro-business chairman Jack Herrity was defeated by growth control advocate Audrey Moore. But even Moore's Board could not put the brakes on the county's continuing growth and prosperity—though it certainly tried. In just a few short years, the Board downzoned development densities in the Route 28 corridor, enacted the highly restrictive Chesapeake Bay Protection Ordinance, and curtailed spending on economic development.[331] Fortunately, as Bill Hazel says, "Audrey [Moore] didn't stop growth as much as everyone else helped it."[332]

The county's prosperity soon caught the attention of national magazines like *Time*, which identified Fairfax in 1987 as a "boom town." Just four months earlier, *The Wall Street Journal* had described it as a "mini-city." *Inc.* magazine also cited the Washington area as having the strongest economy and best-educated population in the country.[333] The county's workforce blossomed further in 1989 when the Berlin Wall came down, marking the end of Soviet-dominated communism and bringing a consequent contraction in the U.S. government. Many technologists on the government's payroll were let go, creating an even wider talent pool for companies eyeing Fairfax as a place to do business.

Among them was Mobil Corporation. With operations in one hundred countries at the time, Mobil was the fifth largest industrial company in America. In 1989, the oil giant moved its headquarters from New York City to the Merrifield section of Fairfax, making it the biggest business in the Metropolitan Washington region by far, with greater profits and sales than the other one hundred largest stockholder-owned companies in the region combined.[334] The move was a good fit for both Mobil and Fairfax. The company saved $40 million a year by exiting the Big Apple, and its $125 million annual payroll was a tax boon for Fairfax. But as *Inc.* magazine reported, in relocating to Fairfax, Mobil had also been seeking something "less tangible than a good balance sheet." The county provided the oil giant with "high quality of life in a cosmopolitan setting, a place where educated, sophisticated people wanted to live and where a multinational corporation could easily carry on international business."[335]

Once Mobil moved to Fairfax, a parade of other major corporations marched behind it, relocating major divisions and business units. Fortune 500 companies General Dynamics and LaFarge also moved their corporate headquarters to the county. "After the Mobil announcement, real estate professionals poured out of the woodwork," says Dave Edwards, a former director of the Fairfax Economic Development Authority. "Coldwell Banker took Fairfax seriously, hiring a cadre of young, hotshot former Xerox Corporation sales representatives to do an exhaustive inventory of all Northern Virginia real estate . . . Armed with a detailed and systematic knowledge of the market, including when all significant tenant leases would be expiring, they began to convince investors and out-of-town business executives that they ought to take a serious look at Fairfax County."[336]

Black Clouds on the Horizon

As the year 1990 debuted, optimism about the future of Fairfax County was at an all-time high. Income earned by its residents was the highest in the nation, and few doubted the good times wouldn't last forever.[337] But in reality, a major real estate recession was brewing. The failure of dozens of savings and loan institutions in the mid-to-late 1980s had set the stage for impending catastrophe. Nationally, fifty-four thrifts had failed in 1985, sixty-five in 1986, and fifty-nine in 1987. By the end of 1988, the S&L crisis had reached its climax when a staggering 190 thrifts failed across the country.

The Bush administration responded by changing federal banking regulations, impelling banks to foreclose properties at a time when real estate values were already plummeting. Altogether, the value of commercial real estate across the nation fell an estimated 30 percent from 1989 to 1992. It was not uncommon for the government's Resolution Trust Corporation, formed to liquidate the assets of failed thrifts, to dump its commercial properties at prices well below 50 percent of their original stated value.[338]

The situation in Northern Virginia was particularly bleak. Many of the region's builders and developers were hit hard, some forced into corporate insolvency and even personal bankruptcy. Others hung on by the barest of threads, hopeful the market would revive. Countless office buildings and residential units on the drawing board were put on hold, some never to materialize. The market for new and existing residential and commercial structures dried up. "The repercussions are brutal for anyone who feels compelled to sell property in today's market," *Fortune* reporter Carol J. Loomis lamented.[339]

For Fairfax, the economic engine that had thrust the county forward in the 1980s had slipped a gear. Yet as time would prove, it was still humming.

CHAPTER 7

From Recession to
Renaissance

When the real estate recession struck, few in Virginia were hit harder than Dwight Schar. Dwight had grown Northern Virginia Homes (NVR) into one of Greater Washington's largest home building organizations—one with nearly one hundred subsidiaries that provided services for construction, land acquisition, home finance, investments, and other real estate development activities. Through this extensive network, NVR generated profits from virtually every aspect of the homebuilding and financing process. By 1990, the company had amassed a homebuilding and land development inventory of more than $600 million and had entered markets in Florida, California, Indiana, Kentucky, North Carolina, Ohio, Pennsylvania, and Virginia.

This skyrocketing growth underwent a dramatic reversal when the real estate recession took hold. From 1988 to 1991, NVR's revenues plummeted from $1.15 to $0.6 billion. The company's assets also lost much of their market value. These reductions in revenues and asset values caused a net income loss of more than $260 million, and NVR's stock fell to a paltry 25 cents a share. The reverberations were unsettling, to say the least. "I went to bed with a net worth of a little more than

$200 million, and when I woke up it had gone to minus $54 million," Dwight says.[340]

In retrospect, the real estate crash was a perfect storm. Convinced that property values couldn't decline, many area homebuilders and developers had gone into debt to purchase land. But then interest rates unexpectedly soured, building slowed and land values plunged. To compound the problem, the confidence of the region's financial institutions plummeted along with property values. "Rather than ride through the recession with the local builders, the banks pulled the plug on everybody," says Skip Coston.[341] "We lost a huge number of local builders."

The banks had their reasons. First American Bank, which had bankrolled so much of Northern Virginia's development, had more than $400 million locked up in bad real estate loans. "Everyone thought that land in the county would run short and they wouldn't have any place left to build, so they started buying up land [on debt] and bought too much," says Milt Drewer, the bank's longtime president. Drewer was fortunate to have retired before the storm clouds gathered. "They were building houses on spec before they had a sale," he remembers. "Suddenly, there were an awful lot of houses on the market, and before long they got to half-price. Still, no one was buying . . . It was unbelievable."[342]

Many builders couldn't meet their loan obligations. Drowning in red ink, NVR was forced to declare Chapter 11 bankruptcy in 1992. "It was horrible," says Dwight. "There were people committing suicide . . . I lost everything; so did everyone else."

Longtime Virginia builder Ed Carr and developer James Lewis were among those battered. "I had to file personal bankruptcy," says Carr. "I lost a lot of money."[343] Lewis did, too. A kindhearted man who ironi-

Dwight Schar, president and CEO of Northern Virginia Homes (NVR), one of the Washington, D.C. metro area's largest home building organizations, 2006.

cally shares a grandchild with growth-control advocate Audrey Moore, Lewis was riding high. He had recently christened Tycon Tower and was in the midst of developing the mixed-use National Harbor project (then known as PortAmerica). Located on the banks of the Potomac River in Prince George's County, National Harbor would claim the tallest structure between New York City and Atlanta.

Lewis had just invested a significant portion of his wealth into an award-winning, architecturally distinctive home on the Potomac Palisades. Then came the crash. "Before the recession I had a net worth of $50 million. During it I was negative more than that," he says.[344] "I had to sell [the house] to meet a payroll or two." National Harbor ended up in the hands of Resolution Trust Corporation, the government agency cleaning up the savings and loan mess.

The big developers and builders weren't the only ones damaged. The Milton Company, a midsize residential builder that constructed about seven hundred units a year, went under and never resurfaced. "We had a fairly large land inventory, so we were affected like other companies,"[345] says former Milton employee Russell Rosenberger, now president of Madison Homes. Firms serving builders and developers also suffered. Billings at Dewberry & Davis fell by almost 20 percent between 1990 and 1992, and Sid Dewberry was compelled to pare the staff from 1,218 employees to 818. "We had clients who went bankrupt and couldn't pay their bills," he remembers. "We had to write off about $5 million in bad debt in 1991. For the first time in our history we were forced to borrow money to ease the pain."[346]

After years of rising employment, jobs were suddenly scarce. "A lot of people who came here had lost their jobs, particularly younger people," says John Ulfelder, senior vice president of West*Group. "They went home to Indiana and North Carolina."[347] The combination of fewer companies moving to Fairfax and fewer available jobs had one unexpected bright spot. As Ulfelder recalls, "You could actually feel the traffic get better."

The bleak period cast a shadow on the county, but the real estate recession was only partly to blame: Board of Supervisors Chairwoman Audrey Moore had also gutted county spending on economic development.[348] With growth seemingly at a standstill, it would be several years before things began to look up for Fairfax County again.

A Modern Day Battleground

West*Group survived the storm better than most, a consequence of the company's "conservatism," says Jerry Halpin. It had little debt and, unlike other developers, it retained ownership of the structures it built. When real estate values fell, West*Group was largely unaffected since it had no intention of selling the buildings anyway.[349]

Hazel/Peterson was another matter. Although it too was direly affected by the recession, the developer had benefited financially from a fortuitous happenstance. In the 1980s, the firm had purchased Williams Center, a 542-acre tract in Prince William County, for $11 million. It planned to develop the property into a mixed-use complex of office buildings and residential houses, many constructed by NVR. Later, the firm negotiated a deal with the Edward J. DeBartolo Corporation to develop a portion of the land into a shopping mall.

Hazel/Peterson applied for and received zoning approval from the Prince William Board of County Supervisors, which was seeking to catalyze employment in the area. There was just one hitch. The property was adjacent to a historic Civil War site: the first and second battles of Manassas in 1861 and 1862, respectively. In the North, these skirmishes—both won by the South—are known as the battles of Bull Run, the name drawn from a nearby creek. While the initial battle is considered the first major engagement of the war, the second inflicted some of its heaviest casualties. More than fourteen thousand Union Army soldiers and 8,500 Confederate Army soldiers perished.

Williams Center was situated on Stuart's Hill, which overlooked the scene of the second confrontation. Confederate General Robert E. Lee had established his headquarters there—and people were not happy about seeing developers set up their own camp next to such sacred ground.

When news about the shopping mall leaked, area preservationists and civic activists joined with members of Congress to condemn the proposed development. On one side were the developers, a few stalwart county officials, and a handful of residents looking forward to rising land values. On the other were the United Daughters of the Confederacy, the National Parks and Conservation Association, the National Trust for Historic Preservation, and the Civil War Roundtable.

These well-funded organizations joined with likeminded groups to create the "Save the Battlefield Coalition." In a paid advertisement, they warned: "If developer John T. Hazel has his way, the tranquil 542 acre tract at Manassas Battlefield will be transformed overnight into a snarling traffic jam adjacent to a huge office park and shopping mall." The top of the ad pleaded, "Without Your Support, the Soldiers Who Died at Manassas Will Be Turning Over in Their Graves." To buttress the point, the ad depicted a bulldozer literally turning the earth.

Til and Milt didn't have a chance. In 1988, the United States Senate voted fifty to twenty-five to condemn the property. Hazel/Peterson subsequently filed a claim against the federal government for remuneration covering the present value of the land, a case won by attorney Grayson Hanes. The property was preserved as an addition to the Manassas National Battlefield Park.

There was a silver lining for Hazel/Peterson, though it did not become clear until the real estate recession hit. "We sold [the property] at peak value," says Til. "We got about $120 million, of which Dwight [Schar] got about $30 million. That money was very comforting to me and Milt once the bad times surfaced. Had it not happened we might have been broke."[350]

What did break, however, was Milt and Til's partnership. In 1991, the firm dissolved, though it had nothing to do with the real estate crash. Both men's families had become increasingly engaged in real estate enterprises, a second generation that would strike out on separate paths. Til had also been invited by his law firm to return to practicing law. The firm was in merger negotiations at the time with Reed Smith, one of the largest international law firms in the world.

Meanwhile, Milt had taken over Jim Lewis's stalled National Harbor project. His efforts would finally pay off when ground was broken on the first phase of construction in 2006. After more than a decade of intensive planning and untold meetings with government officials and financial institutions, four million square feet of hotels, restaurants, retail stores, and condominiums were now in the works. *The Washington Post* called the massive mixed-use project Milt's "biggest and perhaps most indelible mark on the suburban Washington landscape."[351] The Peterson Companies is now one of the largest real estate development firms in the Greater Washington area.

During their nearly twenty years as Hazel/Peterson, Milt and Til changed the landscape of Fairfax County, developing an astonishing twenty-five thousand lots together. Today, ten percent of county residents live in places built by Hazel/Peterson.[352]

The two men remained friends after their parting, and as members of the 123 Club, they still socialize together frequently. Their respective firms also continue to conduct a fair amount of business. In 2007, both companies were engaged in building a new 350,000-square-foot-building in Tysons Corner for the U.S. government. "We have the highest respect for each other," says Milt. "And always will."[353]

Fairfax County: Under New Management

The real estate crash undid more than just various county firms; it also dismantled Audrey Moore's anti-growth agenda. During her term as chairwoman, Moore had challenged the county's spending on economic development, a position that quickly lost favor with much of the public. In 1991, Moore was defeated at the polls by Thomas M. "Tom" Davis III, a Republican who was swept into office on a pro-business platform.

One of Davis's first actions was to evaluate the deepening crisis. For this he turned to a familiar, trusted face: Noman Cole. Davis appointed Cole to chair his own commission and charged it with studying the economic fallout of the crash. The results were heartening. As Til recalls, "The commission reviewed the numbers and the atmosphere and assured the Board of Supervisors and the citizens that no precipitous decline was anticipated [in Fairfax's fortunes] since county revenues were stable and the employment base healthy—there was little to fear."

Buoyed by the report, Davis restored the county's economic spending to levels not seen since the Herrity era. He earmarked $100,000 for the Fairfax Economic Development Authority's advertising budget, overturned several of his predecessor's downzoning measures, and eased the overly burdensome environmental regulations. He also revamped stringent tax rules that had put the county at a competitive disadvantage with other high technology corridors.[354] To corporate onlookers, Davis's moves were a clear indication that Fairfax County was back in business. Davis became so popular, in fact, that three years after becoming chairman of the Board of Supervisors, he was elected to the U.S. House of Representatives.

By late 1992, the real estate recession had whimpered its last. Among the developers and builders who had held tough was Dwight Schar. Dwight had kept NVR alive through innovation and tenacity. After filing for bankruptcy protection, he had personally called all of NVR's major shareholders to solicit their forbearance. "Dwight told me he had a plan to turn around the company, and he asked me and everyone else to stick with him," Sid Dewberry recalls. "We did, and we reaped the rewards for doing so."[355]

In the wake of the crash, Schar reorganized NVR to minimize its exposure to risk. For example, the company no longer speculated on home building; now it would only build a house after the customer had ordered it. This novel approach called for erecting a variety of model homes in each of NVR's planned communities. If prospective homebuyers liked a particular model, they could order a version built to their tastes. NVR also stopped speculating on land values, which had been the cause of its near demise. Rather than use debt to buy a property, it optioned the land: If a customer chose to build a house on the tract, the firm exercised the option. If the property remained idle at the end of the option period, NVR had the first right of refusal to re-option the land. Consequently, the company was on the hook for only the cost of the option.

The 12.5-mile Dulles Greenway Toll Road, designed and engineered by Dewberry & Davis, connected Dulles Airport to Leesburg, Virginia, 2006.

This strategy proved a winner, especially for those shareholders who had held onto their NVR shares. The stock rose like a phoenix, from a trifling $.25 per share to $500 per share in 2006. "We made out like bandits," says Sid. Dwight did, too. His negative $54 million net worth at the height of the recession turned positive, and he became one of the country's wealthiest citizens. The former Ohio schoolteacher is now part owner of the Washington Redskins football team, and in 2004, he bought the Palm Beach, Florida, mansion of billionaire Ron Perelman for a reported $92 million. Dwight is a major donor to the Republican Party and retired in 2007 as finance chairman of the Republican National Committee. He also remains chairman of Reston-based NVR, the largest residential homebuilder in the Greater Washington area. "We've had a nice long run," Dwight acknowledges.

Other builders and developers that weathered the storm included Russ Rosenberger. He survived the dissolution of the Milton Company to found the McLean-based Madison Homes, Inc., a midsize builder of mostly townhouses and condominiums. Ed Carr also made it through intact, although his firm was broken into several segments, each boasting a core competency. "I kept the home building part and survived by the skin of my teeth," Carr comments. "I lost a lot of money, but frankly, we were lucky. We came back reasonably well."

So did Dewberry & Davis. It had been cushioned from the crash by its other enterprises, including its disaster-response work for the Federal Emergency Management Agency and its growing transportation business. During the recession, the firm provided design and engineering services for the Dulles Greenway, a 12.5-mile toll road connecting Dulles Airport to Leesburg, Virginia. The highway was financed by Maggie Bryant, a private citizen who lived in rural Loudoun County and detested the traffic situation. The Greenway nearly cost Bryant her fortune and her health, but she was eventually able to garner a return on her investment through the toll proceeds. (She later sold the road to an Australian company.)

The Greenway had far-reaching benefits. One year after its completion in 1996, 6.3 million cars were counted on the thoroughfare; in 2006, the number soared to twenty-one million cars. Thanks in part to one woman's greenbacks and resolve, Loudoun is the fastest growing county in America today—and Sid Dewberry's engineering and design firm remains the largest of its kind in Greater Washington.

"We got through [the recession]," Sid says, "counting our blessings."[356]

Real Estate Renaissance

Although area builders and developers had been weakened by the real estate slump, many projects were nonetheless under way. One such case was the first twenty-acre phase of the Reston Town Center, which opened to the public in 1990. This remarkable mixed-use project had been on the drawing board since Bob Simon imagined it three decades earlier. When the first phase finally came to fruition, it was comprised of sixteen restaurants, more than thirty specialty retailers, two eleven-story office buildings, a multiplex cinema, a luxury 514-room hotel, and a central plaza with a burbling fountain dominated by a twenty-six-foot-high statue of Mercury.

In succeeding years, the Town Center became what its name intended: the area's focal point. In 1993, a glass-roofed pavilion was erected to accommodate ice-skating in the winter and special events throughout the year—from open-air concerts to the Northern Virginia Fine Arts Festival. Chic high-rise condominiums and townhouses also sprouted in and around the center, luring younger generations and their families. The decade ended with the completion of Phase II: the opening of One

Freedom Square, a mixed-use development of sixteen- and eighteen-story office towers.

Once derided as a "hippie haven," Reston had matured into a residential hotspot and a magnet for visitors. The Town Center was such a stunning success that many companies were compelled to plant roots there, including Sallie Mae, Nextel, Novadyne, Titan Systems, and Unisys. By the time the last lot for a single-family house was purchased in Reston in 1999, the former Sunset Hills Farm claimed forty-five thousand workers and sixty thousand residents. The only evidence of the old bourbon distillery was the bottles of *Virginia Gentleman* ornamenting the bars of posh restaurants.

One mile away, the community of Herndon was enjoying a renaissance of its own. A blue-collar town of scattered dairy farms throughout much of its history, Herndon had burgeoned into a smaller version of Reston. Ironically, the residents of both communities had a history of deriding one another, with Herndon residents calling Reston "Kooksville," and Reston residents calling Herndon "Hicksville."[357] Nevertheless, the former Hicksville's twenty-eight-acre central business district had been revitalized, and a corridor for high-tech companies along the Herndon Parkway was being developed.

These projects helped spur an incredible 500 percent increase in available office and commercial space in Herndon from 1984 to 1989, "transforming country fields into high-technology office parks," *The Washington Post* reported.[358] New developments included the 2.9 million-square-foot Worldgate office complex, located south of Reston Town Center, and the headquarters of PSINet Inc. Herndon had become a veritable high-tech haven, and one nearly equal to Reston. More than twenty-two thousand people live within its 4.3-square-mile radius today.

Meanwhile, Tysons Corner remained Fairfax County's top employer throughout the early 1990s, with massive media conglomerate Gannett Company Inc. moving its corporate headquarters there in 1994. Two years later, Tysons Corner became the fifteenth largest central business district in the United States.[359] Not surprisingly, the area's primary builder was already thinking about the next phase of development. "I wanted Metrorail to extend a link to Tysons," says Jerry Halpin, "and could envisage the area becoming a high-density residential center, a mini-Manhattan, in the next fifteen years."[360] In succeeding years, Jerry would prove himself a visionary once again.

A Place to Live, Grow, and Thrive

By the early 1990s, the county had become what the Blue Ribbon Committee had hoped for two decades earlier: a thriving center of corporate activity. Jack Herrity, who had appointed the commission, recalls, "The vision was to have our own tax base and our own job opportunities. We created an atmosphere and environment that people wanted, so they could establish businesses here, live here, and grow here."[361]

The growth that the committee envisioned was explosive indeed. The county boasted 365,000 jobs in 1993, a figure that had practically doubled since 1980. More than twenty thousand companies and 250 trade associations were in residence—with new ones on the way. And the county's sole employment no longer came from Washington, D.C. Now only 15 percent of county workers commuted to work in the District of Columbia, while 57 percent drove to jobs within the county.[362]

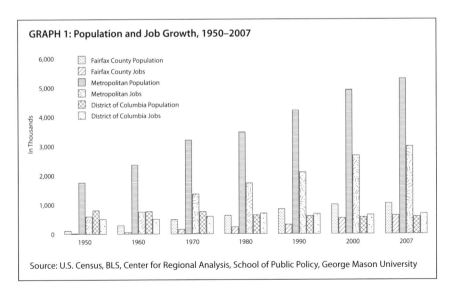

GRAPH 1: Population and Job Growth, 1950–2007

Fairfax County Population
Fairfax County Jobs
Metropolitan Population
Metropolitan Jobs
District of Columbia Population
District of Columbia Jobs

In Thousands

Source: U.S. Census, BLS, Center for Regional Analysis, School of Public Policy, George Mason University

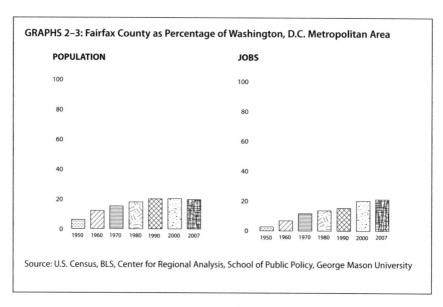

GRAPHS 2–3: Fairfax County as Percentage of Washington, D.C. Metropolitan Area

POPULATION

JOBS

Source: U.S. Census, BLS, Center for Regional Analysis, School of Public Policy, George Mason University

Meanwhile, many of the same people who had sat on the commission continued to suggest and implement various initiatives to keep the county's motor humming. One such effort was the Herndon-based Northern Virginia Technology Council. The group was comprised of technology companies that had split off from the Fairfax County Chamber of Commerce in the early 1990s to focus on high-tech firms

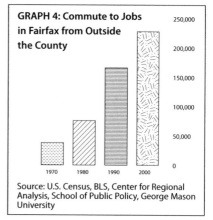

GRAPH 4: Commute to Jobs in Fairfax from Outside the County

Source: U.S. Census, BLS, Center for Regional Analysis, School of Public Policy, George Mason University

and the service companies (such as law and accounting firms) that supported them.

The debut of the Internet also inspired the council to strike out on its own. In 1993, the Pentagon made the historic decision to commercialize the ARPANET (Advanced Research Projects Agency Network), which had been created by the U.S. Department of Defense to allow communication between computers. Suddenly, the people who produced the Internet were transplanting the network to the commercial sector. "Companies wanted to be near the experts who developed the Internet, which made Northern Virginia the on-ramp of the 'Information Superhighway,'" explains Bobbie Kilberg, president and CEO of the Northern Virginia Technology Council. "In the early to mid-1990s, 65 percent of all Internet traffic came through Fairfax."[363]

The Internet wasn't the only technological advance sweeping the region. Other government agencies had developed communications technologies like satellites, cultivating a large contractor base to support these activities. Much of it was oriented toward defense and espionage. "Those early developments put Virginia in a position to capitalize on a profound shift now taking place in the computer industry—networking," the *Los Angeles Times* commented.[364]

The region benefited from a retrenchment in federal spending as well. As federal agencies downsized during the Reagan and Clinton administrations, the government outsourced technology projects worth hundreds of millions of dollars to technology and telecommunications firms located in Northern Virginia. Suddenly, countless people who had been working for Uncle Sam were available for private sector jobs. "Lots of inside-the-Beltway engineers and researchers took their expertise as sophisticated communications specialists, computer innovators and soft-

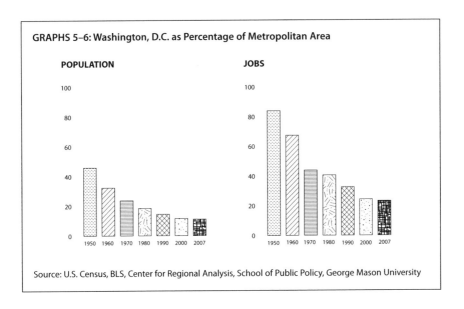

GRAPHS 5–6: Washington, D.C. as Percentage of Metropolitan Area

POPULATION

JOBS

Source: U.S. Census, BLS, Center for Regional Analysis, School of Public Policy, George Mason University

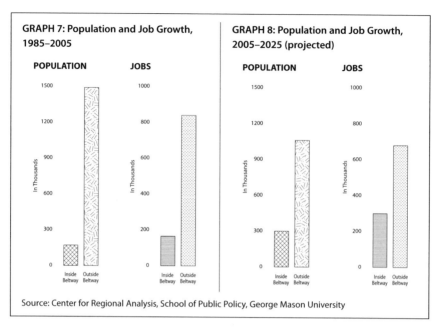

GRAPH 7: Population and Job Growth, 1985–2005

GRAPH 8: Population and Job Growth, 2005–2025 (projected)

Source: Center for Regional Analysis, School of Public Policy, George Mason University

ware designers out on the street," noted *Time* magazine. "Many [people] stayed put where the big cold war consulting firms [like BDM and PRC] had been located, in the low-rent Northern Virginia suburbs."[365]

Today, the Northern Virginia Technology Council consists of more than 1,100 members representing approximately two hundred thousand employees. Sixty-two percent of its members are technology companies; 29 percent are service companies; and 9 percent are non-profit organizations, such as government agencies and universities. The council remains a focal point of the industry and has become a major stop for political candidates, luring presidential contenders Rudolph Giuliani and Mitt Romney to separate breakfast meetings in 2007.

An Alliance of Ideas

Another influential endeavor put forth by the private sector during this time was the Northern Virginia Roundtable. The organization was founded by George Johnson; Earle Williams; Til Hazel; April Young, former head of the state's economic development department; and Ed Bersoff, CEO of BTG, Inc., a systems integrator in Vienna. Johnson had imagined the Roundtable as a forum to enhance Northern Virginia's long-term economic stability and growth. Young remembers, "I was sitting in George's office and mentioned that I wanted to create a business alliance that crossed geographic and industry lines when George told me he was thinking the same thing."[366]

By 1993, the Roundtable was off and running with a membership of more than one hundred area business leaders, many of them CEOs. What brought its members together was the realization that economic development in the new knowledge-based economy would require a different approach. The Roundtable also wanted to ensure that Fairfax County got its fair share of resources from Richmond to pursue its agenda. Over the years, Fairfax had provided the Commonwealth with far more in tax revenue than it received back for public infrastructure needs. For instance, in 1990, only 66 cents of each dollar sent to Richmond made its way back to Fairfax. As Til told a local business newspaper, "We developed an agenda for improvements, and we then told the politicians, 'This is what we need.' That helped bring some focus on the needs of Northern Virginia."[367]

Before solidifying its agenda, the Roundtable spent nearly two years studying Northern Virginia's economy. The study was conducted by the Institute of Public Policy at George Mason University and culminated in several published reports. Based on these findings, the group worked with the leadership of the General Assembly in Northern Virginia to develop and propose a long-term legislative platform. Their strategy addressed such priorities as transportation, tax reform, and education. "Education is the number one issue," Bersoff told a reporter. "There is only one source of revenue [for it]—the taxpayers."[368]

Indeed, state funding for higher education was falling precipitously at the time. Governor L. Douglas Wilder, elected in 1990 as the first African-American governor in American history, had taken a machete to education funds to balance the state's budget. Wilder cut more than $400 million in allocations during his single term in office, reducing Virginia to forty-fourth place among states in spending per student. Meanwhile, tuition skyrocketed as colleges and universities tried desperately to make up for the shortfall. Wilder, said Til, "balanced the budget on the back of higher education."[369]

One viable solution to the education mess was to raise taxes, a move the Roundtable strongly recommended. "People are prompted to say they'll pay more in [taxes] if the money doesn't go into the general treasury [but goes] to education and transportation," said John Tydings, a member of the Roundtable and CEO of the Greater Washington Board of Trade.[370]

Leadership in the Knowledge Age

The Roundtable took tough, courageous stances in putting forth its legislative agenda, and it soon spawned other organizations. One was the Potomac Knowledgeway Project. The project acted as a catalyst, thought leader, and incubator of ideas to ensure the region maintained its leadership in the information technology industry. Mario Morino, a former software entrepreneur and investor in emerging technology firms, presented the project to the Roundtable. Morino had made millions of dollars following the 1995 sale of his technology company, Legent Software, to Computer Associates. His goal was to form an organization that would firmly establish Greater Washington as the global leader in the creation, development, and delivery of information products and intellectual services. "Mario realized that the Internet represented a huge transformation in the ways in which business is conducted globally," says April Young, who helped lead the project's development. "We were blown away by his presentation."[371]

Morino knew that the universal connectivity of computers would change the world, both in terms of commerce and communications. Northern Virginia was already home to hundreds of high technology and telecommunications companies as well as countless government agencies and their hordes of knowledge workers (such as the Central Intelligence Agency's encryption specialists). These companies and individuals were significant assets to Fairfax County—but they "weren't positioned appropriately for the region to take advantage of," comments

Robert Templin, president of the Center for Innovative Technology (CIT). "Companies and knowledge workers were operating in isolation, which didn't make the area attractive to venture capitalists. The vision was to bring all this together by getting everyone connected."[372]

The Roundtable quickly endorsed the formation of the Potomac Knowledgeway Project as an independent, industry-led organization. Both the Roundtable and the CIT were primary partners in the endeavor. Other partners included George Mason University, Northern Virginia Community College, the Northern Virginia Technology Council, the Morino Institute, and the Governor's Regional Economic Development Advisory Council for Northern Virginia.

Under Templin's leadership, CIT matched one dollar for every two raised by the Potomac Knowledgeway Project. A portion of these funds financed a series of documentaries that told the story of the Internet as it related to Northern Virginia's enviable technological and knowledge-based resources. "The metaphor we used in the first film was the 'final spike in the transatlantic railroad,'" Templin recalls. "At the time I thought we were exaggerating to make a point, but as things turned out, we weren't. Our region wasn't becoming an Internet leader; we *were* the dominant leader. Silicon Valley was all about making [semiconductor] wafers, whereas we were all about the convergence of telecommunications, technology, and information."

Like its predecessor, the Potomac Knowledgeway has experienced many successes. One in particular is NetPreneur. Derived from the Knowledgeway project, NetPreneur is an online forum where regional startup Internet firms can share their ideas and receive support for their projects. The program is sponsored by the Morino Institute today.

Another child born out of the Roundtable was the Northern Virginia Project, an industry-driven educational initiative similarly predicated on growing the region's information technology products and services. The Northern Virginia Project established a "learning center" that assisted businesses, educational institutions, and everyday citizens in making the area a world center for innovation in the Knowledge Age. Among the organization's initial board members was Earle Williams, who had retired as chairman and CEO of BDM International in 1992. Earle was highly respected within younger tech groups as one of the pioneering Beltway Bandits. "Earle always saw something bigger [for Fairfax County]," says Templin. "He and others had led the way."

Indeed, in the twenty years since Earle had taken the reins of BDM, he had grown it from a company that employed approximately one hundred people to a major technology firm with revenues of $425 million and a workforce in excess of 4,500 employees. One year after Earle's retirement, he tossed his hat in the ring for governor. Although he had the backing of the Northern Virginia business community, Earle came in second behind George Allen in the Republican convention. Allen, son of the legendary football coach by the same name, went on to win the general election, succeeding Doug Wilder. "It didn't work out the way I had hoped," says Earle, "but it was a great experience nonetheless. I got my whole family involved, and we all enjoyed ourselves immensely."[373]

BDM was later sold to TRW, which was bought by Northrop Grumman in 2002 for $7.8 billion. This acquisition merged the assets of BDM with PRC, which was sold to Emhart in 1986 and went through a maze of acquisitions until it too ended up with Northrop Grumman. "Earle and I used to talk about merging BDM and PRC, and we laugh today that both companies sort of ended up that way anyway," says John Toups, former president and CEO of PRC.[374] Today, both companies' assets are part of Northrop Grumman.

In the mid-1990s, another effort was brought forth by the private sector: the creation of the Northern Virginia chapter of the Virginia Economic Advisory Council. Sid Dewberry was the organization's first chairman and de facto goodwill ambassador. In this role, he sought to strengthen the ties between the state's powerful business interests in the north and those in the south to the benefit of all Virginians.

By ensuring that Fairfax County remained the focal point of the global Internet, these various initiatives effectively made the area the "paver" of the Information Superhighway. By 1996, the county boasted more than two thousand businesses that were directly involved in the information technology industry—companies that employed a staggering forty-two thousand people.[375] "From the largest producer of milk in the Commonwealth of Virginia to the home of the Internet is definitely something upon which to reflect," stated the Fairfax County Economic Development Authority.

Fairfax had truly become the "center of gravity" for the "Washington-area technopolis," asserted *Virginia Business* magazine. With Tysons Corner, Reston, Herndon, and the Dulles Corridor literally teeming with technology firms, county office space was at a premium. In 1995, the office vacancy rate fell to 8.5 percent, the lowest rate since 1984 and a far cry from the 18.3 percent recorded during the recession years.

No office building in the county offered more than fifty thousand contiguous square feet, crimping the expansion plans of many companies. America Online was so flummoxed by the lack of office space in Vienna that it was forced to institute a hiring freeze. The Internet service provider ultimately solved the dilemma, buying a 235,000-square-foot building in Reston in 1996.[376] With the birth of the Internet, the real estate recession in Fairfax County had become a thing of the past.

Educating the Public

As more people migrated to Fairfax to pursue careers in information technology and other businesses of the new age, Til Hazel wanted to be sure their children had the opportunity for a high-quality education. Unfortunately, these aims ran counter to a state government led by Governor Wilder that kept squeezing the spigot of education funding.

Til wasn't alone in wanting to save the public education system. Other Virginia business leaders shared his concerns, including Hays T. Watkins, chairman of CSX Corporation, a large railroad; James W. McGlothlin, president of the United Company, a major coal concern; and Joshua P. Darden, Jr., CEO of Colonial, a large chain of automobile dealerships founded by his father in 1930.

In 1992, George Johnson asked Til to meet with these power brokers in Richmond to discuss the poor condition of Virginia's education funding. "They were sitting around this table talking about doing something for higher education when I walked in for the meeting," Til recalls. "They looked up and said, 'You missed the meeting. And by the way you're the chairman of a new organization we're forming.' I said okay, and then just took it from there."

They called the organization the Virginia Business Higher Education Council. It soon became the most outspoken advocate of public education in Virginia. "Til organized the business community to run roughshod over the troglodytes in [Richmond] that didn't seem to understand we have to do something about education," says former governor Chuck Robb. "To Til's credit, he is serious about education."[377]

Til made the Virginia Business Higher Education Council a thorn in the side of Wilder; his successor, George Allen; and legislators on both sides of the political aisle. The media dubbed Til a "crusader for higher ed," noting that he "doesn't worry about whom he offends."[378] Although Til had donated to Allen's gubernatorial campaign after Allen had defeated Earle Williams in the Republican convention, he did not mince words about the governor's spending priorities. The state's educational bureaucracy, he asserted, had grown "fat, dumb, and happy." He added, "I am not in the business of supporting any particular political leader. I am in the business . . . of doing what I need to do for higher education."[379]

As Til told the *Virginian-Pilot,* there was an "absolutely astounding and appalling decline in support for higher education" in the Commonwealth. The newspaper continued, "Without flinching, Hazel and a few dozen other of the state's business leaders are calling for Virginia to spend hundreds of millions of dollars more on its colleges and universities."[380]

The council bolstered its position through a series of advertisements in major Virginia newspapers and *The Washington Post.* With a membership that included forty top executives from Virginia's largest companies, it was the government's proverbial eight-hundred-pound gorilla. Leveraging its power, the group worked to defeat a tax cut proposed by Allen. Council members also helped defeat state legislative candidates who did not support funding for higher education and helped elect those who did, asking all 140 candidates for the State Senate and the House of

Delegates to sign a "statement of support" for Virginia's public system of higher education. More than three quarters signed. As Til said, "We're pretty aggressive and we make a lot of people nervous."[381]

The Virginia Business Higher Education Council additionally spearheaded the passage of two bond referendums for higher education that made hundreds of millions of dollars in construction money available to the state's two- and four-year institutions. Thanks in large part to the council's efforts, state spending on higher education increased by $230 million between 1995 and 1997. "The [Council] has been enormously successful," acknowledged former Virginia governor Gerald Baliles. "They have provided a bipartisan umbrella of support for legislators in both parties who wanted to support higher education but were concerned about the political consequences."[382]

Yet Til was not satisfied with the council's many successes. At the time, he merely told a reporter, "Things are a little better."[383] Til wasn't trying to be negative; on the contrary, "failure" is simply not a word in his vocabulary. In his office hangs a framed quote from Winston Churchill, given to him by his daughter. It reads: "Never give in, never give in, never, never, never, never—in nothing, great or small, large or petty—never give in." Til applied this sentiment to all he did, including his work on behalf of Virginia's public education system.

Flint Hill Becomes First Class

Til Hazel was equally concerned about the state of the county's private schools. As *The Washington Post* put it, "Hazel has a mission. Convinced that public schools are failing to prepare young people for college and the world at large, Hazel wants to build a first-class preparatory school in Northern Virginia."[384]

For years, Til had been chairman of the board of trustees at St. Stephen's, an exclusive Episcopalian school in Alexandria where his sons had studied and graduated. He had also donated generously to the school. According to figures compiled by the school's development office, Til gave $3.5 million to St. Stephen's from 1981 to 1988, making him the largest donor in its history. "He helped build our second campus, an old parochial school that we bought and tore down," says Tom Whitworth, assistant headmaster of St. Stephen's in the mid-1980s. "It later took the name of the Hazel Campus." Til wasn't concerned with the name of the new facility, though—it was the quality of education that mattered to him. "He was extremely interested in our academic curriculum," Whitworth recalls.

Til later parted ways with St. Stephen's over the future direction of the school. He and his fellow trustees wanted to build more campuses, attract a better faculty, and most divisively, make St. Stephen's a coeducational institution; the Episcopal Diocese of Virginia in Richmond wanted to preserve the status quo. "The issue was control and governance," says Whitworth. The diocese promptly rebuffed the board's suggestion and fired the trustees. Whitworth and other administrators and faculty members then handed in their resignation. The dispute between the board and the diocese ultimately landed in court, and the diocese won.

Til took the defeat in stride, still believing that western Fairfax County would someday become the home of a world-class private school. This goal was brought into focus when Flint Hill Preparatory School fell on hard times. A private school known more for its championship basketball team than its academic record, Flint Hill was in the thick of building a new campus at the corner of Chain Bridge and Jermantown Roads in Oakton. The cost was higher than anticipated, causing its private owner to consider selling. Whitworth and other former St. Stephen's administrators, teachers, and trustees approached Til to lead an effort to buy the school and its new campus. Til felt a strong allegiance to this loyal group of likeminded individuals and was confident the school could be transformed into an academic powerhouse, so he reached deeply into his wallet.

Some parents and teachers initially expressed concerns over the sale, but J. Wade Gilley, a former Flint Hill trustee and the senior vice president of GMU, quickly quelled the anxiety. "[Til's] overall vision," Gilley told a reporter, "is he wants to make Fairfax County one of the premier places in the world to work and live [and that] required first-rate schools."[385]

In January 1990, a deal was struck to buy the school. "It was a momentous day," says Whitworth. He became the new non-denominational Flint Hill School's first headmaster, while St. Stephen's former headmaster, who had also resigned, became its first president. The new campus housed a four-story, eighty-thousand-square-foot academic building now named for Til's late wife, Jinx, who passed away in 1995. It also featured a twelve-thousand-square-foot administration building and dining hall. Eight months after the sale, school began for four hundred students, twenty-five faculty members, and ten administrators.

In succeeding years, the number of buildings, students, faculty and administrators at Flint Hill increased markedly. A gymnasium and performing arts theatre were constructed, and a second campus was built in 1997 on thirty acres a quarter mile away. Today, the original campus teaches kindergarten through eighth grade, while the new west campus houses a secondary school. More than one thousand students enroll at Flint Hill each year, and the number of faculty members and administrators exceeds 220.

Flint Hill's academic record is also strong, with nearly 90 percent of its students completing advanced placement courses. For the past fifteen years, its students have attended the prestigious Governor's School, a range of extremely challenging summer courses only available to top-grade pupils. "Without Til and his friends in the business community, none of this would have happened," says Whitworth, now the headmaster of Darlington School in Rome, Georgia. "When one thinks about Fairfax County and education you have to think 'Til Hazel.'"

Succeeding George Johnson

Just a few years later, the state's other great champion of education, George Johnson, retired in 1996 as the most effective president in George Mason University's history. Alan G. Merten succeeded him on July 1. Merten was a former dean of the business schools at Cornell University and the University of Florida, and a computer scientist who spoke the language of the area's technology companies. He had big shoes to fill. "The shadow of George Johnson was a very large shadow, indeed," says Kathryn A. Maclane, executive vice president of West*Group.[386]

During George's tenure from 1978 to 1996, GMU's enrollment more than doubled to over twenty thousand students. Over thirty degree programs were unveiled, a great number of buildings were constructed, and the university's geographical footprint was substantially widened. When George took over, GMU had been a commuter school. There were no doctoral programs, no law school, no school of information technology and engineering, and no sports or entertainment arena. By the time he left, it had become a major institution of higher learning.

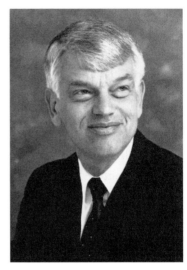

Dr. Alan G. Merten, president, George Mason University

"George was larger than life and the perfect person to grow that university, and it grew like crazy," says Maclane. "Alan's job was to get it more organized, structured, and focused." Merten agrees: "George was the entrepreneur. People said to me when I got here, 'Alan, you're replacing a cowboy, a fellow with guns blazing into the room to get things done.' And George did what was needed. He started a university and it grew enormously. My job was to sustain this growth."[387]

George's imprint on Fairfax County extended beyond the confines of GMU. By uniting business leaders in a variety of organizations to create more commerce and industry in Northern Virginia, he had forged a better life for its inhabitants. Chief among them was the George Mason Institute. More than any other organization in the late-twentieth century, the institute had helped Fairfax County become a major technology corridor.

It is perhaps fitting that the year George announced his retirement was the same year that GMU was chosen to host the biennial World Congress on Information Technology. The conference is considered the premier event for senior-level information technology executives around the world to network, explore global markets, and listen to customer perspectives. When it was announced that Fairfax would be the location for the 1998 conference, no eyebrows were raised. Thanks to George Johnson and the region's business community, the county had earned its stripes.

The County's New Calling Card

Fairfax entered the latter part of the decade as a major global center for information technology and telecommunications. The county had become a chief competitor in telecommunications following the government's deregulation of the industry in 1996. As the first important overhaul of telecommunications in nearly sixty-two years, the legislation forced local telephone companies to share their lines with competitors at regulated rates. "Suddenly, we had these huge communications facilities in the Washington area that were built up over many years that now were open to everyone," recalls Jim Todd, former vice chairman of the Economic Development Authority and currently the president of The Peterson Companies. "There was a boom in the number of new phone companies, and they tended to come here to Northern Virginia."[388]

The digitization of information, fast-growing computer speed, and increasing bandwidth redefined the notion of a telephone call. Now, the Federal Communications Commission (FCC) offered a spectrum in which new phone companies could compete against existing ones in an "infocom" industry—one where computers could formulate digitized information and transmit it over phone lines to other computers. This intersection of the Internet and telecommunications gave birth to hundreds of companies in Fairfax County.

As telecom companies like MCI Communications planted stakes in the county, the industries serving them followed. One such industry was fiber optics, which manufactures fiber optic cables that transmit light through fibers made of transparent materials, like glass or plastic. These cables make up the vital electronic pathway of phone calls and Internet communications. By the end of the decade, Virginia's 650,000 miles of installed fiber optic cable far outranked any other U.S. state,[389] and

Northern Virginia was home to more telecom and satellite companies than any other place on earth.

With Fairfax County's reputation firm as a nexus of technology, telecommunications, and the Internet, venture capitalists descended on the region. From 1996 to 1998, nearly two-dozen high-tech companies in Fairfax went public. In the meantime, the county's marketing outreach to companies grew more global in scope. In 1979, a scant seventeen foreign-owned companies operated in Fairfax.[390] Sixteen years later, more than 110 foreign companies employing approximately 8,200 people were on the scene.

In the meantime, the Economic Development Authority hoped to increase the county's number of foreign businesses via its new international marketing division. The division did so in part by leveraging the 1998 World Congress on Information Technology. The four-day conference featured sixty-four speakers, among them Margaret Thatcher and Mikhail Gorbachev. "We had more than thirty security agencies involved," recalls Alan Merten, co-chairman of the event. More than two thousand executives from ninety-five countries attended, including technology gurus Michael Dell, founder of Dell Computer Corporation; James Barksdale, CEO of Netscape Communications; and Larry Ellison, CEO of Oracle Corporation. Shortly thereafter, Oracle opened its main East Coast office in Reston.

Fairfax was a powerful lure for the corporate sector—and international companies were no exception. "With Dulles International Airport on one side and the federal government on the other, international marketing makes sense," said Gerald L. Gordon, who as president of the Economic Development Authority had been instrumental in bringing the World Congress to Fairfax.[391] By 2005, the number of foreign-owned firms in the county skyrocketed to 332, a near tripling in less than a decade. Assisting the increase was Washington Dulles International Airport, which continued to expand its number of nonstop international markets, from sixty a week in 1988 to 160 a week in 1993. The EDA also opened international marketing offices in Tokyo, Frankfurt, and London in 1998. In succeeding years, the organization would launch several additional marketing offices around the globe.

Land of Wide Open Opportunity

As Fairfax County brought more telecommunications, Internet, and foreign-owned firms into its fold, the volume of available office space dwindled and Loudoun County began to absorb the overflow. To preserve Fairfax County's few remaining large open spaces, community activists quickly joined with environmental groups like the Piedmont Environmental Council to thwart further development. Not surprisingly, the organizations underplayed the number of green spaces that had already been set aside by real estate developers like West*Group and Hazel/Peterson Companies. The developers of Reston in particular had designated enormous parcels of land for its residents to enjoy. In 2001, Reston became the third and largest community in the country to receive certification from the National Wildlife Federation as a Community Wildlife Habitat.

Jerry Halpin had contributed to the environmental effort for decades, planting many of the trees and shrubs in Tysons Corner with his own hands. "I feel blessed to have watched them mature through the years," he says.[392] His efforts extended throughout the county. When West*Group developed a planned residential community in McLean where the Evans Farm formerly stood, Jerry made sure as many trees as possible were saved.

"Neighbors were outraged that someone would take this property that they had used as their backyard and develop homes on it," recalls Alice Starr, the vice president of marketing at West*Group. "But we kept all the old trees, every single one of them, at great expense. We also measured every tree more than twelve inches in diameter, assessed [its] health and type, and made an effort to save as many as possible."[393] Today, the Evans Farm community is a highly desirable place to live.

In 1998, *The Washington Post* and the Fairfax County Federation of Citizens Associations named Jerry the "Fairfax County Citizen of the Year," extolling his work as an "environmentally conscious and fiscally responsible real estate developer." *The Post* went on to say, "He has created office parks and other developments that have generated thousands of jobs in Fairfax County, while preserving the trees and beauty of the land.

. . . As a conservationist, he has donated parkland and invested heavily in saving trees and wildlife."

Where preservationists saw a dwindling quantity of land, Jerry and others saw beautifully landscaped communities. "Most experts agree the Washington area probably has many more trees today than it did 50 years ago," *The Washington Post* affirmed in 1997. "Developers increasingly see advantages to preserving vistas and trees as selling points that raise the value of a given parcel."[394] Til explained it this way: "The land is a resource for people to use, and the issue is whether you use it well."[395]

Indeed, many developers and business leaders had put their collective energy behind promoting industry and commerce, creating jobs, and then building homes in fine communities with abundant green space. From their point of view, such quality of life prerogatives took precedence over preserving land merely for the sake of preservation. As Til said in a 2006 speech, "Washington is now the world's capital. Land in this region is needed for the essential provision of housing and employment." Denying such accommodations for people in the Washington region would be "contrary to the best interests of American society. Provisions for people who are required to populate the national government are a need of national importance."

Besides, curbing development would not solve the county's pressing need for new schools, libraries, fire stations, roads, and other infrastructures. Doing so would only reduce the sorely needed tax base provided by the private sector. Fairfax County required more than $1 billion to meet the needs of the one-million-plus people expected by the beginning of the new millennium, and it was reportedly $300 million short of the target. The county also called for additional roads in its outlying areas, where new development would likely occur.

Propelled by this data, Fairfax business leaders urged the Commonwealth to build a collection of eastern and western highway bypasses to recharge the region and thereby bolster the tax base. The proposition did not sit well with the preservationists, but business leaders had good reason for requesting new roads. Despite having a comparatively high percentage of carpool and transit use, the Greater

Washington region had the second longest commuting time in the nation in the late 1990s and the third greatest number of workers commuting more than sixty minutes each day.[396] The Greater Washington Board of Trade concluded in a 1997 regional transportation report: "It is clear that the removal of highway and bridge projects from previous regional plans has produced the fifth smallest highway network [in the country] and is directly responsible for the region's commuting times and congestion costs being among the nation's highest."

The Board of Trade endorsed both the western and eastern bypasses, as well as the widening of Interstate 66 and the building of a new highway called the InterCounty Connector. The latter, a six-lane, eighteen-mile highway between the Interstate 270 and Interstate 95 corridors, would join Prince William County in Virginia with Prince George's County in Maryland via a new Potomac River crossing.[397] The Washington Airports Task Force also backed the proposed connector. It noted in a 2000 study: "A parkway connection from I-270 to Dulles Airport and its Potomac River crossing could improve the region's efficiency and the airport's service to Montgomery County, while embellishing both [Fairfax County] and the National Capital Region."[398]

Despite such strong endorsements, politicians bowed to a different transportation agenda, one less divisive among the public: rail service. Legislators focused on extending Washington's Metrorail system within the county, putting stops in major hubs like Tysons Corner, Reston, Herndon, and the fast-growing Dulles Corridor. The Metropolitan Washington Council of Governments posited that 51 percent of the household growth and 55 percent of the job growth in Fairfax and Loudoun counties would occur in the Dulles Corridor.[399] But even the subject of rail proved divisive, and several years elapsed before actual plans were drawn up.

Whether or not rail will solve the county's traffic congestion remains an open question. As Bob Chase from the Northern Virginia Transportation Alliance notes, "Rail is great for large groups of people who move to a particular place during certain hours, which is why it works in New York City. But it is not a suburban mode of transit anywhere in America for the same reason. Nevertheless, public officials believe it is the wave of the future."[400]

Til is more to the point: "Rail will provide little, if any, substantial relief for existing gridlock or future needs."

Center of Cyberspace

Its transportation problems aside, Fairfax continued to march to the new era's techno beat. By the dawn of the twenty-first century, the county had one of the most dynamic office markets in the nation, with more than 12.5 million square feet of office space completed since 1990 and another 8.65 million square feet under construction. The 8.5 percent office vacancy rate recorded in 1995—a vast improvement after the recession years—seemed almost bearish when the vacancy rate hit 3.45 percent in 2000, the lowest in the country. With an office inventory of 93.5 million square feet, Fairfax now ranked tenth among the country's largest suburban office markets.[401]

Information technology was largely responsible for the surge in commercial activity and the constant hum of construction. Fairfax was the indisputable epicenter of the Information Age—second only to Silicon Valley in resident high-tech companies—with more than 2,600 firms employing 237,000 workers in 2000.[402] Two-thirds of the world's Internet traffic passed through Northern Virginia, and the Greater Washington area claimed the most phone lines and fiber optic cables in the country. It was also home to the country's largest grouping of Internet service providers. Dollars now seemed to fly in from venture capital firms, with

A Virginia "Internet C@pital" license plate design was issued to celebrate Fairfax County's rise to epicenter of the Information Age.

thirty listing their address in Fairfax in 2000. That year, such firms provided more than $1.2 billion to 107 high-tech companies in Fairfax.

The county now confidently billed itself as "E-country," and the state's license plates sported a new moniker: "The Internet Capital of the World." To the chagrin of Silicon Valley and other technology corridors, the *Los Angeles Times* dubbed Northern Virginia "the world's electronic nerve center," adding, "with its wealth of tech jobs and skilled candidates, [it] is poised to cash in on a profound shift taking place in the computer industry."[403]

The following year, the *Dallas Morning News* asked, "Where do you dock in cyberspace?" Once again, the answer was Northern Virginia. "America Online, MCI WorldCom, Oracle Corporation, PSINet and 2,500 other technology companies call it home," the newspaper explained.[404]

Even the head of the Federal Communications Commission considered the state to be the citadel of the Information Age. "Virginia continues to lead the nation into the future," said FCC Chairman William E. Kennard. "Tech companies are falling all over themselves to find technology-skilled workers." Kennard predicted that by 2003, there would be 112,000 jobs in Virginia "awaiting qualified applicants."[405] Among the likely employers would be 190 foreign-owned companies, such as Cable & Wireless and Hitachi Data Systems—a testament to the Economic Development Authority's success in luring overseas firms to the county. A different story was playing out in Silicon Valley. Between 2000 and 2003, jobs in the region fell by 18 percent, with technology jobs dropping by 25 percent. Per capita income also decreased by 7.4 percent.[406]

Such national and international success boded well for the county's residents. Fairfax now enjoyed the highest median household income in the nation, $90,939, a direct result of the high-paying jobs provided by the information technology sector.[407] "You can't miss the new economy entrepreneurs in their Lexuses and Land Rovers doing deals on cell phones as they zip around I-66 and Routes 7, 50 and 123," reported *Time* magazine.[408] Once a "sleepy" and "remote" place, Fairfax had become a magnet for "hundreds of new dotcoms, telephone companies, wireless firms, Internet service providers and venture capitalists."

People now drove to Fairfax County, rather than through it. The region was, according to *Time*, "home to everything that makes the new economy the powerhouse that it is." The magazine added: "Fairfax County, VA, [that's] where the real money is."

And the county's million citizens knew it.

With redevelopment plans underway such as Metrorail's expansion, more residential housing, and better accommodation for pedestrians, Tysons Corner may become the country's first successful "surburban city."

CHAPTER 8

Nexus of
Prosperity

A t the dawn of the new millennium, Virginia's *Times-Community* newspaper selected three people as Fairfax County's "Citizens of the Century." One was Bob Simon, who sold his inheritance, the family-owned Carnegie Hall in New York, to build the "New City" of Reston. The second was Catherine Filene Shouse, who donated the land upon which the Wolf Trap National Park for the Performing Arts was erected. The third was Til Hazel. More than any other person, he had recognized what Fairfax County could become and worked throughout his lifetime to realize that vision. "[Til] has done more to shape the Washington area than any man since Pierre L'Enfant, the Frenchman who designed the District of Columbia," wrote author Joel Garreau.[409]

When Til glimpsed construction on one of the county's first postwar subdivisions at Pimmit Hills as a teenager, Fairfax had been a patchwork of dairy farms and scrubland. There was no Beltway, let alone Beltway Bandits. Tysons Corner was a rural crossroads. And Reston, George Mason University, Northern Virginia Community College, and the Inova Health System did not exist. Neither did Washington Dulles International Airport, Dulles Toll Road, or Dulles Corridor. Fairfax had yet to become Washington's bedroom community, much less a booming center of its own commerce and industry.

No other jurisdiction in America had gone from so little to so much in such a short period of time, and very few could credit their prosperity to such a small group of people. Fairfax now possessed everything a twenty-first-century community could want: high-paying jobs, a first-class private and public school system, relatively large homes in close-knit neighborhoods, abundant parkland and green spaces, the highest or next to highest median household income in the United States, a superior health care system, a highly-skilled and educated workforce, a growing array of cultural institutions, and a constellation of leading companies in the new knowledge industries. While the county's population grew a strong 60 percent from 1980 to 2000, its job base increased by 147 percent.[410] Fairfax offered what most other counties did not: the exhilaration of entrepreneurial activity and a resulting better life for all.

Traffic congestion remained a sore spot, but plans were in the works to widen Interstate 66, as well as improve Interstate 495 and extend the Dulles Toll Road. Hopes were also high that several roads on the drawing board would be constructed. One was the Techway, a thoroughfare that would connect the booming Dulles Corridor to the Interstate 270 technology corridor in Gaithersburg, Maryland, via a bridge over the Potomac River. The highway would reduce Beltway congestion and facilitate the evacuation of the capital region in the event of a terrorist attack.

Virginia governor Mark Warner, a Democrat supported by the county's business community in large part because he backed the Techway's construction, pledged to build the road. But like many of the area's planned roads, it fell prey to the usual NIMBY and slow-growth resistance. When Warner asked Virginians to vote on a referendum to raise the sales tax by half a penny per dollar to pay for transportation improvements such as the Techway, the measure was killed by an improbable coalition of anti-tax conservative Republicans and anti-growth liberal Democrats. Nevertheless, some citizens like Sid Dewberry remain confident it will be built someday. "We'll also see further improvements made to I-66, the Beltway and the Dulles Toll Road, and routes 50 and 7," Sid projects.[411]

An Explosion in Military—and Monetary—Activity

Fairfax County's economy remained strong even during the global recession that occurred in the wake of the terrorist attacks on September 11, 2001. The United States government responded to the attacks by waging a "war on terror" both domestically and internationally, which required a steep increase in military spending. More than $9 billion in government procurement contracts poured into the coffers of Fairfax companies that year.[412] Between 1983 and 2001, the Greater Washington area experienced a 359 percent increase in federal procurement outlays, with Northern Virginia companies reaping the greatest share of funding. Los Angeles, a major competitor for federal dollars, experienced a 28 percent decrease during the same period. While federal contracting monies spent in the Greater Washington area accounted for only 36 percent of the total awarded the Los Angeles area in 1983, by 2001 the numbers were reversed, with the Greater Washington area's federal procurement awards double that of Los Angeles.[413] Of the $12 billion in federal procurement contracts in 2003, the Greater Washington area tallied two-thirds.[414]

"This region is showing notable resilience, as its unique cluster of longtime defense contractors, telecom pioneers, Internet firms and tech consultants reap the benefits of proximity and strong ties to the federal government," the *Mercury News* reported. "The ten largest defense contractors all have a major presence in the region, including Northrop Grumman and SAIC, which also have large information technology divisions."[415] As economist Stephen Fuller, director of the Center for Regional Analysis at George Mason University, put it, "War is good for the Washington economy."[416]

It was even better for Fairfax County. In 2002, the value of goods and services produced in the county exceeded that of the District of Columbia, the region's historic economic center, for the first time ever.[417] "From 1980 to 2000," says Fuller, "the county's economy grew at a 291 percent clip (in inflation adjusted dollars), a rate more than double the gain in the entire Greater Washington region, of which it is a part." Fuller predicts that Fairfax will expand at triple the economic growth rate of

Greater Washington through 2020. He also projects a 35 percent increase in the county's population by that time, with the employment base growing by 63 percent—an increase reflecting 474,100 new jobs.[418]

Gateway to Growth

Other technology corridors were reeling from the dotcom bust in the early part of the new century, but not Fairfax County. Its economy flourishing, unemployment in Northern Virginia was 2.9 percent in 2003, compared to 6 percent nationally. Silicon Valley in Santa Clara, California, and the Route 128 corridor in Boston each lost thirty thousand jobs between October 2001 and October 2002, and unemployment in Silicon Valley hovered around 8.3 percent.[419] Meanwhile, Fairfax added 6,100 new jobs, most in information technology.[420]

New industries such as bio-informatics, a merging of biotechnology and information technology, also made the scene. To promote the nascent industry, the Fairfax County Economic Development Authority unveiled the BioAccelerator. The 7,500-square-foot facility was constructed in Springfield in 2002 to spur the development of young biotechnology, biomedical, and bio-informatics companies. Early tenants of the BioAccelerator included JIRIS, a South Korean biometrics company; ProImmune of the United Kingdom; and Germany-based JPT Technologies—just a few of the 260-plus foreign-owned companies the county listed in 2002. "We want to help innovative growth companies from around the world use Fairfax County as a gateway to the U.S. market," said Gerald Gordon, president and CEO of the Economic Development Authority.

The BioAccelerator's proximity to the federal government's research and regulatory agencies, Northern Virginia Community College's new biomedical campus, and Inova Health Systems's new medical center all made it a nexus for the burgeoning field. And the county's highly-educated workforce, pro-business climate, and enviable quality of life were other draws.

These attractions lured an increasing number of foreign-born people, making the county a veritable gateway for immigrants. From 1990 to

2000, the number of Hispanic residents more than doubled to 107,000, making up 11 percent of the total population. The county also counted 127,000 Asian residents in 2000.[421] While only 16,139 Fairfax residents or 3.5 percent were foreign-born in 1970, by 2004 there were 259,227 foreign-born residents—roughly 20 percent of the population, compared with a national average of 12 percent. This mass migration of immigrants made up 73 percent of the county's total population increase from 1990 to 2000.[422]

A *Washington Post* headline from 2001 captured the county's demographic shift, stating, "A Global Village Takes Root."[423] A symphony of languages, including Spanish, Urdu, Farsi, Vietnamese, Korean, Kurdish, and Somali, could now be heard on the streets of Fairfax.

Many of these new residents worked in the region's information technology sector or were proprietors of small businesses. The county was home to six Fortune 500 companies (NVR among them) in 2004, but the vast majority of its companies—97 percent—were small businesses with fewer than one hundred employees and under $1 million in revenues.[424] "We have fifty thousand Korean-Americans and forty thousand Indian-Americans who own their own businesses here," Gordon says, referring to 2007 figures. "Of the top five hundred Hispanic-owned businesses in the U.S., twelve are in Fairfax County. Of the top one hundred African-American companies in technology, we have six."[425]

Only New York City has a foreign-born population as diverse as Northern Virginia—and these new residents feel a strong connection to their communities. A study by the Fairfax County Department of Systems Management for Human Services indicates that although only 48 percent of immigrants own homes in Fairfax, 91 percent feel that the county is "home," and 83 percent say their neighbors made their families feel welcome.[426]

These families embrace the county's emphasis on higher education. An impressive 41 percent of its foreign-born adults have a four-year college degree, significantly more than the 24 percent of all adults nationwide.[427] Fairfax County's immigrants have made George Mason University a veritable multicultural institution—the "most diverse" university in the nation, according to the *Princeton Review*. "You walk on campus and the world passes by," says Alan Merten, who succeeded George Johnson as GMU's president.[428]

At Northern Virginia Community College, students from more than 150 countries are represented. "Diversity is one of our strong suits," says Robert Templin, president of the college and former director of the Center for Innovative Technology. "Many of our students are new Americans who have come here to live the American Dream. Most understand that the dream is achieved through education. We're transforming these new arrivals so they not only are productively engaged in our economy, they contribute to our community."[429]

John W. Ryan, chairman of the board at NVCC, agrees: "Diversity has brought a richness to the campuses. You grow up in Annandale and the kid next to you is Ethiopian, you learn a lot about each other. We've come a long way from the Confederate flag."[430]

Looking Ahead—and Up

As the county's economy prospered and its population increased and changed demographically, traffic congestion became an even more pressing concern. The much-hoped for solution—more roads—was still a question mark. But after many years of stalled attempts, a 23.1-mile extension of Metrorail to Tysons Corner, Reston, Herndon, and other business hubs in the county was under way.

The rail extension was approved in November 2002 by the Washington Metropolitan Area Transit Authority, the agency in charge of managing Metrorail. The following month, the project was endorsed by the Commonwealth Transportation Board, which establishes policies and allocates funding for Virginia's transportation system. One by one, other agencies and jurisdictions required for the rail extension to move forward lined up to support it, and by 2006 the preliminary engineering was completed.

Most of the extension would be constructed in the median of the Dulles Access Road, which had been set aside for that purpose decades earlier. Construction was expected to begin in 2008, with a completion date of 2015. The project would lengthen the existing Metrorail system on the Orange Line from the East Falls Church station in Fairfax County through Tysons Corner to Washington Dulles International Airport, ending at Route 772/Ryan Road in Loudoun County. Along the way there would be eleven stops, with some at Reston and Herndon. Four stations were planned at Tysons Corner alone.

Jerry Halpin had engaged two popular former governors, Chuck Robb and Linwood Holton, to lobby for the rail extension. "We got a whole new generation of corporate leaders and some very civic-minded younger people to join our committees and come to meetings," says Robb.[431]

Jerry had big plans for Tysons Corner as well. He saw it as a denser urban environment where people worked, lived, and entertained—a "mini-Manhattan," he says.[432] Today, West*Group is preparing to tear down many of the modest two-story office buildings it erected there in the 1960s to make way for taller structures in their place. Several luxury high-rise condominiums were under construction in 2006 in anticipation of this transformation, with the Long Companies breaking ground on a series of nearly 1,500 units.

William D. Leics, president of the Fairfax County Chamber of Commerce, predicts that Tysons Corner will become "the country's first successful suburban city."[433] National Public Radio commented in 2008 that when the rail system arrives, "Tysons could be a model for change across the country. . . . People want walkable, construction, livable urban environments. That will be possible as Metrorail makes its way from D.C. to the airport."[434] This positive outlook is shared by many. Lecos and the chamber surveyed 1,800 Fairfax residents to solicit their views on the area's future. "They saw it as another Boston, Bethesda, or the west side of Alexandria around King Street, places they had strong familiarity with," he says. "The buzzwords today are 'high-density living,' 'compact development,' 'mixed-use,' 'transit-oriented,' and 'pedestrian friendly.' It all gets back to the concept of connectivity—people want to feel connected. Jerry realizes all this; he's a visionary. He envisioned Tysons Corner in its current iteration—the world's most successful office and shopping venue—and is now looking toward the next twenty-five years."

As Jerry understands, denser development pares driving distances, lessens traffic congestion, curbs automobile emissions, and controls sprawl. "It's either we continue to sprawl into Loudoun and Stafford counties or we go up and get more dense," says Chuck Ewing, co-founder of West*Group.[435] Former Fairfax County planner Rosser Payne likes the concept. "The future is what Jerry is doing: taking down [small] buildings to create densities," he says. "Going out into the country and putting houses on quarter-acre lots is a waste of real estate. Fairfax still has lots of room to grow—upwards."[436]

Current county officials are sanguine as well about the ability of denser live-work environments to alleviate highway overcrowding. "More than 150,000 people commute every morning at the same time to Tysons Corner and leave in the evening at the same time," says Gerald Connolly, chairman of the Fairfax Board of Supervisors. "The mall alone gets twenty-one million visitors a year, more people than visit any single monument in downtown Washington. Meanwhile, only seventeen thousand people live there." Connolly compares the area with his hometown of Boston: "[It] easily fits into Tysons' 1,700 acres with plenty left over, and think of its density and multimodal transportation. Jerry is right about the need for more residents, changing the imbalance to improve [traffic] congestion."[437]

A Successful Suburban City

More people living and working in Fairfax demands more diverse accommodations. In January 2004, the county's population was gauged at 1,022,298, making it more populous than the states of Alaska, Delaware, Montana, North Dakota, South Dakota, Vermont, and Wyoming.[438] Between 1970 and 2004, the percentage of employed residents working in Fairfax jumped from 35.6 percent to 52.5 percent.[439] This percentage increased to 55 percent two years later.[440]

Many newcomers were either single or young married couples with no children. If they were willing to hike a few blocks to work or take the Metro a couple stops, reasoned the area's business leaders, they also might purchase a condominium or townhouse somewhere with nice streets, good restaurants, and other amenities. Many cities, including Washington, Seattle, Portland (Oregon), and Palo Alto—the intellectual heart of Silicon Valley and home to Stanford University—were building higher-density, mixed-use developments in their downtown business districts. Palo Alto, for example, had grown into an urban mecca, with a downtown core featuring more than eight hundred businesses, thousands of residences, and a vibrant shopping center, restaurant scene, and nightlife. Why not Tysons Corner? For one thing, more jobs were on the way—another 106,900 positions projected by 2010, and an additional 90,600 from 2010 to 2020.[441] Altogether, the county expected nearly another five hundred thousand residents within a generation.[442] As Connolly commented to *The Washington Post*, "Where are we going to put these people?"[443]

Ted Lerner, who with Jerry Halpin has been responsible for much of the area's development, sees a day when Tysons Corner will be a mixed-use mecca similar to Palo Alto and Reston. In 2004, Reston's last six-acre parcel of land was sold for $35 million, three times what Bob Simon paid for the entire 6,750 acres in 1961. "We're planning two thirty-five-story residential structures at Tysons II, and I'm hoping they're completed by 2010," Lerner says. "I don't think we'll get it all residential, but twenty-five years from now who knows? Obviously, what Jerry is thinking is down the road."[444]

He and others acknowledge that despite the opportunities, transforming an area originally developed as office and retail space into a livable, walkable "city" will not be easy. Tysons Corner has more retail activity than any city or jurisdiction on the East Coast outside of New York City, as well as the thirteenth largest daytime office population in the country. But bringing in residents will give it what it lacks: a "soul," says Bob Templin. "If it could develop into a place where people live, play, and learn as well as work, it could be a place like Reston, which certainly has a soul."[445]

Metrorail is the area's best bet at creating this new identity. "Look what Arlington [County] has done, building up a tremendous residential and economic base around its Metro stations over the years," says developer Russell Rosenberger, president of Madison Homes, Inc.

"The same possibilities exist along the planned Metro stops in Fairfax and Loudoun."[446]

Fairfax Supervisor Catherine M. Hudges shares his optimism. "By increasing the density around the rail stations," she projects, "we can create a pedestrian-friendly community where people will be able to live, work, and play."[447]

Commutes, Congestion, and the Cost of Living

In addition to accommodating the influx of new residents and alleviating traffic, there is another compelling reason for creating higher densities in Fairfax: the county's rising affluence and dwindling land supply have conspired to make the purchase of a traditional home out of reach for many people. "Area workers seeking affordable houses are forced further and further from where they work," wrote Til Hazel in a *Washington Post* op-ed. "The suburbs are dragged further out from employment centers. With a lack of new highways, those same workers must make longer commutes in worse traffic."

Til's solution was to finish the two additional circumferential highways that had been planned decades before. The so-called eastern and western transportation corridors, one of the planned highways, would migrate East Coast thru-traffic off the Beltway, easing congestion. He further recommends construction of the Techway connecting Montgomery County and Northern Virginia. His proposals are in tune with much of the public. A 2005 survey by the Northern Virginia Transportation Alliance indicates that 85 percent of the public support the use of state general fund tax dollars for transportation, as long as the money doesn't reduce core program funding. Another 66 percent support a regional tax dedicated to regional transportation policies.[448]

Til does not believe higher-density building patterns will ease the gridlock of cars on the highways—but he doesn't think Metrorail will solve the dilemma either. Instead, he argues that the solution lies in building affordable housing in the undeveloped portions of the county. As of 2004, there remained twenty-four thousand zoned acres of vacant land in Fairfax County.[449] "Trains and dense housing at Metro stations did not build this region; highways and affordable houses did," stated Til. "If new housing is not built, the cost of existing housing goes up—good for existing residents but only in the short run."

Gordon of the Economic Development Authority agrees that the lack of affordable housing ranks with traffic as one of the county's most pressing problems, but he believes Metrorail can have a positive effect on traffic congestion. "Mid-level professional employees cannot afford to live here, [and] that will cost us," says Gordon. "If people can live in Loudoun County, drive to their local Metro station, and then take that into Tysons Corner instead of sitting on the [Greenway] toll road, we [will] reduce traffic."

As for building more highways, Gordon thinks people might accept the idea of new roads, but that they would be unwilling to accept the costs. "One foot of lane construction is $20,000," he says, "and that's a figure from ten years ago."[450] He proposes a multimodal transportation solution intertwining Metrorail, light rail, buses, and more roads "where economically feasible." Gordon also advocates shifting work hours to ease the rush hour effect, whereby groups of employees would travel to and from work at different intervals.

Til isn't so sure. He says it's not commuters causing traffic congestion, it's so-called soccer moms taking their kids to sports practices, ballet lessons, and the mall. His position is backed by the Greater Washington Council of Governments, which indicates that only 25 percent of all daily trips in the region are for home-to-work purposes.[451]

Obviously, the solution will not come easy, and it is something that other large metropolitan areas are struggling with as well. Fortunately, the county has seen one answer to its transportation woes: the 2006 dedication of the first half of a two-span, twelve-lane bridge named for former president Woodrow Wilson. The bridge carries Interstate 95 and Interstate 495 (the Beltway) traffic across the Potomac River between Maryland and Virginia. The second span is scheduled for completion in late 2008.

The new bridge replaces another by the same name built in 1962. The old bridge was in disrepair and unable to handle the region's mounting private automobile and commercial truck traffic—two hundred thousand vehicles a day, far more than the seventy five thousand it was originally designed to accommodate. The Beltway's eight lanes of traffic had also created a massive bottleneck at the now-demolished six-lane bridge.

At the dedication ceremony for the first new span, Virginia governor Timothy Kaine greeted Maryland governor Robert Ehrlich Jr. in the middle of the $2.4 billion bridge to shake hands. The gesture signified the states' cooperative effort in building the structure and the unifying link it represented. While Kaine acknowledged the bridge would not bring an end to the region's traffic congestion, he stated that it would "make a difference."

The first vehicle to cross the new bridge was Woodrow Wilson's 1923 Rolls Royce Silver Ghost, on loan from the late president's family. The sight of the vintage automobile on the modern bascule bridge reminded the 1,400 people there how much the region had changed since the 1920s. And no place had changed more so than Fairfax County.

Clear Skies Ahead

Fairfax had become an economic powerhouse, the juggernaut of the Greater Washington area and the Commonwealth of Virginia. From 2001 to 2004, the county added 49,980 jobs to its service sector, more than any other county besides King County in Washington state.[452] With an inventory of 103 million square feet in 2005, the county represented the largest office market in the state and one of the biggest in the country. That year, Fairfax even outpaced the nation in economic growth and job creation, adding over twenty-two thousand jobs to its economy.

Another nine companies chose the county as their corporate headquarters in 2005. Not all were high technology firms; new businesses spawned from post-911 homeland security concerns pitched their tents, too. "A county that lies just outside the nation's capital is reaping the economic windfall of rapidly expanding defense contractors and research organizations," stated *Site Selection* magazine.[453] In 2005, the *Washington Business Journal* listed the fifty fastest-growing companies in the Greater Washington area. Twenty-six of them were based in Fairfax. "By any pos-

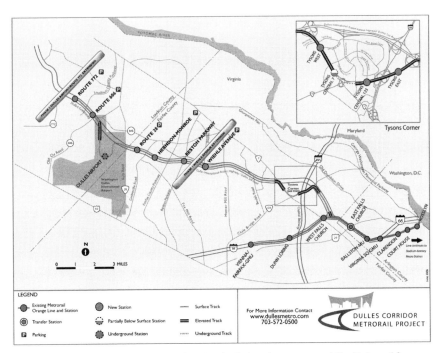

Phase I of the Dulles Corridor Metrorail Project includes plans to extend the Metrorail from the East Falls Church Metro Station through Tysons Corner and out to Wiehle Avenue in Reston.

sible measure, Fairfax is an economic success story," concluded Harvard University's Joint Center for Housing Studies.[454]

Fairfax County had truly become a global nexus of commerce and industry. By 2005, 332 foreign firms operated there, up from seventeen in 1979. A good number of them were lured by the Economic Development Authority, which now listed offices in London, Tokyo, Bangalore, Seoul, Frankfurt, and Tel Aviv. These international companies stimulated the economy further, generating over fourteen thousand new jobs.

The Clear Skies Agreement reached by the United States and the European Union in October 2005 promised the region more global business. The pact replaced the numerous bilateral agreements between the U.S. and many European countries, effectively making the European Union a single transatlantic air service entity. A study by George Mason University's School of Public Policy forecasted that the agreement would create more nonstop international flights from both Dulles and National airports to Europe, ultimately increasing high technology business along the Dulles Corridor.[455]

The federally mandated Base Realignment and Closure Act (BRAC) of 2005 promised another spike in employment, a positive sign for Fort Belvoir. Located in the southeastern corner of the county, the 8,656-acre Fort Belvoir was founded during the First World War as Camp A. A. Humphreys. It was renamed in the 1930s to honor William Fairfax's historic home, Belvoir Manor, which stood on the land before accidentally burning to the ground in 1783.

Today, the base is home to the U.S. Army Materiel Command and several U.S. Department of Defense agencies and Army reporting units. With the implementation of the BRAC Act, Fort Belvoir will soon comprise a variety of other military and intelligence-related enterprises, as well as medical care facilities currently located at Walter Reed Medical Center in Maryland. An estimated twenty-one thousand people—five thousand military personnel and sixteen thousand civilian employees—and their families are projected to move to the base by 2011, a doubling of the twenty-two thousand civilians and military personnel already employed there. "We expect an additional eighty thousand people in all at the base," says Gerald Connolly. "The many new agencies at the fort will attract private sector companies that do business with them, promising an economic boom in the Route 1 corridor, which will see much construction in the years ahead."[456]

The Quality of Life Report

By the twenty-first century, Fairfax County offered far more than just jobs. While the 1970s-era Blue Ribbon Committee had set out to boost commerce and industry to lessen the tax burden on residents, members like Til Hazel, Earle Williams, and Jerry Halpin further endeavored to make the county as desirable as it could be. Together, they put their efforts and estimable clout to work on behalf of education, health care, and transportation, and lobbied for a fairer share of the state's funding.

These private-sector led initiatives spawned an extraordinary quality of life in Fairfax County. Even with its increasingly diverse population, the county still had the highest median family and household income in the nation in 2004 at $88,133.[457] Fairfax also claimed one of the most educated populations in the U.S. More than 25 percent of its residents has earned a master's degree or better, and 57.4 percent have completed a bachelor's degree—the second and fourth highest figures in the country, respectively, for counties with more than 250,000 residents.[458]

With the lowest crime rate of any jurisdiction in the country containing more than one hundred thousand people, Fairfax also was one of the safest places in America. In 2006, its residents were less likely to be the victim of violence or a property crime than at any other time in the previous three decades. "People make assumptions because of our racial and ethnic diversification about our crime rate and schooling, and yet we fare among the best in both categories throughout the nation," says Connolly. "In 2006, we had the highest SAT scores in our history, and every single one of our high schools was ranked 'best' by *Newsweek*."

Higher education in Fairfax County had indeed come a long way. In the aftermath of the Second World War, residents had to travel south of the Rappahannock River or north to Washington, D.C., if they wanted to attend college. Today, George Mason University has an enrollment of thirty thousand students and is expected to reach forty thousand in the next ten years. Its School of Public Policy—which began as an institute in 1991—has grown to become one of the largest in the country. GMU even boasts two Nobel laureates on its faculty: James Buchanan, who won the award in 1986 for economics, and Vernon Smith, who was honored in the same category in 2002. Meanwhile, its basketball team made it to the Final Four in 2006, and its Center for the Arts, which recently hosted the Royal Philharmonic Orchestra, draws more than one hundred thousand patrons each year.

George Johnson's wife, Joanne, who used to cook dinner for the members of the 123 Club, is largely responsible for nurturing the arts center to maturity. "She was the guiding light," says A. George Cook III, distinguished fellow at the School of Public Policy. "She raised private money, and ran it in the beginning without pay and without staff."[459]

Fairfax County can also take pride in its local government, which was named among the best in America by *Governing* magazine in 2002. Standard & Poor's and other ratings agencies have given the county's government a AAA bond rating for its sound financial management and stringent debt service. And to its great benefit, the strident anti-growth mentality of 1970s-era Boards of Supervisors has given way to more collaborative, congenial relations with area businesspeople. "We've got a civic-minded private sector with a vision," says Connolly, "a smart electorate and an enlightened form of government."

As the seat of seemingly endless development since the end of the Second World War, Fairfax County could easily be a concrete jungle of roads, buildings, and parking lots. Yet the county is home to more parkland than many other jurisdictions its size. "We're pro-growth here, but our environmental record is strong," says Connolly. "We've got twenty-five thousand acres of parkland here, and that excludes state and federally-held land and the [land held by the] regional park authority. If you add it up, my guess is that 20 percent of the land mass in Fairfax is protected."

The Fairfax County Park Authority alone manages more than twenty-three thousand acres of parkland—approximately twenty-three acres of open space per one thousand residents. "When people look out across the county from the Tower Club, they are amazed at how green Fairfax is," says Lecos from the Chamber of Commerce. "Right now I'm in Mason District Park sitting under the trees, looking at an amphitheater and listening to the Army band and the cicadas. Only six miles away is the nation's capital." Lecos chuckles. "Where else can someone say that?"

A Few Good Men

The men who built Fairfax into America's County are now in their sixties, seventies, and eighties. All are still active and engaged in civic and charitable duties. Jerry Halpin goes to work every day at West*Group and stays well into the evening. It's not uncommon for him to be the only employee there, other than the cleaning crew. His company has been responsible for the development, redevelopment, and construction of more than twelve million square feet of office, retail, residential, and industrial space in the county. More is on the way, too, as older structures are torn down for tomorrow's denser environments.

One can be certain that under Jerry's watchful eye, ample room will be set aside for green spaces. A true lover of the land, he recently received a Lifetime Achievement Award from the Urban Land Institute. It's just one of many awards that this son of an elementary school custodian from Scranton, Pennsylvania, has received over the years.

Jerry and his wife, Helen, own considerable property in Wyoming, where they've built a beautiful ranch overlooking the Grand Teton Mountains. They travel to the ranch often, and Jerry can't help but ask almost everyone he meets to come visit. He is chairman of the Grand Teton National Park Foundation's board of directors, and a director of the National Fish and Wildlife Foundation. With Jerry at the helm, the Grand Teton National Park Foundation raised $12.6 million to fund the new Craig Thomas Discovery and Visitor Center at the park in Moose, Wyoming.

As George Hartzog, former director of the National Park Service, puts it, "He's a treasure to mankind."

Meanwhile, Milt Peterson is as hardworking as ever, putting the final touches on the Potomac River's massive National Harbor project. His firm, the Peterson Companies, owns more than two thousand acres of land spanning two dozen locations in eleven jurisdictions in Virginia and Maryland. This property is in various stages of planning, zoning, and development, and could ultimately provide more than six million square feet of office/industrial space, 4.5 million square feet of retail space, and seven thousand residential units.

Milt's company has won more than seventy awards for preservation, marketing, and design excellence, but he would rather talk about his charitable work. Milt, his wife, Carolyn, and their children are major benefactors of the Life with Cancer program at Inova Health Systems (formerly the Fairfax Hospital Association), which provides vital support and information about cancer to afflicted individuals and their families at no cost. Carolyn, a two-time cancer survivor, chaired Life with Cancer's first board of directors in 1988. Today, their daughter Lauren Peterson Fellows is a director on the board.

The family's unstinting support helped Life with Cancer open an $8.5 million, sixteen-thousand-square-foot Family Center in 2007. The facility houses outpatient programs and services, and is dedicated to providing a comfortable environment for cancer patients and their families. The Petersons donated a good portion of the money themselves; the rest came from friends like John and Nina Toups, and Sid and Reva Dewberry, who provided the land upon which the facility is built. The building is officially called the Dewberry Life with Cancer Family Center—but to all who have appreciated Carolyn's selfless work over the years it is "Carolyn's House." As Lauren Peterson Fellows said at the dedication ceremonies, "Friendship, loyalty, and a sense of giving back have made this center possible."

Boosted by the support of individuals like Milt, Til, and John, and the leadership of its longtime executive director, Knox Singleton, Inova Health Systems itself has matured into a major medical institution. Inova was the first hospital in Virginia and the Greater Washington region to perform a heart transplant, and it is now a major leader in organ transplant and donation. With Inova, the days of traveling to Arlington County or Washington for health care services are long gone.

Sid Dewberry continues to preside over his firm, Dewberry, each day. He takes special pride in his office's collection of historical and antique surveying equipment—some dating from the days of Virginia surveyor George Washington. For more than half a century, his firm has been a leader in the planning, design, and program management professions. It now boasts thirty-six offices across the country and a truckload of awards for architectural merit and construction excellence.

He also continues his involvement in civic duties. When George Johnson retired as the chairman of the 123 Club in 1997, the same year that he stepped down as president of GMU, Sid became the unelected chairman—a role that he remains in today. In addition, he is the founding member of the Engineers & Surveyors Institute and the key person behind GMU's civic engineering program. He has given generously of himself to higher education, too, chairing the "Campaign for George Mason University," the university's first-ever comprehensive initiative for private support. The campaign raised a remarkable $142 million in 2005. More recently, he served as rector of GMU's Board of Visitors.

Sid's ongoing fund-raising efforts for the university prompted the Association of Fundraising Professionals to give him its highest honor in 2007. In addition, he was named "Northern Virginian of the Year" by *New Dominion* magazine and was elected to the Washington Business Hall of Fame in 2007. But Sid considers his highest achievement to be the George Mason Medal, which is given to those whose character mirrors the author of the Virginia Declaration of Rights. "He's just an incredible man," says John Fowler, a member of Dewberry's board of directors.[460]

John Toups has spent a good deal of his retirement bettering education and health care in the county. He and his wife, Nina, provided both financial and fund-raising support to expand and renovate the laboratories at GMU's College of Nursing and Health Science, transforming them, as GMU officials stated, into "state-of-the-art showplaces." The new labs were named in their honor as the "Mr. and Mrs. John M. Toups Nursing Clinical Simulation Laboratories."

Dwight Schar has stepped down as CEO of NVR, although he is still chairman. He actively raises funds for education and for the Republican Party, of which he is a former finance chairman. The former school-teacher has not forgotten his alma mater either, donating sizable sums to Ashland University over the years. Ashland has since named its College of Education after the steadfast homebuilder. Today, the Dwight Schar College of Education is one of the largest schools of its kind in the country, offering teaching licenses to students interested in all levels of education, from pre-kindergarten to post-graduate posts.

Bill Hazel remained president and CEO of William A. Hazel, Inc., until 2008. His company has been engaged in all aspects of site development and road construction in Northern Virginia for nearly fifty years. Like his older brother, Til, Bill believes businesspeople have an obligation to give something back to their communities. He has been a member of many important organizations reshaping Fairfax County, from the Washington Airports Authority to the 123 Club. Bill's son, Dr. William A. Hazel Jr., followed in the footsteps of his grandfather Dr. John T. Hazel Sr., and became an orthopedic surgeon. In 2008, Bill received the George Mason University Gold Medal for his long efforts on behalf of the institution.

Earle Williams was awarded the prestigious James M. Rees Award by the Fairfax County Chamber of Commerce in 2005. The award is named for former chamber chairman Jim Rees, who died in a tragic plane crash in 1986. Earle was recognized for his contributions to the Blue Ribbon Committee—which gave wings to the area's economy—and his invaluable leadership of the Economic Development Authority at a pivotal time in the county's history. Receiving the award along with him was Jerry Halpin. "They are two of the most revered business leaders in Fairfax County," the chamber stated, "true pioneers in their respective industries who have made invaluable contributions to the economy and quality of life in Northern Virginia."

The following year, Til Hazel and George Johnson were honored with the Rees award. The chamber cited their unflagging zeal in building GMU's academic and research capabilities and reputation, and their efforts in forging the enduring bonds that exist between the university and the region's business community. "For more than three decades," stated the chamber, "George Mason University has been a valuable partner in the growth of Northern Virginia's powerhouse economy and world-class quality of life."

Under George's leadership, GMU blossomed from a moderately sized liberal arts college of ten thousand students into a nationally recognized institution with an enrollment of twenty-four thousand students and a reputation for innovation and excellence. "Johnson attracted prestigious faculty; developed an engineering school based on information technology; and opened the region's first performing arts center," the chamber stated. "He also helped start the Northern Virginia Roundtable, a group of corporate and civic leaders dedicated to the region's economic growth."

But no one had done more for GMU than Til Hazel. Til had served as rector of the Board of Visitors in the school's early years, and was the first recipient of the university's Mason Medal in 1987. He was a trustee of the George Mason University Foundation from its creation in 1966 until 1997, and its president from 1984 to 1988. Most importantly, he lobbied tirelessly for a school of law. In recognition of his efforts, the George Mason University School of Law Building was renamed John T. Hazel Jr. Hall in 2005. Til gave generously to GMU—but as university president Alan Merten says, his money "wasn't nearly as massive as his influence or his willingness to lead and fight."[461] In all likelihood, George Mason University would still be a commuter college were it not for George and Til.

These men all made money the hard way, tirelessly building businesses that prospered with the county. What sets them apart, however, is not their financial success. Each imagined a future for Fairfax County and endeavored to realize it, utilizing their talents to create a remarkable place bustling with entrepreneurial energy next to the capital of the world. "The amount they have done, thinking about what was needed in this community and then going out and doing it, was extraordinary," says Kathryn MacLane, executive vice president of West*Group. "We've all learned at the knees of Til, Milt, Jerry, Dwight, and the rest of them about the need to give back, how to fight for good causes, and how to ask for money."[462]

Developer Henry Long agrees: "It was a depth of love and concern that these people had for this region, and their willingness to work together that has made Fairfax County what it is today."[463]

From Good to Great

What is Fairfax County today? It's a region where thousands of people commute to work, earn excellent salaries, and live in nice homes on shady streets. Their children attend some of the finest public schools in the country, and their parents are cared for at superb medical facilities. They shop at Reston's Town Center and the mall in Tysons Corner. They congregate in the area's 391 parks, attend performances of the Fairfax Symphony Orchestra, and join the audience at Wolf Trap. They marvel at the holdings of the National Air and Space Museum, Steven F. Udvar-Hazy Center—the largest aviation museum in the world—and visit the county's historic attractions, from the celebrated courthouse built in 1800 in the old City of Fairfax to George Washington's home at Mount Vernon. On occasion they drive into Washington for monument gazing, the theatre, and five-star dining. What Fairfax *isn't* any longer is a bedroom community, much less a loose collection of dairy farms.

Few jurisdictions can compete with Fairfax County when it comes to employment in modern industries, a rich talent base, top quality public and private education, high levels of educational attainment, superior health care, high incomes, low tax rates, and other elements of the good life. Need a job? Fairfax is a spigot for federal defense, intelligence, and homeland security funds. Eighteen of the top twenty federal contractors are based in the county, as well as thirteen of the twenty largest technology employers in the Greater Washington area. There are more technology companies and workers in and around Fairfax than any other metropolitan area in the U.S. The county is also one of America's most wired— more than 80 percent of households have at least one computer with Internet access.

With over one hundred million square feet of office space and zoning for another forty-five million square feet, Fairfax represents one of the largest office markets in the country. Its population soared to almost 1.1 million people in 2007, doubling in size since 1970. That year, unemployment was just 1.9 percent.[464] Over the same period the number of jobs increased by five-and-one-half times.[465] Another two hundred thousand jobs are expected by 2020. "Northern Virginia is the crucible for tomorrow's world in terms of technological evolution," says Leo Schefer of the Washington Airports Task Force.[466]

The Washington Times reported on the county's growth patterns in 2007, citing a study by the U.S. Department of Labor. "Fairfax County, Va., has become the economic center of the Washington area, generating professional and business management jobs at a substantially higher rate than the rest of the region and the country," the paper stated. "[Fairfax] generates high-paying jobs for software designers, lawyers, accountants, architects, engineers, and other professionals at 2.57 times the rate of the rest of the United States [and] created nearly half the 230,000 such jobs that opened in the area between 1990 and 2005."[467] As Gerald L. Perrins, co-author of the study, said, "Fairfax is a magnet—nationwide and world-wide. This is the top rung. There is no other place to go."

Were it a city, Tysons Corner would be the sixteenth largest in the country today just based on office space density, while Reston-Herndon would be the nineteenth. Back in 1960, no one other than Jerry Halpin and Bob Simon could have imagined that a dusty intersection and farmland noted for its bourbon distillery could emerge as such. Now Reston comprises four lakes, fifty-five miles of walking paths, and a seventy-two-acre nature education sanctuary within 1,300 acres of permanent open space. More than four hundred species of wildflowers sprout in fifty-one naturalized meadows, and 184 varieties of birds, including bald eagles and ospreys, have been tallied. Deer, foxes, otters, beavers, bobcats, and coyotes have been spied in Reston's protected areas, and the community is one of only three in America to be certified as a Community Wildlife Habitat by the National Wildlife Federation. Reston could have simply stayed an unimpressive dairy farm with good local spirits, but Simon, Jim Todd, Chuck Veatch, and others had something more dignified in mind.

People born in Fairfax County no longer have to leave their homes and venture across the river to find their future. So robust is the county's employment that the number of new jobs in Fairfax will eventually exceed the supply of qualified workers to fill them, according to GMU's Fuller. By 2030, Fuller predicts that the county will add 829,000 jobs and 454,000 people.

Not only are employment opportunities right there for the taking, so is an exceptional quality of life. "If you want a funky, urban place near a Metro station to live, we'll have it," says Connolly. "If you want a detached home with a picket fence, garage, and dog, we've got several hundred thousand units. If you're a senior citizen and want to downsize but stay in the community where you raised your family and have friends, [you can have] that, too."

The county has challenges, certainly. The Board of Supervisors has identified seven geographic areas ripe for revitalization. For the most part, they are places that grew up in the aftermath of the Second World War on the county's eastern side closest to Washington, before more pedestrian friendly and livable mixed-use developments were born.

"They're 'strip-type' retail outlets in older buildings in places like Annandale and Seven Corners," says Gordon. "And the county and the Economic Development Authority are doing things to change it."

Traffic will remain a problem unless cars can fly someday, which is about as likely as the state building all the major highways that myopic anti-growth proponents quashed long ago. The extension of Metrorail into Fairfax and Loudoun counties will hopefully ease the congestion, as will the more recent decision by the Virginia Department of Transportation to create fifty-six miles of high-occupancy toll lanes on both Interstate 95 and Interstate 495. Until then, it is something that Fairfax residents, like citizens from most other metropolitan areas, will just have to deal with.

It's a small price to pay. Although Silicon Valley still claims the most technology jobs in the country—209,274 versus 132,337 in Fairfax—both regions are tied at first place (24.6 percent) in the percentage of total technology-oriented jobs. Meanwhile, Fairfax boasts higher median income, per capita income, and educational attainment than Santa Clara, Boston, and Seattle, and it has a lower unemployment rate to boot.[468] In terms of aesthetic appeal, Santa Clara County is an "archetypal slurb, a sprawling confusion," *Business Week* observed. "Growth came so fast . . . and with such disastrous results that the experience serves as a dire warning," *Newsweek* concluded.[469]

How did Fairfax turn out so differently? While many hardworking, visionary public servants like Carlton Massey, J Hamilton Lambert, Rosser Payne, and Jack Herrity assisted the county's economic growth and high living standards, it was the private sector that led the way. Individually and collectively as members of the Blue Ribbon Committee, the Roundtable, the 123 Club, the Washington Airports Task Force, and other civic-minded organizations, they battled slow-growth factions; mended fences; built businesses, airports, health care institutions, highways, homes, and schools; and never, ever gave up the cause.

It is amazing to compare the county's current brimming prosperity to the way things were before the Second World War. People have their theories on how the transformation came about. Kathryn MacLane attributes it to men and women who were "happy they made it back alive from the war, and moved to a region they thought had some upside. It was a wonderful crossroads of circumstances." Ed Carr has a similar perspective: "We were in the path of economic development."

Dwight Schar sees things differently. "A hundred years from now," he says, "people will look back and think, 'It was a lucky time: a gold rush in Fairfax.' But it really wasn't. It took a lot of hard work, collaboration, trust, and integrity. It took a group of guys pushing and moving this thing in the right direction, and always doing our best to keep things from derailing."[470]

Still Leading the Way

Til Hazel no longer practices law, although he is still involved with his children in real estate development. These days he is something of an elder statesman, the legendary lawyer and developer contacted frequently by the media for his views on such county concerns as education and transportation. He takes umbrage when the new generation of NIMBYs, no-growthers, and populist politicians blame traffic congestion on developers when it was their spiritual ancestors who caused the problem through lack of planning and political will. "The prosperity generated in Fairfax County and the Washington region is so robust that it is now taken for granted by the antis and their political supporters as though it was some God-given right or maybe a Constitutional right," Til says. "I have found no reference in either the Bible or the Constitution to prosperity such as we have enjoyed in Fairfax."

He is as honest, opinionated, and dynamic as ever, putting his unvarnished reputation behind the issues he has always supported. He recently fought plans by Dominion Virginia Power to stretch 500,000-volt power lines across the Virginia Piedmont, a stretch of pristine farmland known locally as the "hallowed ground." He has also stayed involved with his alma mater, serving on numerous Harvard committees and councils over the past fifty years. Til is happier, too, having married a wonderfully bright, articulate lady, Anne Barnett Merrill (now Hazel), whom he met on a Yale/Harvard-sponsored trip to China. Anne likes many of the same things her husband does, such as travel and current events, although she wishes his golf game were better. Til, of course, never had the time to hone this skill, preferring more important fields of conquest.

Their leisure time is spent at homes in North Carolina and Fauquier County, where Til and his brother, Bill, each own two thousand bucolic acres containing one of the largest cattle farms in Virginia. On this land is the splendid red brick Georgian Palladian mansion that Til and his late wife, Jinx, built in 1987. Til calls the home "Huntley Hall"—a nod to the eighteenth-century land descriptions that referred to the 750 acres he originally purchased as "Huntley." The driveway curls 1.3 miles, bending around a manmade pond and waterfowl habitat before arriving at the house, which rests on a hill. The first-floor library is paneled in walnut, much of it logged on the property, and in the kitchen squats a Vermont Castings Resolute wood stove. The dining room is big enough to host sixteen-plus people. A short drive from the house is a small lodge that the Hazel children frolicked in as youngsters, its dated furniture still bearing the scuffs of childhood and the memories of old family dogs.

The land recalls the history of a bygone era. A Civil War barn has been rebuilt and restored, as has a rough-hewn cabin, estimated to be the second-oldest structure in Fauquier County. Til hopes the land will be preserved in perpetuity, but he is, as always, a pragmatist. Ever since he baled hay as a boy, watching the Pimmit Hills subdivision burst from the ground, he has recognized that land is a resource for the people's purposeful use. As Fairfax and Loudoun counties brim with commerce and fill with people, the overflow must go somewhere.

Outside the lodge, his eyes scanning acres and acres of unspoiled woods and pastures, Til imagines a city the size of Tysons Corner or another Burke Center or two in its place. He smiles, buttons the top of his coat against the chill, and heads down the hill toward home.

Afterword

As this book neared printing a global economic crisis had reared, marked by a severe housing crunch, rising unemployment rates, and anemic business and consumer spending. While certainly affected by the economic crisis, Fairfax County miraculously escaped the worst and, in fact, has performed far better than other counties its size and scope. As Dr. Stephen Fuller, professor of public policy at George Mason University, puts it, "Fairfax has not only survived the downturn, it has grown through it."

Statistics back him up. National unemployment figures in March 2009 were 8.5 percent of the working population. Unemployment in the District of Columbia alone was 9.9 percent, and in the tech-haven Seattle metropolitan region it was 8.8 percent. Fairfax County—a paltry 4.1 percent by comparison. While the value of many homes has fallen on par with other parts of the country, government services have been reduced, and jobs certainly have been lost (the county's unemployment rate was 2.6 percent in April 2008), Fuller notes that, "The jobs being added in Fairfax are paying two-thirds more on average than the jobs lost. In effect, low wage jobs are being replaced by high wage jobs."

Business also remains brisk. While Gross Domestic Product nationally is expected to shrink 3.5 percent for the entirety of 2009, Fuller projects Fairfax's GDP will expand by 1.6 percent over the period and achieve a net gain of 4.5 percent in 2010. "The county has felt the downdraft on retail and construction, but it is adding businesses and professional services in a range of industries, thanks to current and expected federal spending going into the economy to mitigate the economic crisis," Fuller explains. "Fairfax is the epicenter for federal procurement dollars in the United States, with one-third of the money going to the Greater Washington Area spent in the county. In 2008, federal procurement spending in Fairfax actually increased by 17.7 percent from the year before—a total of $20.7 billion going the county's way. More federal money and higher paying jobs are in the offing."

Economics isn't the only factor continuing to make Fairfax a desirable place to live. *U.S. News and World Report* in 2008 recognized George Mason University as the number one "up and coming" college in the country, and Thomas Jefferson High School as the nation's number one high school. Regarding the housing crisis at the center of the storm, in Fairfax the inventory of unsold new homes is four and one-half months in March 2009, compared to a national average of one and one-half years. Sales of new homes in Fairfax were up 14 percent from February 2009 to March 2009. Says Fuller, "The housing sector is recovering in the county."

Not many other places in America could say the same thing.

Chapter
Endnotes

CHAPTER 1 NOTES:

[1] Interview with John Tilghman Hazel Jr.

[2] Marion Meany, Mary Lipsey, *Braddock's True Gold* (Fairfax, VA: County of Fairfax), 75.

[3] Interview with Edward Carr Jr.

[4] Fairfax County Chamber of Commerce.

[5] Interview with Edward Carr Jr.

[6] *The Washington Post*, February 15, 1953, R2.

[7] *National Geographic*, May 2007, 34.

[8] *Ibid*, 45.

[9] Nan Netherton, Donald Sweig, Janice Artemel, Patricia Hickin, and Patrick Reed, *Fairfax County, Virginia: A History* (Fairfax, VA: Fairfax County Board of Supervisors, 1992), 218–220

[10] *Ibid*, 32.

[11] *Ibid*, 64.

[12] Ross and Nan Netherton, *Fairfax County: A Contemporary Portrait* (The Donning Company, 1992), 15.

[13] *Ibid*, 17.

[14] U.S. Bureau of the Census, U.S. Census of Population, 1900.

[15] Fairfax County Board of Supervisors, *Industrial and Historical Sketch of Fairfax County, Virginia* (Fairfax, VA: County Board of Supervisors, 1907), 4, 6, 8–9.

[16] Ross and Nan Netherton, *Fairfax County*, 24.

[17] Grace Dawson, "No Little Plans: Fairfax County's PLUS Program for Managing Growth," 1976.

[18] *The Washington Post*, March 20, 1955, E1.

[19] First Report to the Arlington County Planning Commission, Arlington County, 1938.

[20] Robert A. Alden, "Omer Hirst Is Key Figure in Real Estate, Politics," *The Washington Post*, December 10, 1970, H5.

[21] Dawson, "No Little Plans," 14.

[22] Supreme Court of Virginia, *Board of County Supervisors of Fairfax County, Virginia v. G. Wallace Carper, et al.*, 200 Virginia, 653, S.E. 2nd, P. 390 (1959).

[23] Interview with John McClain, deputy director, George Mason University Center for Regional Analysis.

[24] Netherton, Sweig, et al, 639.

[25] Office of Management and Budget, 1940–2002, *Budget of the United States Government Historical Tables*.

[26] *The Washington Post*, November 22, 1953, M25.

[27] Interview with James Wilding.

[28] "What Fairfax County Offers," Fairfax County Board of Supervisors and Fairfax County Chamber of Commerce, 1956, 13.

[29] Netherton, Sweig, et al, 639.

[30] Interview with Rosser Payne.

[31] Interview with Ralph Louk.

[32] Interview with Harriet Bradley.

[33] Fairfax County Economic Development Authority, 1995 Annual Report.

[34] *The Washington Post*, November 22, 1953, M25.

[35] *The Washington Post*, May 21, 1955, 15.

[36] *Ibid.*

[37] *The Washington Post*, March 20, 1955, E1.

[38] *The Washington Post*, February 15, 1953, R2.

[39] Fairfax County Industrial Authority, Fairfax County Prospectus, vol. 3, September 1971.

[40] *The Washington Post*, March 20, 1955, E1.

[41] Netherton, Sweig, et al., 24.

[42] Lucille Harrigan, Alexander von Hoffman, "Happy to Grow: Development and Planning in Fairfax County, Virginia," Joint Center for Housing Studies, Harvard University, February 2002, 9.

[43] Joel Garreau, "Life on the New Frontier," *The Washington Post Magazine*, July 21, 1991, 26.

CHAPTER 2 NOTES:

[44] Interview with Gerald T. Halpin.

[45] Letter from Fairfax County Executive Carlton C. Massey to the Northern Virginia Center, June 27, 1957.

[46] Mark Frankel, "George Mason's Call to Revolution," *Regardie's*, February 1984, 75.

[47] Fairfax County Board of Supervisors, Fairfax County Chamber of Commerce, "What Fairfax County Offers," 1956.

[48] Interview with A. George Cook III.

[49] Interview with J. Knox Singleton.

[50] W.T. Woodson High School, "W.T. Woodson High School: 38 Years of History," http://www.fcps.edu/WTWoodsonHS/woodhistory.htm (last accessed on June 6, 2007).

[51] Nan Netherton, Donald Sweig, Janice Artemel, Patricia Hickin, and Patrick Reed, *Fairfax County, Virginia: A History* (Fairfax, VA: Fairfax County Board of Supervisors, 1992), 577.

[52] W.T. Woodson High School, http://www.fcps.edu/WTWoodsonHS/woodhistory.htm.

[53] Library of Virginia, "What Was *Brown v. Board of Education*," http://www.lva.lib.va.us/whoweare/exhibits/brown/whatwas.htm (last accessed on June 6, 2007).

[54] *Crabgrass Frontier: The Suburbanization of the United States*, Kenneth T. Jackson, ISBN 0195036107

[55] Fairfax County Board of Supervisors, "An Industrial and Historical Sketch of Fairfax County," 1907.

[56] Alexander Potter Associates, "Fairfax County, Virginia Comprehensive Water Supply Plan, Preliminary Report," March 16, 1955.

[57] Interview with Fred Griffith.

[58] Fairfax Water, "Fairfax Water Loses Its Founding Father," www.fairfaxwater.org/corbalis_obit.htm (last accessed on June 6, 2006).

[59] *The Washington Post*, December 10, 1981, 2.

[60] Times Community Newspapers, January 19, 2000, 6.

61 Sidney Dewberry, *The Dewberry Way* (Fairfax, VA: Spectrum Publishing Group, 2006), 4.

62 Ibid, 97.

63 Interview with Rosser Payne.

64 *The Washington Post*, April 22, 1956.

65 Fairfax County Board of Supervisors and Fairfax County Chamber of Commerce, "What Fairfax County Offers," 1956.

66 *The Washington Post*, September 7, 1956, 23.

67 Federation of American Scientists, Director National Intelligence http://www.fas.org/sgp/news/2007/10/dni103007.pdf

68 Minutes from the Fairfax County Board of Supervisors meeting, October 10, 1956.

69 "What Fairfax County Offers," 14.

70 Interview with William B. Wrench.

71 *The Washington Post*, July 2, 1960, D1.

72 *The Dun & Bradstreet Reference Book*, November 1956.

73 Interview with William B. Wrench.

74 Netherton, Sweig, et al, 643.

75 Margaret C. Peck, *Images of America: Washington Dulles International Airport* (Charleston, SC: Arcadia Publishing, 2005), 8.

76 Interview with James Wilding.

77 *The Washington Post*, November 22, 1959, E4.

78 *The Washington Post*, January 1, 1960, A17.

79 Supreme Court of Virginia, *Board of County Supervisors of Fairfax County, Virginia v. G. Wallace Carper, et al.*, 200 Virginia, 653, S.E. 2nd, P. 390.

80 *Ibid.*

81 Census, http://www.census.gov/prod/2002pubs/censr-4.pdf, p. 33

82 Census via University of Wisconsin-Milwaukee, http://www.uwm.edu/Dept/CED/publications/milwecon/chap1.html

83 *The Washington Post*, February 20, 1977, 21.

84 *The Washington Post*, January 27, 1962, C1.

85 Fairfax County Economic Development Authority newsletter, vol. 4, no. 1, January 1973.

86 *The Washington Post*, July 13, 1980, K1.

87 R.G. Seeley, *History of Maplewood Farm* (Fairfax County, VA: R.G. Seeley, 1950).

88 Diane N. Rafuse, *Maplewood* (Fairfax County, VA: May 1970), 36.

89 Seeley, *History of Maplewood Farm.*

90 Interview with Charles Ewing.

91 *Industrial Development*, August 1965, 22.

92 *The Washington Post*, October 13, 1961, C2.

93 Rafuse, 41.

CHAPTER 3 NOTES:

94 Interview with John T. Hazel.

95 Interview with William Wrench.

96 *The Washington Post*, December 24, 1969, B1.

97 Interview with James H. Dillars.

98 Interview with Audrey Moore.

99 Interview with Joseph Alexander.

100 Interview with Harriet Bradley.

101 Interview with Rosser Payne.

102 Zoning Procedures Study Committee, "Planning and Zoning for Fairfax County, Virginia," September 1967.

103 John T. Hazel, "Growth Management Through Litigation," *Urban Land*, November 1976, 8.

104 *The Washington Post*, December 18, 1967, B6.

105 Interview with William A. Hazel.

106 Interview with Robert E. Simon.

107 *The Washington Post*, August 16, 1999, A1.

108 Grace Dawson, "No Little Plans: Fairfax County's PLUS Program for Managing Growth," 23.

109 *The Washington Post*, August 16, 1999, A1.

110 Interview with Charles A. Veatch.

111 http://www.census.gov/const/soldann.pdf

112 Interview with Jim Todd.

113 *Ibid*, 10.

114 "The Socio-Economic Impact of the Capital Beltway on Northern Virginia," Charlottesville, Virginia, 1969, 35.

115 Margaret C. Peck, *Images of America: Washington Dulles International Airport* (Charleston, SC: Arcadia Publishing, 2005).

116 JFK Library http://www.jfklibrary.org/NR/exeres/140FB99E-2B4E-4A76-A384-A9BC041D234D.htm

117 Interview with Leo Schefer.

118 *The Washington Post*, November 27, 1962, B23.

119 Peck, *Images of America*, 32.

120 Interview with Jim Wilding.

121 Interview with Lee Ruck.

122 *The Washington Post*, March 20, 1955, E1.

123 Interview with Millard Robbins.

124 *The Washington Post*, February 28, 1964, B1.

125 Interview with William Wrench.

126 Interview with Abe Pollin.

127 *The Washington Post*, April 9, 1970, A13.

128 William Nye Curry, "Mason Neck, Virginia" (draft article), May 1971, 4.

129 Archives of Noman M. Cole Jr., "A River Revived," 9.

130 Interview with Sidney O. Dewberry.

131 Interview with Jimmie Jenkins.

132 Noman M. Cole Jr., "A River Revived," *The Washington Post Magazine*, May 18, 1980.

133 Hazel, "Growth Management Through Litigation," 9.

134 *Ibid*, 8.

135 "Til Hazel," *PowerLine*, Spring 1987, 6.

136 Interview with Gordon Smith.

137 *The Washington Post*, March 30, 1970, C1.

138 *The Washington Post*, July 31, 1970, C1.

139 Senate Congressional Record, July 30, 1970 (S12445).

140 Census, www.bellevuewa.gov/pdf/PCD/census_VOL2_6.pdf

141 Hazel, "Growth Management Through Litigation," 8.

142 http://www.opm.gov/feddata/html/ExecBranch.asp

143 National Capital Regional Planning Council, "The Regional Development Guide 1966–2000," June 30, 1966, 61.

144 Lucille Harrigan and Alexander von Hoffman, "Happy to Grow: Development and Planning in Fairfax County, Virginia," Joint Center for Housing Studies, Harvard University, February 2004, 12.

145 Interview with Doug Fahl.

146 Interview with Dave Edwards.

147 Interview with Bob Chase.

148 The Harvard Crimson, http://www.thecrimson.com/article.aspx?ref=494054

149 Interview with A. George Cook III.

150 *George Mason*, Fall 1987, 8.

151 Interview with John W. Ryan.

152 Wikipedia/white flight

153 Interview with John Tydings.

154 Interview with Theodore N. Lerner.

155 *Fairfax Prospectus*, vol. 1, no. 2, June 1970.

156 *Ibid*.

157 *Fairfax Prospectus*, vol. 2, no. 3, September 1971.

158 *The Washington Post*, October 2, 1988, A16.

CHAPTER 4 NOTES:

159 Interview with Stan Harrison.

160 Interview with Earle Williams.

161 *The Washington Post*, March 31, 1981, B4.

162 *The Washington Star*, Mar 30, 1981

163 Nan Netherton, Donald Sweig, Janice Artemel, Patricia Hickin, and Patrick Reed, *Fairfax County, Virginia: A History* (Fairfax, VA: Fairfax County Board of Supervisors, 1992), 649.

164 John T. Hazel, "Growth Management Through Litigation," *Urban Land*, November 1976, 9.

165 *The Washington Post*, October 18, 1987, 59.

166 Grace Dawson, "No Little Plans: Fairfax County's PLUS Program for Managing Growth," 30.

167 Interview with Grayson Hanes.

168 E-mail from Jean Packard, August 13, 2006.

169 Interview with Jean Packard.

170 Interview with Joseph Alexander.

171 Interview with J. Hamilton Lambert.

172 Interview with Bob Chase.

173 Interview with Doug Fahl.

174 Interview with Shiva Pant.

175 *The Washington Post*, January 14, 1973, A1.

176 http://209.85.207.104/search?q=cache:UNZlPi9CbakJ:web.dcp.ufl.edu/ebartley/urp6131/Assignments/Petaluma.pdf+san+francisco+%2B+1972+development+limit+500+permits&hl=en&ct=clnk&cd=3&gl=us

177 E-mail from Jean Packard, 2006.

178 Interview with Rosser Payne.

179 *Board of Supervisors of Fairfax County v. Allman*, 215 Va. 434, 211 S.E.2d 48 (1975), Supreme Court of Virginia.

180 Hazel, "Growth Management Through Litigation," 9

181 *Planning* magazine, April 1990

182 Interview with Jean Packard.

183 Interview with Gordon Smith.

184 Interview with John T. Hazel.

185 Interview with Dave Edwards.

186 E-mail from Jean Packard, 2006.

187 Interview with Fred Griffith.

188 *The Washington Post Magazine*, July 21, 1991, 28.

189 Netherton, Sweig, et al, *Fairfax County, Virginia: A History*, 650.

190 Grace Dawson, "No Little Plans: Fairfax County's PLUS Program for Managing Growth," 28.

191 *The Washington Post*, August 9, 1972, C1.

192 *Ibid.*

193 *Ibid.*

194 *Ibid.*

195 Dawson, "No Little Plans," 28.

196 *Ibid*, 30.

197 *The Washington Post*, November 2, 1978, VA1.

198 *The Washington Post*, May 30, 1973, D1.

199 "Proposal for Implementing an Improved Planning and Land Use Control System," Task Force on Comprehensive Planning and Land Use Control (Final Report), Fairfax County Board of Supervisors, May 1972, 1.

200 *Ibid*, 4.

201 *The Washington Post*, June 9, 1972.

202 E-mail from Audrey Moore, December 13, 2006, 1.

203 Fairfax County Board of Supervisors, "Proposal," 5.

204 *Golden v. Ramapo*, Supreme Court of New York, 1972.

205 *Board of Supervisors v. Horne*, 216 Va. 113, 215 S.E.2d 453 (1975), Supreme Court of Virginia, 2.

206 Interview with Rosser Payne.

207 Dawson, "No Little Plans," 61.

208 Interview with William Berry.

209 Interview with William A. Hazel.

210 Interview with Chuck Ewing.

211 Interview with Alice Starr.

212 Interview with Jean Packard.

213 "Santa Clara Valley's Appointment with Destiny," Leonard Downie, Jr., *The APF Reporter*

214 Fairfax County Office of Comprehensive Planning, 1975 Countywide Plan.

215 *The Washington Post*, January 4, 1974, G1.

CHAPTER 5 NOTES:

216 Interview with Earle Williams.

217 *The Washington Post*, October 18, 1987, 59.

218 Interview with Shiva Pant.

219 Interview with Charles Veatch.

220 Interview with Jim Wordsworth.

221 County of Fairfax, "Committee to Study the Means of Encouraging Industrial Development in Fairfax County, Final Report," 1976.

222 *Scientific American*, September 1980, 2.

223 http://query.nytimes.com/gst/fullpage.html?res=9C0DE4DC123EF935A15752C1A9609C8B63&sec=&spon=&pagewanted=2

224 Interview with J. Hamilton Lambert.

225 Interview with Earle Williams.

226 Interview with Dave Edwards.

227 Interview with Jim Todd.

228 Interview with John Tydings.

229 *The Washington Post*, October 18, 1987, 59.

230 http://seattletimes.nwsource.com/special/centennial/november/lights_out.html

231 "Fairfax Prospectus, Fairfax County Economic Development Authority," vol. 8, no. 5, November 1977, 1.

232 "Fairfax Prospectus, Fairfax County Economic Development Authority," fourth quarter 1996, 1.

233 "Final Report of the New Millennium Occoquan Watershed Task Force," January 27, 2003, 5.

234 Interview with Millard Robbins.

235 Interview with A. Linwood Holton Jr.

236 Noman M. Cole Jr., "Chronology of Major Events Associated with the Development of the State Water Control Board's Occoquan Policy and Development of the Upper Occoquan Sewage Authority Project," February 1, 1979, 42.

237 Interview with Milton Peterson.

238 *The Washington Post*, April 8, 1976, 167.

239 *Ibid.*

240 *The Washington Post*, November 8, 1979, VA1.

241 *The Washington Post*, May 28, 1988, E1.

242 Interview with Otis D. Coston.

243 http://www.fostercity.org/, Foster City Historical Society http://books.google.com/books?id=NerPoI0sWjIC&pg=PA35&lpg=PA35&dq=%22foster+city%22+first+residents&source=web&ots=13Wu83UWBH&sig=B6U3cHPn89qMAQOFhAJ3acNyNoY#PPA8,M1

244 Virginia Power, *PowerLine*, Spring 1987, 6.

245 *The Washington Post*, February 20, 1977, 21.

246 *The Washington Post*, June 26, 1976, F35.

247 *The Washington Post*, February 20, 1977, 21.

248 Interview with Dwight Schar.

249 http://www.washingtonpost.com/wp-dyn/content/article/2008/02/09/AR2008020900157.html

250 Nan and Ross Netherton, *Fairfax County: A Contemporary Portrait* (The Donning Company: 1992), 50.

251 Interview with Frederick Lee Ruck.

252 Mark Frankel, "George Mason's Call to Revolution," *Regardie's*, February 1984, 76.

253 Interview with George Johnson.

254 Frankel, 79.

255 *Ibid*, 74.

256 *Ibid*, 76.

257 *The Washington Post*, November 11, 1985, A1.

258 *Ibid*.

259 Interview with Milton Drewer.

260 Frankel, 76.

261 Interview with Harriet "Happy" Bradley.

262 Interview with L. B. "Bud" Doggett.

263 Interview with Alice Starr.

CHAPTER 6 NOTES:

264 Interview with Earle Williams.

265 Interview with John T. Hazel.

266 Interview with George Johnson.

267 Interview with Dwight Schar.

268 *Virginia Business*, September 1994, 65.

269 *Virginia Business*, January 1990, 46.

270 Ross and Nan Netherton, "Fairfax County: A Contemporary Portrait," 42.

271 Interview with Chuck Robb.

272 Fairfax County Economic Development Authority, "Fairfax Prospectus," vol. 15, no. 3, July 1984, 1.

273 Joel Garreau, "Edge City: Life on the New Frontier," *The Washington Post Magazine*, July 31, 1991, 30.

274 http://www.fairfaxcounty.gov/ service/pdf/DemoTrends2004.pdf

275 http://www.britannica.com/bps/ topic/544409/Silicon-Valley#tab= active~checked%2Citems~checked% 3E%2Fbps%2Ftopic%2F544409%2 FSiliconValley&title=Silicon%20

Valley%20--%20Britannica%20 Online%20Encyclopedia

276 Interview with Stan Harrison.

277 *Virginia Business*, January 1990, 40.

278 Interview with Leo Schefer.

279 Interview with Chuck Robb.

280 *Richmond-Times Dispatch*, January 18, 1987, B1.

281 Interview with Stan Harrison.

282 Washington Airports Task Force, "All Aboard! The Case for Rail in the Dulles Corridor," December 1993, 3.

283 Interview with Sid Steele.

284 *The Washington Post*, December 2, 1982, B1.

285 *The Washington Post*, April 16, 1983, E14.

286 *The Washington Post*, March 20, 1979, A3.

287 Interview with Sidney O. Dewberry.

288 *The Washington Post*, February 21, 1985, 11.

289 Lucille Harrigan and Alexander von Hoffman, "Happy to Grow: Development and Planning in Fairfax County, Virginia," Joint Center for Housing Studies, Harvard University, February 2004.

290 http://www.ccis-ucsd.org/ publications/wrkg17.PDF

291 *Virginia Business*, January 1990, 40.

292 Fairfax Economic Development Authority, Directory of Business and Industry, 1988.

293 *Regardie's*, February 1984, 76.

294 Interview with April Young.

295 http://www.ncpc.gov/UserFiles/File/ PDF_files/FedProcurement.pdf

296 Interview with George Johnson.

297 *The Washington Post*, September 13, 1981, A1.

298 *The Washington Post*, October 17, 1981

299 *The Washington Post*, September 15, 1981, A1.

300 *The Washington Post*, September 19, 1981, A1.

301 Interview with Milton V. Peterson.

302 Interview with Philip Yates.

303 Interview with Otis Coston.

304 Interview with Milton V. Peterson.

305 *The Washington Post*, October 25, 1978, A1.

306 Virginia Power, *PowerLine* magazine, Spring 1987, 3.

307 *The Washington Post*, February 14, 1988, B1.

308 Noman M. Cole Jr., "Fun and Games with Sewers in Fairfax County" (unpublished), October 19, 1983, 9.

309 Fairfax County Chamber of Commerce, "Mission and History," 2.

310 "Northern Virginia Major Thoroughfare Plan," vol. 1, 1969.

311 *The Washington Post*, August 4, 1986, C1.

312 *Ibid.*

313 *Ibid.*

314 *Richmond-Times Dispatch*, January 18, 1987, B1.

315 *Ibid.*

316 Interview with James T. Lewis.

317 *Virginia Business*, January 1990, 34.

318 Interview with Henry Long.

319 *The Washington Post*, October 18, 1987, 59.

320 Interview with Henry Long.

321 *First National News*, September 1986, vol. 2, no. 9, 5.

322 *Dolan's Virginia Business Observer*, November 8, 1999, 13.

323 Interview with L. B. "Bud" Doggett.

324 The *Vienna/Oakton Connection*, October 11, 1995, vol. 9, no. 41, 4.

325 Interview with Hank Hulme.

326 Interview with Sidney O. Dewberry.

327 *Virginia Business*, September 1994, 66.

328 *The Washington Post*, April 3, 1989, B1.

329 *Virginia Business*, January 1990, 38.

330 Joel Garreau, *The Washington Post Magazine*, July 21, 1991, 12.

331 *Virginia Business*, September 1994, 59.

332 Interview with William A. Hazel.

333 Joel Kotkin, "The Future Is Here," *Inc.*, June 6, 1989.

334 *The Washington Post*, May 3, 1987, A15.

335 Joel Kotkin, "The Future Is Here."

336 Interview with Dave Edwards.

337 Fairfax County Economic Development Authority, 1993 Annual Report, 5.

338 Carol J. Loomis, "Victims of the Real Estate Crash," *Fortune*, May 18, 1992.

339 *Ibid.*

CHAPTER 7 NOTES:

340 Interview with Dwight Schar.

341 Interview with Otis "Skip" Coston.

342 Interview with Milton Drewer.

343 Interview with Edward Rutledge Carr.

344 Interview with James Lewis.

345 Interview with Russell Rosenberger.

346 Sidney O. Dewberry and Kathi Ann Brown, *The Dewberry Way* (Fairfax, VA: Spectrum Publishing Group, 2006), 59.

347 Interview with John Ulfelder.

348 *Virginia Business*, September 1994, 59.

349 Interview with Gerald Halpin.

350 Interview with John T. Hazel.

351 *The Washington Post*, April 22, 2007, A1.

352 *www.Washington.Bizjournals.com*, April 19–25, 27.

353 Interview with Milton V. Peterson.

354 *Virginia Business*, September 1994, 59.

355 Interview with Sidney O. Dewberry.

356 *Ibid.*

357 *The Washington Post*, May 11, 1989, PVA1.

358 *The Washington Post*, March 25, 1989, B1.

359 Fairfax Prospectus, Fairfax County Economic Development Authority, fourth quarter 1996, 1.

360 Interview with Gerald Halpin.

361 Fairfax County Economic Development Authority, 1995 Annual Report, 5.

362 Washington Airports Task Force, "All Aboard! The Case for Rail in the Dulles Corridor," 8.

363 Interview with Bobbie Kilberg.

364 "The Internet Capital," *Los Angeles Times,* April 20, 1998, B5.

365 *Time*, August 14, 2000, vol. 156, no. 7.

366 Interview with April Young.

367 *Dolan's Virginia Business Observer*, November 8, 1999, 12.

368 www.washingtontechnology.com, June 12, 1997.

369 The California Higher Education Policy Center, vol. 5, no. 2, Spring 1997.

370 *Ibid.*

371 Interview with April Young.

372 Interview with Robert G. Templin.

373 Interview with Earle Williams.

374 Interview with John Toups.

375 Fairfax County Economic Development Authority, Fairfax Prospectus, fourth quarter 1996, 4.

376 www.washingtontechnology.com, March 21, 1996.

377 Interview with Charles S. Robb.

378 *Ibid.*

379 *Ibid.*

380 *Ibid.*

381 The California Higher Education Policy Center, vol. 5, no. 2, Spring 1997.

382 *Ibid.*

383 *Ibid.*

384 *The Washington Post*, February 3, 1990, B1.

385 *Ibid.*

386 Interview with Kathryn A. Maclane.

387 Interview with Alan G. Merten.

388 Interview with Jim Todd.

389 "High-Tech Hub," *the Dallas Morning News*, June 13, 1999, H1.

390 *The Washington Post*, July 17, 2005, CO1.

391 *The Washington Post*, March 4, 2004, EO1.

392 Interview with Gerald Halpin.

393 Interview with Alice Starr.

394 *The Washington Post*, March 23, 1997, AO1.

395 *Ibid.*

396 Greater Washington Board of Trade, Transportation Study 1997, Executive Summary, 1.

397 *Ibid.*

398 Washington Airports Task Force, "The Case for a New Potomac River Crossing and Parkway between Montgomery County and Northern Virginia in the Vicinity of the Washington Dulles International Airport," January 2000, 6.

399 Washington Airports Task Force, "A Proposal for an Innovative, Multimodal, Phase Transit System for Northern Virginia's Dulles Transportation Corridor," January 1998, 1.

400 Interview with Bob Chase.

401 Fairfax County Economic Development Authority, 2000 Annual Report, 13.

402 *Time*, August 14, 2000.

403 "The Internet Capital," *Los Angeles Times*, April 20, 1998, B5.

404 "High-Tech Hub," *Dallas Morning News*, June 13, 1999, H1.

405 "High-Tech Hub," *Dallas Morning News*.

406 http://staff.haas.berkeley.edu/kroll/Colliers%20BlkWht.pdf

407 Fairfax County Economic Development Authority, 2000 Annual Report, 4.

408 *Time*, August 14, 2000.

CHAPTER 8 NOTES:

409 Joel Garreau, *Edge City: Life on the New Frontier* (Anchor Books), 351.

410 Dr. Stephen Fuller, "The Evolution and Future Structure of the Fairfax County Economy," George Mason University, 2.

411 Interview with Sidney O. Dewberry.

412 Dr. Stephen Fuller, George Mason Center for Regional Analysis, George Mason University.

413 http://staff.haas.berkeley.edu/kroll/Colliers%20BlkWht.pdf

414 Fuller, "The Evolution," 2.

415 "Tech Funding Boosts Virginia," *Mercury News*, June 11, 2003, A1.

416 *Ibid.*

417 Fuller, George Mason Center.

418 Fuller, "The Evolution," 3.

419 "Tech Funding," A1.

420 Fairfax County Economic Development Authority, press release, January 20, 2003 (quoting U.S. Bureau of Labor Statistics).

421 *The Washington Post*, March 16, 2001, BO1.

422 Fairfax County Department of Systems Management for Human Services, "Anticipating the Future: A Discussion of Trends in Fairfax County," 15.

423 *The Washington Post*, March 16, BO1.

424 Lucille Harrigan, Alexander von Hoffman, "Happy to Grow: Development and Planning in Fairfax County, Virginia," Joint Center for Housing Studies, Harvard University, February 2004.

425 Interview with Dr. Gerald Gordon.

426 *Ibid*, 53.

427 *Ibid*, 16.

428 Interview with Alan Merten.

429 Interview with Robert G. Templin.

430 Interview with John W. Ryan.

431 Interview with Charles "Chuck" Robb.

432 Interview with Gerald Halpin.

433 Interview with William D. Lecos.

434 NPR, December 11, 2008, www.npr.org/templates/story/story.php?stpruOd+9801149

435 Interview with Chuck Ewing.

436 Interview with Rosser Payne.

437 Interview with Gerald Connolly.

438 Fairfax County Department of Systems, "Anticipating the Future," 3.

439 Fairfax County Department of Systems, "Anticipating the Future," 7.

440 *Ibid.*

441 *Ibid*, 9.

442 Fairfax County Chamber of Commerce, "Doing Business," December 2005, 3.

443 *The Washington Post*, December 12, 2004, CO8.

444 Interview with Theodore N. "Ted" Lerner.

445 Interview with Robert Templin.

446 Interview with Russell Rosenberger.

447 *Ibid.*

448 Northern Virginia Transportation Alliance, NVTA Alliance Report, September 2005.

449 *Ibid.*

450 Interview with Gerald Gordon.

451 Transportation Alliance, Alliance Report, October 2005.

452 GMU Center for Regional Analysis, George Mason University, "Fairfax County Peer Count Analysis," August 2005, 1.

453 Fairfax County Economic Development Authority, "Fairfax Prospectus," third quarter 2005, 1.

454 Harrigan and von Hoffman, "Happy to Grow," 3.

455 Kenneth Button and Jonathan Drexler, "The Implications of Economic Performance in Europe of Further Liberalization of the Transatlantic Air Market," School of Public Policy, George Mason University, September 2005.

456 Interview with Gerald Connolly.

457 American Community Survey, U.S. Census Bureau.

458 *Ibid.*

459 Interview with A. George Cook III.

460 Sidney O. Dewberry and Kathi Ann Brown, *The Dewberry Way* (Fairfax, VA: Spectrum Publishing Group, 2006), 97.

461 Interview with Alan Merten.

462 Interview with Kathryn A. Maclane.

463 Interview with Henry Long.

464 *Time*, February 19, 2007, 48.

465 U.S. Census Bureau.

466 Interview with Leo Schefer.

467 *The Washington Times*, January 30, 2007, AO1.

468 Fairfax County Economic Development Authority, 2008 comparative facts and figures.

469 "Santa Clara Valley's Appointment with Destiny," Leonard Downie, Jr., The APF Reporter, October 1971.

470 Interview with Dwight Schar.

List of Illustrations
Sources and Credits

Page x. U.S. Highway 1 Intersection with Gum Springs Road, 1930. Library of Congress.

Page 2. John Tilghman "Til" Hazel Jr. on tractor. Courtesy of Til Hazel.

Page 4. Harrowing a cornfield on a dairy farm in Fairfax County, c. 1940. Library of Congress.

Page 5. Aerial view of Pimmit Hills subdivision. Star Collection, D.C. Public Library; © Washington Post.

Page 9. A painting of Thomas, Sixth Lord Fairfax by Sir Joshua Reynolds. Library of Congress.

Page 10. Mount Vernon. Mount Vernon Ladies Association.

Page 16. Original airport proposal site map, Burke, Virginia. *Washington Star,* June 14, 1951, reprinted by permission of the D.C. Public Library, © Washington Post

Page 18. Fairfax County Executive Carlton Massey raising a flag during the 1959

Fairfax Hospital construction ceremonies. Photo by Wilkins. Star Collection, D.C. Public Library; © Washington Post.

Page 20. Seven Corners Shopping Center. Photo by Paul Schmick. Star Collection, D.C. Public Library; © Washington Post.

Page 21. Rosser Payne. Courtesy of Rosser Payne.

Page 26. Traffic on Capital Beltway (Route I-495), 1970. Photo by Bernie Boston. Photographic Archive, Fairfax County Public Library.

Page 35. Opening of the Capital Beltway in 1964. Star Collection, D.C. Public Library; © Washington Post.

Page 40. Aerial view of Shirley Highway (Route I-395) with the Pentagon in the background, 1970. Photo by Bernie Boston. Star Collection, D.C. Public Library; © Washington Post.

Page 42. Laying the cornerstone for the Central Intelligence Agency headquarters in Langley, Virginia, 1959. C.I.A., Langley.

Page 51. Tysons Corner looking south on Chain Bridge Road, c. 1935. Photo by Samuel R. Pearson. Photographic Archive, Fairfax County Public Library.

Page 56. Fairfax County residential subdivision. Star Collection, D.C. Public Library; © Washington Post.

Page 65. Early rendering for Reston, Virginia. Reston Collection, Special Collections & Archives, George Mason University Libraries.

Page 66. Statue of Robert E. Simon Jr. in Reston, Virginia. Photo by Gregory F. Maxwell.

Page 77. Fairfax County Board of Supervisors, Fairfax County Government, 1977. Star Collection, D.C. Public Library; © Washington Post.

Page 78. Fairfax County Board of Supervisors, Harriet F. Bradley speaking, 1968. Star Collection, D.C. Public Library; © Washington Post.

Page 80, 81. A 1965 Major Streets and Highways Plan. Fairfax County Virginia Planning Office.

Page 83. Northern Virginia Regional Plan for transit lines and residential development. Northern Virginia Transportation Alliance.

Page 84. Year 2000 Plan map of projects deleted to control growth. Northern Virginia Transportation Alliance.

Page 85. Vintage Northern Virginia Regional Plan, Year 2000. Northern Virginia Transportation Alliance.

Page 89. Corridors, Clusters, and Open Space Map. Northern Virginia Regional Planning District Commission. Star Collection, D.C. Public Library; © Washington Post.

Page 104. Rufus Phillips chairs a meeting of the Comprehensive Planning and Land Use Control Task Force, Fairfax County Board of Supervisors, 1973. Office of the County Executive, Fairfax County, Virginia.

Page 108. Annie Lauler, Til Hazel, and Mary Howard. Courtesy of Til Hazel. Photo by Mattox Commercial Photography.

Page 119. Protesters at a Fairfax County Supervisory Board meeting, 1974. Star Collection, D.C. Public Library; © Washington Post.

Page 127. Tysons Corner, 1955. Photographic Archive, Fairfax County Public Library.

Page 128. Old Fairfax County map, c. 1742. Library of Congress.

Page 129. Dirt road alongside a dairy farm in Fairfax County, c. 1940. Library of Congress.

Page 130. Centreville, VA, streetscape, c. 1904. Photographic Archive, Fairfax County Public Library.

Page 130. Maplewood. Jerry Ellison photographer. Library of Congress.

Page 131. Aerial, Fairfax County. Photographic Archive, Fairfax County Public Library.

Page 132. Muddy road conditions. Photo by Auto Manufacturers Association. Photographic Archive, Fairfax County Public Library.

Page 132. Erecting a telephone pole, 1950. Photographic Archive, Fairfax County Public Library.

Page 133. Fairfax Car Wash, 1956. Photographic Archive, Fairfax County Public Library.

Page 133. Shirley Highway paving, 1948. Photographic Archive, Fairfax County Public Library.

Page 134. Sully Plantation, 1972. Photo by Robert Lautman. Metropolitan Washington Airports Authority.

Page 134. Inset: Terminal and tower at Washington Dulles International Airport, 1960. Metropolitan Washington Airports Authority.

Page 135. President John F. Kennedy and former President Dwight D. Eisenhower at the opening of Washington Dulles International Airport. Metropolitan Washington Airports Authority.

Page 135. Interior, Washington Dulles International Airport, 1960s. Metropolitan Washington Airports Authority.

Page 136. Architectural rendering of George Mason College of the University of Virginia, Stage I construction. George Mason University Facilities Planning. Special Collections & Archives, George Mason University Libraries.

Page 136. Groundbreaking at George Mason University. Special Collections & Archives, George Mason University Libraries.

Page 136. George Johnson, GMU President, c. 1980. Special Collections & Archives, George Mason University Libraries.

Page 136–137. Donald L. Wilkins, Fairfax County Hospital and Health Center Commission chairman, and Franklin P. Iams, Fairfax Hospital administrator, at the Fairfax Hospital site, 1958. Star Collection, D.C. Public Library; © Washington Post.

Page 138. Gerald T. "Jerry" Halpin. Courtesy Gerald T. Halpin.

Page 138. Atlantic Research. Star Collection, D.C. Public Library; © Washington Post.

Page 139. Above: U.S. Geological Survey Building. Middle: General Technologies Corporation. Below: Motorola. Planned Community Archives, Special Collections & Archives, George Mason University Libraries.

Page 140. Inauguration of the Fairfax County Board of Governors, 1964. Office of the County Executive, Fairfax County, Virginia.

Page 140. John Tilghman "Til" Hazel, Jr., and Milton V. Peterson. Courtesy of Til Hazel. Photo by Hill Signature Portraits.

Page 141. Zoning protestors jam the lobby of the County Office Building during a hearing, 1974. Photo by Wellner Streets. Star Collection, D.C. Public Library; © Washington Post.

Page 141. The Fairfax County Board of Supervisors in the studios of Channel 53 WNVT, 1972–73. Office of the County Executive, Fairfax County, Virginia.

Page 141. Earle Williams. Courtesy of Earle Williams.

Page 142. Yates Village, Springfield. Photo by Arnold Taylor. Star Collection, D.C. Public Library; © Washington Post.

Page 142. Traffic near Tysons Corner, 1975. Star Collection, D.C. Public Library; © Washington Post.

Page 142. William A. "Bill" Hazel. Courtesy of William A. Hazel.

Page 143. Fairfax County Zoning Administrator Philip Yates at Burke Centre with planning map. Photo by Bernie Boston. Star Collection, D.C. Public Library; © Washington Post.

Page 143. Aerial of Tysons Corner under construction, 1967. Photo by Blue Ridge Aerial Surveys. Star Collection, D.C. Public Library; © Washington Post.

Page 144. Sid Dewberry, Jim Nealon, and Dick Davis of Dewberry, Nealon & Davis. Reprinted from *The Dewberry Way: Celebrating 50 Years of Excellence.*

Page 144. Inset: Sidney O. "Sid" Dewberry. Courtesy of Sid Dewberry.

Page 145. The "Mixing Bowl", Shirley Highway, 1973. Photo by Geoffrey Gilbert. Star Collection, D.C. Public Library; © Washington Post.

Page 146. Rendering of Reston. Reston Collection, Special Collections & Archives, George Mason University Libraries.

Page 146. Dwight Schar. Courtesy of Dwight Schar.

Page 147. Aerial of Reston. Star Collection, D.C. Public Library; © Washington Post.

Page 148. Advertisement designed to draw businesses to Fairfax County, 1979. Star Collection, D.C. Public Library; © Washington Post.

Page 148. 2008 Techtopia fanciful map. Northern Virginia Technology Council.

Page 149. Dulles Greenway Toll Road. Dewberry.

Page 149. CIT building, Herndon, Virginia. The Center for Innovative Technology.

Page 150–151 spread. Interior, Tysons Corner Center. Tysons Corner Center/ Macerich.

Page 150. Aerial of Tysons Corner. Photo by Scott Boatwright. Photographic Archive, Fairfax County Public Library.

Page 152. Northern Virginia Community College Campus. Northern Virginia Community College.

Page 152–153. Aerial of George Mason University Campus. Photo by Nicolas Tan. George Mason University.

Page 153. John Toups. Courtesy of John Toups.

Page 154. Washington Dulles International Airport. Metropolitan Washington Airports Authority.

Page 154–155 spread. National Air and Space Museum, Steven F. Udvar-Hazy Center. Photo by Dane Penland. Smithsonian National Air and Space Museum, Steven F. Udvar-Hazy Center.

Page 156–157 spread. Reston Town Center. Photo by Marcella Drula-Johnston. Spectrum Creative, LLC.

Page 158. Inova Fairfax Hospital Campus, 2008. Inova Health System.

Page 162. Noman M. Cole Jr., 1973. Photo courtesy of Janet Cole.

Page 167. Old process schematic, Regional Water Reclamation Plant. Upper Occoquan Sewage Authority (UOSA).

Page 169. The Upper Occoquan Sewage Authority Water Reclamation Facility. Photo by Helmuth "Tom" Humphrey, Apertures, Inc.

Page 174. The Fairfax County Board of Supervisors inauguration, 1972. Office of the County Executive, Fairfax County, Virginia.

Page 179. Doug Fahl. Courtesy of Doug Fahl.

Page 187. Til Hazel receiving the first George Mason Medal, 1987. Courtesy of Til Hazel.

Page 189. The Filene Center at Wolf Trap National Park for the Performing Arts in Vienna, Virginia. Dewberry.

Page 194. Route 123 sign. Star Collection, D.C. Public Library; © Washington Post.

Page 208. Sign at the entrance to Fair Lakes at the Fairfax County Parkway. The Peterson Companies.

Page 211. Map showing a signalized ramp plan for the Fairfax County Parkway near Fair Lakes. Virginia Department of Transportation.

Page 222. J Hamilton Lambert presenting Fairfax County budget proposal, 1981. Photo by Paul Schmick. Star Collection, D.C. Public Library; © Washington Post.

Page 230. Dwight Schar, 2006. Ashland University, Ashland, Ohio.

Page 236. The Dulles Greenway Toll Road, 2006. Dewberry.

Page 239–241. Graphs 1–6. Source: U.S. Census, BLS, Center for Regional Analysis, School of Public Policy, George Mason University.

Page 242. Graphs 7–8. Source: Center for Regional Analysis, School of Public Policy, George Mason University.

Page 252. Dr. Alan G. Merten, President, George Mason University. Special Collections & Archives, George Mason University Libraries.

Page 258. Virginia "Internet C@pital" license plate design. Virginia Department of Transportation.

Page 260. Aerial of Tysons Corner Center. Tysons Corner Center.

Page 273. Metrorail extension design plan, 2008. Dulles Corridor Metrorail Project.

Index